D1532077

Academic Capitalism
and Literary Value

Academic Capitalism

Literary Value

· · · · · · ·

Harold Fromm

The University of Georgia Press

Athens and London

© 1991 by the University of Georgia Press

Athens, Georgia 30602

All rights reserved

Designed by Betty Palmer McDaniel

Set in ten on fourteen Linotype Walbaum

The paper in this book meets the guidelines for
permanence and durability of the Committee on
Production Guidelines for Book Longevity of the
Council on Library Resources.

Printed in the United States of America

95 94 93 92 91 C 5 4 3 2 1
95 94 93 92 91 P 5 4 3 2 1

Library of Congress Cataloging in Publication Data

Fromm, Harold.

Academic capitalism and literary value / Harold Fromm.

p.   cm.

Includes bibliographical references and index.

ISBN 0-8203-1350-5 (alk. paper)

ISBN 0-8203-1399-8 (pbk.: alk. paper)

1. Literature—History and criticism—Theory, etc.   2. Criticism.

I. Title.

PN81.F69   1991

801'.95'0904—dc20   90-22246

CIP

British Library Cataloging in Publication Data available

William Carlos Williams's "This is Just to Say" is reprinted by permission
from Collected Poems 1909–1939, vol. 1. Copyright 1938 by New
Directions Pub. Corp.

For Gloria

Contents

PART THREE
Academic Capitalism

Preface

Most of the chapters of this book are concerned with the ways in which politics and professionalism have taken over literary studies, alienating nonspecialist readers while throwing various forms of pseudorevolutionary virtue in their faces. Since this takeover is almost entirely academic and since the revolutionary aura is almost entirely specious—the real agenda being power and success in the academy—I see much of it as a pretentious counterpart to the ordinary everyday exchange of mundane commodities. And just as many of today's literary theorists reject the New Criticism for its separation of literature from history, politics, and nonaesthetic values, I reject much of today's criticism and theory for their own separation from the ethics of everyday life. Thus, if I sometimes avoid quarreling with theorists and critics about specific doctrines and truth-claims (though I generally *do* quarrel with them), it is because I am less concerned with the unprovable truth or falsity of what they say than with the ethical character of their whole enterprise.

In many cases, I take these critic-theorists more seriously than they take themselves, seeing their writings as a form of intellectual and ethical autobiography that is frequently more revealing than they could have intended. Without knowing anything substantive about their private lives or their characters as persons-in-the-world, I find that their writings alone often sufficiently project an "ethical subject" (to jargonize in the Marxist fashion) about whom a good deal can be—and ought to be—said. For my own position is that it is not just what intellectuals say (in the sense of "intend") that matters, but what they *do* (in the sense that their writing expresses a mode of being and doing in the world). This is bound to be extremely irritating to the self-protective critical monopoly that functions at the vanguard of "academic capitalism." Eager as these monopolists may appear to be to overturn "patriarchy," "the canon," and "capitalism," they will certainly not cooperate in allowing me to overturn them and will most likely accuse me of violating all kinds of rules, even though their numbingly repetitive argument is that "the rules" are a form of oppression by one interest group over another. I treat them as they treat so much else—as oppressive forms of a self-aggrandizing industry, much like their own versions of capitalism and patriarchy.

Some of the chapters that follow have been published previously in one form or another, while others have been written specifically for this volume. Although the book does not press a thesis from beginning to end as in a monograph, it hovers around a cluster of themes that keep reappearing in my handling of the problems dominating literary-critical studies for a decade or longer. The chapter on Leonard Woolf's fiction, however, is included for its continuation of the discussion of "Recycled Lives: Portraits of the Woolfs as Sitting Ducks" as well as for its attempt to reclaim Woolf's novels as "literature" from those who would use them merely as instruments for other ends.

If I have raked some academics over the coals, it should not be taken to mean I esteem the species any the less. Whom am I to esteem more highly: politicians? automobile manufacturers? baseball players? It is because I do esteem them that I am disappointed by shabby or hypocritical performances. And though at present an independent scholar, in essence I am still an academic myself, for which I feel no shame.

To friends and colleagues, as well as critics and scholars I have met through the mails, my gratitude is considerable for their readings of various portions of my book in manuscript or in earlier published versions. I offer particular thanks to Martha and Albert Vogeler of California State University—Fullerton; Peter J. Rabinowitz of Hamilton College; Gerald Graff of Northwestern; Alan G. Gross of Purdue—Calumet; Joseph Prescott, retired from Wayne State, and Art Berman of Rochester Institute of Technology. Sanford Pinsker of Franklin and Marshall College and Frank McConnell of UC Santa Barbara have prodded me into worthwhile revisions. Another kind of thanks is due Karen K. Orchard, associate director and executive editor of the University of Georgia Press, for her editorial support.

I am most grateful also for the continuing editorial encouragement I

have had over the years from Frederick Morgan of *The Hudson Review*
as well as Stanley Lindberg and Stephen Corey of *The Georgia Review.*
Staige Blackford of *The Virginia Quarterly Review* provided moral as
well as editorial support when the going got thick.

My greatest debt—to my wife, Gloria G. Fromm—exceeds any possible inventory, which would be superfluous in any case.

Earlier versions of some chapters have appeared as follows:

"Sparrows and Scholars: Literary Criticism and the Sanctification of
   Data," *The Georgia Review* 33 (1979): 255–76.
"Literary Professionalism's Pyhrric Defense of Poesy," *Centennial Review* 25 (1981): 435–47.
"Public Worlds/Private Muses: Criticism, Professionalism, and the
   Audience for the Arts," *Massachusetts Review* 28 (1987): 13–29.
"Recycled Lives: Portraits of the Woolfs as Sitting Ducks," *Virginia
   Quarterly Review* 61 (1985): 396–417.
"Leonard Woolf and His Virgins," *Hudson Review* 38 (1986): 551–69.
"The Lives and Deaths of Charlotte Brontë: A Case of Literary Politics," *Hudson Review* 40 (1987): 233–50.
The first half of Chapter 8 derives from "The Hegemony of 'Hegemony': Criticism, Capitalism, and Being in the World," *The Georgia
   Review* 42 (1988): 183–93.
Chapter 9 makes use of a number of passages from "The Hegemonic
   Form of Othering; or, The Academic's Burden," *Critical Inquiry* 13
   (1986): 197–200; republished in *"Race," Writing, and Difference* (Chicago and London: University of Chicago Press, 1986).
"Real Life, Literary Criticism, and the Perils of Bourgeoisification,"
   New Literary History 20 (1988): 49–64.

Academic Capitalism
and Literary Value

Introduction

It seems like a very long time ago—though it was only the early fifties—
that Randall Jarrell, who was not intimidated by respectable scholarly conventions, could write: "Yet, often, how plain and actual the
poem or story itself seems, compared to those shifting and contradictory and all-too-systematic 'readings' that veil it as clouds veil the rocks
of a mountain. Luckily, we can always seek refuge from the analyses in the poem itself—*if we like poems better than we like analyses.*
But poems, stories, new-made works of art, are coming to seem rather
less congenial and important than they once did, both to literary and
not-so-literary readers." [1]

Today's theorists, reading such lines, can hardly avoid a sneer, as if
they had passed a sylvan vista affording a glimpse of Adam naming
the animals. *Sancta simplicitas!* Was there ever a time, they would ask,
when people actually talked about "the poem itself," a time before the
poem was seen as totally implicated in the web of language, politics,
culture, and the individual or social psyche? Were Jarrell alive today,
he would doubtless not put the matter in quite these same terms, since
even tough-minded iconoclasts do not want to be trounced more than
necessary, but it is hard to suppose that he would simply give up and
throw his hat into the ring of "theory." Rather, he might find himself
writing in the vein of another relatively untheoretical academic, Helen
Vendler, as in her most recent book:

> Paraphrase, interpretation (in the usual sense), and ideological polemic
> are legitimate preliminary activities putting the art work back into the
> general stream of statements uttered by a culture. All of these statements
> (from advertising to sermons) can be examined for their rhetorics of per-
> suasion and their ideological self-contradiction or coherence, but such
> examinations bracket the question of aesthetic success. . . .

It is natural that people under new cultural imperatives should be impelled to fasten new interpretations (from the reasonable to the fantastic)
onto aesthetic objects from the past. But criticism cannot stop there. The
critic may well begin, "Look at it this way for a change," but the sentence
must continue, "and now don't you see it as more intelligibly beautiful
and moving?" That is, if the interpretation does not reveal some hitherto
occluded aspect of the aesthetic power of the art work, it is useless as
art criticism (though it may be useful as cultural history or sociology or
psychology or religion).[2]

Vendler knows the hurdles she must overcome in making such remarks as these in defense of an aesthetic criticism that has been institu-
tionally pushed to the margins of eccentricity. So she has thrown necessary sops to the various Cerberi who guard the gates of the academy
and raced right past. If Jarrell found it necessary to overcome the
New Criticism's pretension to scientificity, a pretension that now seems
absurd, Vendler is faced with a comparable problem: what to do about
the theoretical critic who must *master* the literary text in order to prove
his (or her) virility. To master the text one no longer uses "science," in
the primitive biophysical sense of the New Critics; other pretensions
are needed in order to wrestle the literary work right down to the mat—
and then kick its teeth out. After that, a few love pats may be tolerable,
but too much "literary response" is apt to be regarded as "sentimental"
or even "credulous."

Of course, this is a bad way to introduce a book about politics and
professionalism in the humanities. Can you imagine Fredric Jameson
reading this far without bursting into laughter or finding prime materials for his next Olympian dismantling of the text? But I am in such
deep trouble already, simple-mindedly using words like *literary work*
and *book* without quotation marks, that perhaps Jamesonian scorn is
the least of my worries. Since I have introduced the subject of Jameson
(who will be taken up later on), perhaps it is appropriate to note that
what has replaced the old scientific claims of criticism is something
more global and grand. If Freudian psychoanalyzing of the poet or
novelist is now considered jejune, what has taken its place is the psychoanalyzing of nothing less than the entire "political unconscious" that
underlies everything whatever. Yet the analyst himself has the temerity

to believe that he can avoid the net cast by his own wizardry. Even scholars sympathetic to the New Historicism are beginning to complain that the "readings" and unmaskings that characterize this genre are in reality fully contemporary creations, imposing today's needs upon the writings of yesterday. Although a reader can never escape the fact that he is situated in the present, New Historicists not only seem uncertain as to whether they are *representing* history or attempting to *reconstruct* it, but they seem to glory in their imposition of ideological order upon the subjects they chose to "historicize." Indeed, a reader of Stephen Greenblatt's brilliant essays is apt to feel they are fictitious creations that use old texts as raw materials for producing new ones, critical counterparts of the old-fashioned historical novel.

Today's methodologies, however, despite fancying that they are already in sight of the much-heralded Marxian Realm of Freedom, march to mundane drummers whose tattoos can be heard without elaborate sensing equipment. Deconstruction, Marxism, feminism, black studies—even with all the valuable insights and techniques they have given us—operate in accordance with their own aggressive, some-times covert, agendas, which often have a way of being much less pure than their practitioners are willing to let on. The gradual disappearance of the man of letters, the takeover of the arts and humanities by the academy, the relative dearth of public intellectuals, and the uses of the arts to further professional careers—all these have produced a situa-tion in which poems and novels seem to exist almost entirely for the purpose of being dismantled and reconstituted for political ends, ends that are often not quite as high-minded as the stated ones. Given the nature of today's favored methodologies, we tend to know in advance what everything will turn out to mean anyhow, since the method deter-mines the meaning. Can Sandra Gilbert or Fredric Jameson or Stanley Fish still say anything that would really surprise us? Once in a while, perhaps, because of their skill, they *do* say something that catches us unawares and justifies their preeminence. But in the main we know how their stories will end before we even begin to read, because their tropics of discourse invariably give away the show. In spite of all the revolutionary bravado and the veneer of skepticism, somehow it always ends up that God's in his heaven and everything makes the right sort of sense in the critic-theorist's world, provided you can see it from the point of view of a Marxist, a feminist, or a deconstructionist. The center continues to hold, even in a deconstructed and decentered universe, because the stories being told are already so familiar and reassuring, the orthodoxies so willingly assimilated by the well-prompted intellectual superego, that every acolyte graduate student can recite them like nursery rhymes.

The center keeps on holding because, even with all the proscriptions against words like "book," "self," "poem," in everyday practice the concepts connected with these words are used as if there had been no prior deconstruction of their meanings; they are used by the selfsame people who pretend to ridicule their use. In a truly shocking performance in *Critical Inquiry*, for example, Derrida rages at two critics of his writing for misreading his work, for failing to recognize and honor the conventions that convey the meaning of *an intending author*, even while he satirizes traditional categories of Western essentialism and intentionalism.[3] Such attacks on "logocentrism" are similar to many of the attacks on capitalism, hegemony, and patriarchal power: the attackers are arch-virtuosi at extracting every possible benefit from the smooth and dependable operation of systems they denounce as wicked, undependable, obsolete, or purely phantasmal. Their careers could not flourish without them. For what would be left as objects of desire, now that "knowledge for its own sake" has been laughed out of court as the hegemonic rationalization of the ruling class?

All of this professionalism and ideological appropriation undermines the confidence of nonspecialist readers, who fear they can no longer trust their own feelings. Even though many of these readers may themselves be academics and intellectuals (in fields other than literature), they are inclined to think that experts must be sought who will tell them what everything *really* means, even in a decentered universe where nothing *really* means anything. As for feelings, they begin to seem atavistic, suited to an unevolved primitive like Randall Jarrell, who just enjoys reading Frost, makes us feel we have not experienced him deeply enough, and spurs us on to read the poems all over again. Practically speaking, we seem to be caught in the middle of a new dissociation of sensibility, much worse than the supposed episode that Eliot discovered in the Enlightenment. But today's dissociation is caused not by the poet or his milieu but by the cultural critic who allegorizes all reading. To read Balzac "correctly" today means not to respond to literary power but to defuse it by identifying the unconscious cultural engine, the local ideology, the particular pathology, that produced his work. Jean-François Lyotard's distinction between "scientific knowledge" and "narrative knowledge" provides an ironic commentary on this kind of cultural criticism: "The scientist questions the validity of narrative statements and concludes that they are never subject to argumentation or proof. He classifies them as belonging to a different mentality: savage, primitive, underdeveloped, backward, alienated, composed of opinions, customs, authority, prejudice, ignorance, ideology. Narratives are fables, myths, legends, fit only for women and children [and one's more obtuse academic colleagues]. At best, attempts are made to throw some rays of light into this obscurantism, to civilize, educate, develop."[4]

Fortunately, there are signs of a developing backlash against the current anti-aesthetic hauteur. Ralph Rader, for example, writes: "But the vitality of the new interpretational modalities for their practitioners must be measured against the fact that the freight of accumulating interpretation lies on literature increasingly now with a weight heavy as frost and deep almost as life. Interpretation need not but often now does alienate us from the literary work and insulate us from its power to move, so that our experience of the work is attenuated and impoverished."[5] He notes that "literary works are made of words ordered by a meaning which, when we grasp it, moves us in the physical bodies inseparable from our humanity" (10). He concludes:

> The interassured confidence of mutual understanding offered by the author and accepted by the reader in a full experience of the work compares unfavorably with the exploitative relationship of interpreter to text in so much current criticism where the critic seeks conceptual mastery through whatever tricks and turns of domination are required to tame the writer in his text regardless of the cost to its felt integrity. These critics—often supremely literate and articulate—don't so much write texts of their own as write *over* the texts of the dispossessed authors, nesting in them like cuckoos. (14)

In a less direct way than Rader or Vendler, Peter J. Rabinowitz resists current alienating tendencies by questioning, for all its virtues, the long term rule of New Critical "close reading."

> Different authors, different genres, different periods, different cultures expect readers to approach texts in different ways.
>
> The bias in academe toward close reading reduces that multiplicity. While all close readers obviously don't read in exactly the same way, the variations have a strong family resemblance. Their dominance in the aristocracy of critical activity—virtually undiminished by the critical revolutions of the last 20 years—can skew evaluation, distort interpretation, discourage breadth of vision, and separate scholars from students and other ordinary readers. . . .
>
> Once you give priority to close reading, you implicitly favor figurative writing over realistic writing, indirect expression over direct expression, deep meaning over surface meaning, form over content, and the elite over the popular.[6]

This reassertion of the variety of literature's means and ends is an attempt to dislodge the literary work from an insatiable academic machine that destroys the poem or novel as it "reveals" it.

The alienating effects of academic criticism and theory are by no means confined to the professoriate itself or its own specialized audience. As textbooks like the Norton anthologies and critical editions come more and more to reflect current academic approaches and preferences, greater numbers of students at all levels are subjected to the belief that poems and novels exist in order to be deconstructed, in the broadest sense of the term, and that reading is a game of one-upmanship over the author, who is necessarily an unfree simpleton whose political unconscious needs to be bared. To be taken in by the power of the text is to betray one's putty-like malleability and uncritically dimwitted faculties. In a dissatisfied review of some recent "English" textbooks, Mark Walhout assesses this takeover: these textbooks "represent an ambitious attempt to rewrite the discourse of the humanities classroom, as a glance at the glossaries demonstrates: 'Decentered,' 'discourses,' 'ideology,' 'indeterminacy,' 'intertextuality,' 'naturalization,' 'overdetermined,' 'political unconscious,' 'site of struggle,' 'strong reading'—the list reads like a dictionary of contemporary theory. This, presumably, is the language our students will be speaking by the turn of the century."[7] He feels, however, that more important literary values are being slighted.

The vivacious critical mentality of the past twenty years has certainly been exhilarating and a great deal of good has come of it. But like most orthodoxies, not only does it take itself too seriously, it appears to think it represents a finality of truth and value, even though we recognize that ideologies do not last very long in our consumer economy based on obsolescence. Yet while these orthodoxies flourish, important human capacities are consecrated to atrophy. Fortunately, there are still people who think that poems, novels, and plays have a lot to offer that is not nourished by today's politics and professionalism. Nor is it really an either/or question: cultural theory or else maundering impressionism, but a matter of multivalent inclusiveness. In an interesting, if circuitous, essay, Robert von Hallberg[8] contrasts the criticism written by academics with the criticism written by poets since World War II. He discusses critics like Jarrell, who have much to teach us about poetic sensitivity, despite their sometimes hard to take god-terms and gut-terms and flights of enthusiasm. Insofar as they resist academic critical conventions, they can still speak of beauty, pleasure, poetic skill, and most daring of all, the intentions of the author. But poet-critics have their own limitations. Von Hallberg is very catholic in his ability to tolerate even such ragamuffin critical essays as those of the poet Robert Hass, who makes academic criticism look almost considerate by contrast. But when one turns to some of the writings of Geoffrey Hartman or Houston Baker, Jr., to use two academic examples among many, one is apt to have second thoughts. Between a casual Hass and a doctrinaire Baker, a reader might begin to decide in favor of abandoning the literary enterprise altogether. Does one want to spend one's life reading stuff like that? But what von Hallberg's essay ultimately communicates is the need for a rich multiplicity of both "aesthetic" and academic critical styles and responses, since neither sensibility is adequate by itself and each requires the correction of the other. Chapter 13, "Critical Situations," takes up this need at length.

Although I have spoken harshly elsewhere about some of the theories of Frederick Turner because they seem to me dangerously conserva-

tive, his writings also offer valuable departures from current dogma
that could well serve as curatives to some of today's literary maladies.
Most striking of these is his conception of "Reading as Performance,"
the title of one of his essays. Although he tends to stress actual performances of drama, more appropriate in my context is his treatment of
private reading as a figurative performance, that is, as a counterpart
to the performance of a printed musical score. Reflecting on the rela-
tivity, multiplicity, ambiguity, contextuality, subjectivity, temporality,
locality, and undecidability that we nowadays connect with the act of
reading, in which subject (reader), object (text), and environment are
in flux, he comes to the striking conclusion that "the critics give us
a divine plenum of possible interpretations, but this divine plenum is
quite impossible to perform."[9] "[T]o become flesh the text must take to
itself the tragic limits of particularity and exclusive being" (157), which
is what it does in any given performance or reading. Speaking of the
free play and indeterminacy that today's criticism cultivates, he suggests that "once reading is separated from the other senses and from
the values of personal life and social activity, it becomes, paradoxically,
free to interpret how it wills [i.e., by a conscious, willful, purely cerebral act], while at the same time the text, as a mere hermeneutic system
of differences, loses all its relevance to actual human concerns" (159).
In sum, "*Any* group of words has anarchic proclivities toward tedious
ambiguity: to make them mean something definite is the miracle. . . .
The chief virtue of poetry is to perform a definite act within the indeterminate potentiality of the world. . . . Art realizes a concrete act
out of the unreality of the physical universe" (160).

What Turner is getting at here is that when we are overwhelmed
by music or the other arts, we experience a unifying emotion that is
absolute, unambiguous, and prepossessing while it is occurring, that
is, during the concrete realization of reading, listening, or seeing. This
is what we mean by an aesthetic experience, something that overcomes
volition and the resistance of intellect, taking us out of ourselves. When
the experience is over, we may think about it, dismantle it, evaluate it,
but it is the ability of "art" to produce these *experiences in time* that
makes us want to bother with further analysis in the first place. When
analysis becomes a substitute for affect so that we are no longer able to

relinquish our selves emotionally, then the raison d'être for spending time on art ceases to exist. Art is valuable because it involves a forgetting, an abandonment of one's own customary narrow consciousness, a union with a rich and overflowing Other. If the aesthetic experience is now to be regarded as simple-minded, however, and if the ideal condition is one of resistance toward and domination of the artwork by "culture critics" who see it solely as a "document" revealing the artist to be less intelligent than they, there is no further justification for the traditional preeminence of art. Rather, the professionalized, politicized academic analyst is a new sort of colonialist, exploiting the "primitives" for profit, promotion, and prestige. (See Chapter 9, "Literary Politics and Blue-Chip High-Mindedness.")

In saying these things, I have no intention to promote philistinism or unreflective stupidity. Consciousness cannot be halted or reversed, nor the consolations of eternal verities resuscitated. The consciousness industry is one among many and it really has few grounds for feeling privileged. It can be as blind and self-interested as the automobile industry. It can be destructive, crass, colonialist, careerist, and in its own way philistine as well, by treating art as essentially infantile. It flourishes on a basis of moral superiority often as flimsy as that of politics or conventional religiosity, and its attacks on everything bourgeois are hollow at the core.

The chapters that follow attempt to trace some of criticism's and theory's ethical and aesthetic failures through specimen texts taken from the dominant schools of the past fifteen or twenty years. Most of the examples are academic because most criticism being done today is academic, but there are a few texts drawn from critics with little or no university connection. Feminism, deconstruction, New Historicism, Marxism, reader-response criticism, and black studies are examined at very close range with a particular eye for the relation between what the critic-theorist says and what his or her texts actually seem to be doing—in essence, an informal sociology of criticism. It is interesting to observe that one full pendulum swing has taken place over the course of the last two decades, from an exaggerated estimate of the value of critical subjectivity—as seen in the early texts of the reader-response movement—to a belief in the magisterial objectivity of the culture critic who unmasks whole epochs, not to mention mere texts, because he alone of all mankind escapes the partisanships of ideology and the finitudes of temporality. If my protest in "Sparrows and Scholars" (Chapter 1) is that the communal cognitive world of the late seventies was being dismantled by reader-response critics, a process that would render *all* literary responses valuelessly subjective, my complaint in most of the later chapters is that the inflated truth claims of more recent cultural theorists, as well as their reduction of literature to politics, is destroying the concrete, personal, and sensuous foundation of the literary experience altogether.

In these chapters, with their multiple readings of current critical practice, several themes prevail:

—That once the "search for truth" and "knowledge for its own sake" have been disallowed as rationalizations for scholarly activity, most academic "production" (and here the Marxist term is fully apposite) must be considered as just one form of industry among others, with self-interest, success, and profit as the final goals—in sum, as academic capitalism. (I venture to say, however, that men and women can still be found who simply take pleasure in scholarly, aesthetic, or creative activity, apart from any possible external rewards, but they are increasingly in the position of eccentrics courting starvation, unless they have other sources of income.)

—That many critics and theorists, more interested in political goals than intellectual activity or aesthetic response, malappropriate literary works toward these ends. What is so curious about this development is that the political goals are likely to be purely theoretical, because the real aim is personal success and power, not genuine ethical reform in the world. Very few risks are taken that might jeopardize a rising academic career.

—That once literature is devalued to the role of political instrument (both for the writer and the critic), the cultural rationale for justifying the creation, appreciation, or profession of literature disappears. Literary study becomes just another social science, while novelists and poets appear as more cunningly unscrupulous versions of ourselves, using their gifts for the same grubby vanities as the rest of us. That Virginia Woolf, for example, is known by many students solely through *A Room*

of One's Own and some of the critical/biographical works about her—
but not from a reading of her novels—discloses a good deal about the
current uses of literature. This shift to politics and sociology has resulted in an alienation of the reader, not just in the sense of turning
him or her away from literary works except as ideological documents,
but in the deeper sense of separating the reader as thinker from the
reader as affective consciousness, as someone who *feels* what he reads
as lived emotion. Not only can the reader be confused into self-distrust
when skillful novels and poems are dragged down into social patholo-
gies by culture critics reading them as symptoms of their time—he can
be baffled into incomprehensibility by the way in which inept, third-
rate performances like *Frankenstein* have been cried up by feminist
politics into "masterpieces." The critical literature on this novel over
the past ten years, with its Lacanian obsessions and feminist political
agenda, can only be described as preposterous and must be sampled
to be believed—or disbelieved. Treated in a similar way, the obscurer
Jacobean dramas (Mary Shelley's Renaissance kin) would appear to
be a potential goldmine for academic capitalists on the lookout for
neglected dregs for alchemical recycling.

These themes surface again and again in the book's main sections.
Part One, "Literary Professionalism," emphasizes the influx of continental philosophy upon the more orderly and rationalized world of
Anglo-American literary studies during the seventies. Nietzsche, Heidegger, Derrida, and Saussure collaborate in a rejection of metaphysics
that results in structuralism and deconstruction and that contributes
to the disintegrating subjectivities of the reader-response movement.
The ill effects of these influences, discussed in the first two chapters,
include a growing diffidence about aesthetic response that has only
served to augment the power and prestige of "professionals" who appropriate the arts for their own purposes. The inward-looking character
of this professionalism is so great that even when an earnest attempt
is made to counteract its damage, the act of repudiation itself turns
into yet another instance of the malaise it sets out to cure. This quick-
sand effect is the subject of the second chapter, "Literary Professionalism's Pyhrric Defense of Poesy." Here we see a well-intentioned critical
theorist in action, desperately weaving a web of textuality out of Witt-

gensteinian language games and speech-act theory in order to counter
the ills that result from Derridean indeterminacy. We wince in pain as
he elaborately constructs a metaphysical octopus that will squeeze to
death any residues of literary pleasure that might happen to remain
for a reader already reeling from deconstruction. In "Public Worlds/
Private Muses," other professionals are seen engaging in similar mis-
chief in behalf of public sculpture and the citizens who must view it
as they pass through streets, plazas, and public buildings, but there is
a lesson here for literary studies as well, which is taken up again at
greater length in Chapter 13, "Critical Situations": far from existing
just for the academic specialists who have appropriated them, literature, music, and the visual arts have a potentially large audience of
educated people who venture outside their professional specialities for
aesthetic gratification.

Part Two, "Literary Politics," pays close attention to a range of currently favored literary and critical texts in order to reveal the ethical
violations that result when literature is used for political ends. Some
of the most influential critical schools of the eighties, as well as a few
sui generis individuals, are examined and challenged for the terrible
things they have done to the Woolfs and the Brontës. In later chapters,
several Marxist and black theoreticians are charged with being unwitting doubles of the traditionalists and reactionaries they themselves
have condemned as counterrevolutionary.

Finally, in Part Three, "Academic Capitalism," the concluding chapters on public intellectuals, specialist critics, and literary power
struggles in the academy pull together in more global fashion the
themes pervading the book, summing up the consequences, both ethical and aesthetic, of current critical practice and suggesting a holding
pattern for the immediate future, as we await the uncertain denouement of academic politics and professionalism.

My inclination throughout is not to offer panaceas, because my outlook is anti-utopian. Utopias, in fact, form a large part of the current
problem. Cultural crises work themselves out better in casual practice
than in the planned execution of pie-in-the-sky theories, for one can
hardly anticipate what the plotted revolutions of bemused intellectuals would produce. Today, the manufacture of utopias has become a

glamorous substitute for ethical action: it is much easier to invent ideal worlds that shift moral obligations onto other people's shoulders (preferably in the future, when none of *us* will be inconvenienced) than to incur the bother of altering one's own actual behavior. This is why there are so many "revolutionary" superstars at American universities, earning high salaries that depress the salaries of their less entrepreneurial colleagues, those same academic proles whom in fancy they are out to "save" along with capitalist mankind. The intellectual's planned revolution always begins tomorrow, not yesterday. Today one negotiates for a Chair in the sun at Irvine or La Jolla.

Part One

· · · · · ·

*Literary
Professionalism*

1

. . . . . .

Sparrows and Scholars:
Literary Criticism and the
Sanctification of Data

At the present stage of history, when literature's link with the divine must be regarded as irrevocably severed along with every other formerly transcendent connection, and when the basis for valuation derived in the past from God's revelation no longer obtains, the very value of literature is thrown into question. At the same time, a curious but nonetheless logical development has come to pass: dominant critical methodologies—particularly the structuralist, poststructuralist, reader-response, deconstructive,[1]—reject the notion that works of literature have a determinate or even a determinable meaning. Such a development is understandable enough, since it is a consistent offshoot of the general trends in sociology, anthropology, linguistics, psychology, and other fields that see meaning, value, and substance as psychologically projected by man and his cultures. But it is also rather bizarre, because it undermines literary criticism as a self-consistent discipline while simultaneously encouraging a multiplicity, a "plurality," of critical readings whose lack of theoretical justification renders them practically worthless.[2]

If works of literature (now called "texts," in order to convey their lack of the intrinsic unity and wholeness implied by "works") are in constant movement like everything else, and if the readers of these texts are themselves in motion (i.e., undergoing physical and psychological change from moment to moment), we are in a predicament in which a critical counterpart of "one man, one vote" has come to prevail in literary hermeneutics. Indeed, the motto is inaccurately applied and should read instead, "multiplex reader, manifold readings." As the number of published readings increases, a reflection of the seemingly infinite possibilities of reader-text "transactions," the problem arises: what is one going to do with them? In the past, when knowing instead of being was considered the basis of the humanistic sciences, it was assumed that literary works had real existence and that multiple readings would contribute to the formation of composite readings, very adequate readings, which would be shared by many readers. These readings would then in some sense come to constitute the work itself. If the work itself could never in fact be reached, then at least the *notion* of a work could serve as an ideal toward which composite readings might aspire. But today, the multitude of published readings can be seen as contributing materials toward the production of additional unique readings, valid only for particular readers (i.e., their authors).

The limits of this validity are even further narrowed by the current variations upon the familiar notion of "play," inspired by Kant's purposiveness without purpose, developed by Schiller in his Aesthetic Letters, and then extended by Derrida to the point of anarchy.[3] Added to the familiar concept of play as intense experience of the moment for its own sake is the newer idea of "free play," a phenomenon resembling loose gears in a transmission: the "fit" of language is so poor and approximate that a good deal of leeway is possible before the cogs of reader and text engage. This leeway, in fact, turns out to be practically infinite and the "engagement" doubtful. Among the playful French theorists and their English-speaking disciples, the current critical style involving word-play, punning, tropes, and operatic overstatement produces an effect resembling dizzying inattentiveness on the part of the author, as though he were unable to stick to the train of his thought without myriad distractions en route, however intentionally indulged. Such critiques have hovering and unfocusable meanings. As Geoffrey Hartman observes, in an almost completely opaque debate with Wallace Martin, "In Derrida the line play wishes to be undecidable. Derrida is not a Kierkegaard who seeks to transcend the aesthetic position with its ironic or playful infinitization and to arrive at a religious position with its tragic or decisive understanding of eternity. His infinitizing of meaning hovers between playing and . . . not reality, but an as yet undefinable allegoresis."[4] The problem is compounded, of course, by the fact that even some of the most democratically transactive and subjective literary critics secretly or publicly believe, however playful, that their own readings have things to say that really do apply to the works themselves, even if the works themselves are believed not to exist except in particular psychological realizations. Naturally, critics like Norman Holland, David Bleich, and Stanley Fish exert considerable ingenuity in order to extricate themselves from this embarrassing epistemological bind.

The production of an ever-increasing number of readings of works of literature suggests a troubling question: is it possible, or even desirable, for any reader or scholar to attempt to read a large number of interpretations of any given text, no matter how great that text is esteemed to be? In other words, can the scholarly ideal of mastery of a body of criticism still be justified as a legitimate part of literary study if knowledge of these criticisms is no longer believed to narrow the gap between reader and text? Seen from outside the narrow professionalism that initiates behavior within the professions, what justifications made in accordance with generally accepted ethical or heuristic values could possibly be offered for reading a large number of accounts of *Paradise Lost,* or Joyce's *Ulysses,* or *Songs of Innocence and Experience*—not to mention lesser works—if no amount of critical insights will even begin to lead one to the phantom "work itself"? Even when so many critical essays can be clever, stimulating, or sheer fun to read, doubts must surely arise.

Although, for instance, it is not an especially troubling question to ask whether Barthes's *S/Z* is a production of great brilliance, it *is* troubling to ask whether even as a mere vehicle of its demonstration, Balzac's "Sarrasine" is worth two hundred and fifty pages of critical attention (or, for that matter, whether the story is even worth reading). Very troubling indeed is the fact that Barthes's reading of "Sarrasine" produces a virtually original new work, an artifact of the critic as artist. Are such artifacts more accessible to the reader's understanding than the original "inaccessible" texts out of which they are created?

If in our lives we are afforded only a limited number of pulsebeats, it is not frivolous (however unfashionable) to ask about the priorities for the use of those beats; and *within* the professions, questions of priority need to be raised as much as do questions from without concerning the validity of the activities of these professions as a whole. So the current democratization of readers' responses to literary works together with the imaginative new works based upon them that have resulted from the repudiation of the substantial reality of texts necessarily leave us with practical and ethical dilemmas. How can one hope to read all of those proliferating responses to literary works (when ultimately they do not apply to oneself anyhow)? How can an individual or a profession justify even trying to do so without, however unwittingly, also justifying what amounts to an insidious sort of idolatry?

It may seem quaint, in this last quarter of the twentieth century, to introduce so curious a concept as idolatry into such a sophisticated professional world, but as I understand it, the term refers to the placing of virtually infinite valuation upon the individual and finite productions of man and then regarding those productions as possessing transcendent importance. The usefulness of such a concept as a lens through which to view ethical behavior does not seem to be curtailed merely because our objects of belief have undergone radical transformation. Even the setting up of what appear to be purely aesthetic or professional priorities is dependent, however unconsciously, on the tacit recognition of the physical and mental limitations imposed upon human existence in the world. Acts of any kind achieve at least part of their valuation from the relative amounts of time and energy that are required to perform them, as well as the position of importance that they occupy in relation to the rest of one's life and to other human interests. In medical education, for example, there is now the objection that a purely technical training drains the moral and affective life of the medical student so that he or she is apt to be emotionally crippled in his or her role as physician relating to flesh and blood patients.

In literary studies one can see how a comparable misappropriation

of value could occur as a result of the way we talk about and probably think about such phenomena as *Hamlet,* "Tintern Abbey," and
Dubliners. When literary (or any other) works are seen and treated as
incarnations of the *Creator Spiritus* (as indeed they have been since the
romantic period—and often before), i.e., when they are thought of as
expressions of the "infinite I AM," then it becomes easy and eventually
habitual, especially after the disappearance of God, to take such figures
of speech both functionally and emotionally as literal statements about
reality. When the tremendous energies and anxieties once turned upon
God turn themselves, in the absence of God, upon the incarnations
of the imagination (helped along by the lack of self-reflection encouraged by professionalism), it is not surprising that there should result a
certain amount of going overboard. Naturally, if sophisticated literary
specialists were to be asked if they *really* believed that given works of
literature were the productions of "God," even in a purely analogical
sense, they would probably say, "No." But since we do not generally
accept as indisputable truth the explanations that people offer for their
own behavior in other areas, there is no reason that we should accept
a "no" as faithful to the operating realities of the situation in this one.
Rather, it is hard for a dispassionate observer not to see current expressions of professionalized attention to literary works as one more
instance of misplaced—or at the very least, insufficiently justified—
valuation.

When a scholar or critic chooses once again to present us with still
another reading of a Shakespeare play, a Joyce story, a Wordsworth
poem, in the face of the hundreds of readings that already exist in print,
he may very well have no conscious (or even unconscious) suppositions
about the transcendent value of his subject. In this sense, he does not
mistake a given work of literature for the transcendent, but the very
absence of reflection in the matter, the lack of any doubt or questioning
of what one is doing by writing yet another lengthy piece on "The Sisters" or *To the Lighthouse,* constitutes another sort of indictment. For
absence of reflection amounts to an attribution of value, assuming as it
does *without question* that certain things are both worth doing and self-
justifying. If the appearance of one more full-length book on *Ulysses*
does not produce utter incredulity, then it is likely to produce the sort

of unreflecting assent that one might have granted five hundred years ago upon hearing yet another sermon on "The Gospel According to St. Matthew." Sacred texts, one might then have thought, if one thought about it at all, proffer inexhaustible wisdom, coming as they do from God. This form of idolatry in the arts, however, becomes particularly startling when one realizes that, unlike "God" (whom idols purport to transfix in matter), literary works are now widely believed to have no essence of their own or—at least, no recoverable essence of their own. The difference between "sacred texts" and literary works (which seems to be generally overlooked) is that the infiniteness of sacred texts results from the inexhaustibility of their supposedly infinite wisdom; the infiniteness of literary texts now can be seen to result from the infinite regress that is involved in trying to recover them. In other words, the infiniteness of literary texts is not their presence but their absence. Can an infinite regress pretend to transcendent value?[5]

This functional idolatry, as far as I can determine, has come about as a gradual and unperceived result of the evolution of biblical hermeneutics into literary criticism. Given the literary character of sacred texts, it was an organic development for the methods of understanding them to be applied first to devotional and then to purely secular literature, especially when the secular literature comes to function as religious literature in the absence of God. Once the romantic writers and critics—Blake, Wordsworth, Coleridge, and Shelley, to use a few English examples only—began to see art as the expression not merely of inspiration but of the God-in-the-Self, it was inevitable that works of romantic art, and then all art, should come to generate the same sort of reverence that traditional sacred texts and devotional literature had enjoyed before the disappearance of God.

While the *methods* of biblical and literary hermeneutics have much in common, the *assumptions* behind the two kinds of texts are vastly dissimilar. Although Wordsworth and Coleridge (among many others) could still make a convincing case for the poet as micro-deity, there nevertheless remained an insuperably great difference between sacred and secular texts: to wit, that sacred texts have been assumed to be "written" by God. The constant interpretation and reinterpretation of familiar religious texts, the attendance upon every word and locution, the concern for the accuracy and purity of their transmission and translation hardly required justification. The texts were by God, and nothing in human life could be considered more important than an accurate understanding of God's word. The effects of such understanding were not merely professional or aesthetic—they involved the nature and consequences of mortality itself. If God could care about the fall of every sparrow, the numbering of every hair, the being of every blade of grass, then surely he could be supposed to care about the texts whereby he transmitted his gospel to mankind.

But when God can no longer be regarded as a transcendent presence behind every word of "His" or any other text, the methodological and ontological assumptions of literary hermeneutics fall apart. When the guarantee of ultimate value behind the words of a literary text has been removed as a consequence of the disappearance of God, it requires more than an assertion of the presence of an infinite I am to get that value back again. The transitional numinosity of art during the romantic period could hardly be expected to last indefinitely. Now we must face the problem that either literary texts are *really* transcendent, in which case it would be impossible to spend too much time on them; or literary texts are *really not* transcendent, in which case every individual act of attention directed toward them must be the object of careful scrutiny in order to avoid the charge of triviality or idolatry.

A desperate attempt to supply this lost numinosity has, however, been made throughout contemporary Western life in the form of the sanctification of data and the democratization of the worth of individual consciousness. Though God may not be present to validate the worth of every sparrow, the modern obsession with data has endeavored to make up through sheer plenitude the basis for evaluation that has been lost through what is nowadays called "absence." On the popular scene, we are bombarded with endless collections of data (either as opinion polls or sociological studies) purporting to provide us with general insights derived from the transitory states of consciousness of large (but never large enough) numbers of interviewees. The sexual fantasies of women during intercourse, the meditations of auto workers on the assembly line, the poems written by children in kindergarten and the elderly in nursing homes have all been presented and re-presented in the forlorn hope that the sheer data alone, the sheer indications of intelligent life, can supply the guarantee of meaning and worth that the loss of transcendence has taken along with it. The current interest in "oral history," the success of books like Studs Terkel's *Working*, the ubiquitousness of tape recordings and photographs, the emergence of aleatory and trash art—all appear to be saying that by a sort of *nouvelle alchimie* the act of recording the inconsequential will transmute the commonplace into the infinite. Notation, recording, and publication serve to eternalize transitory acts of emotion and cognition and to lift them above the void of lost transcendence. This elevation to the stars was a difficult enough feat when its vehicle was the consciousness of a Shakespeare or a Wordsworth. When its vehicle is the sensibility of a factory worker, the feat indeed seems transcendent. This is not to say that one doubts that auto workers have thoughts too deep for tears. It is, rather, to say that everybody has them and that simply believing that "everything that lives is Holy" leads neither to knowledge nor to value of the sort on which humanistic disciplines can be constructed. Andy Warhol's famous remark that someday everybody will be famous for fifteen minutes has as its commentary the equally famous remark, "When everybody is somebody, nobody is anybody."

Along with the spewing forth of unlimited data that has resulted from the loss of transcendence is a loss of the basis for valuation that could give meaning to that data. Thus, the very cause of the data is also the cause of their worthlessness. In the past, the data of daily life were seen as The Book of the World, a book written by God, in which all of the substances of nature derived their value from their infinite author. Even as the authority of this author began to fail, the value of the data retained external supports: to Wordsworth, the meanest flower that blows could seem precious because it served as an occasion for self-consciousness. Unable to attend for very long upon daffodils, leech-gatherers, or even the sublime Alps, Wordsworth was very quickly precipitated into an *O Altitudo* by the commonplaces of daily life. For Carlyle, data acquired their value not as occasions for self-consciousness so much as for their revelation of the ultimately miraculous nature of the humdrum, their natural supernaturalism. But by the twentieth century, all of these props had failed. The Book of the World, having lost its transcendent connection, is now mere data. It is no longer a "book," but simply "writing." When Derrida speaks, in *Of Grammatology*, of the "End of the Book and the Beginning of Writing," he has described the present situation. But when the integrative whole symbolized by the book turns into the indeterminate and open-ended "text" of "writing," we are in a world without value. Of what possible interest can those data be, whether as stored "information" or as "readings" of classic "texts"? They are merely the expressions of noisy desperation, the cacophony of absence, the squawkings of what is not there.

In contemporary literature, this view of reality as data has already produced its own genre: the "nonfiction novel." The philosophic presuppositions of this literary mode are examined by Mas'ud Zavarzadeh in his study, *The Mythopoeic Reality:*

> The changes in the empirical and cultural realities in the postwar years (which have historically canceled the role of the totalizing novel) and the internal dynamics of the literary tradition . . . have brought about a shift of the narrative "dominant" in contemporary American literature. . . . The shared epistemology of these new kinds of narrative is their noninterpretive stance toward external reality. . . . The nonfiction novel replaces "interpretation" with a "transcription" of naked facts. The various modes of transfiction employ a variety of strategies to avoid hiding the reality of chaos and the invading entropy in contemporary life under an imposed interpretive order. . . .
>
> Epistemologically, the nonfiction novel is rooted in the idea that the experiencing mind, confronted with the impossibility of reaching a total view of contemporary life and the unavailability of any communal values which could endow experience with a shared significance, is left with a stripped reality: the facts of the phenomenal world of events, its surfaces and appearances. Thus, the nonfiction novel uses transcription, not interpretive analysis, as the most authentic way to deal with a reality which has no precedent and defies all established norms. This stance, however, should not be taken to imply that the nonfiction novelist believes in the existence of an "objective" reality "out there," independent of the consciousness of the human perceiver.[6]

This lack of an objective reality out there can be seen as the non-fiction novelist's counterpart of the literary theorist's indeterminate text. For both, "reality" and "meaning" have been replaced by "facts" and "data."

In the world of current literary theory, facts and data have as their source the cognitions of the reader: these are assumed to be the givens of literary experience. In this light, a contemporary locus classicus, Stanley Fish's "Literature in the Reader: Affective Stylistics,"[7] is worth looking at yet again. In this celebrated essay, Fish takes us word by word through a difficult sentence of Sir Thomas Browne in order to show us the kinds of psychological visions and revisions that Fish claims to take place during the act of reading. With considerable ingenuity, Fish points out each place in Browne's sentence where the reader must quickly produce a new projection of the whole in order to proceed with his reading. This sort of reading experience is not a mere act of understanding but rather a series of contretemps on a psychological battlefield:

> The category of response includes any and all of the activities provoked by a string of words. . . . Obviously, this imposes a great burden on the analyst who in his observations on any one moment in the reading experience must take into account all that has happened (in the reader's mind) at previous moments, each of which was in its turn subject to the accumulating pressures of its predecessors. (127)

> Essentially what the method [Fish's analysis] does is *slow down* the reading experience so that "events" one does not notice in normal time, but which do occur, are brought before our analytical attentions. . . . Of course the value of such a procedure is predicated on the idea of *meaning as an event.* . . . It is more usual to assume that meaning is a function of the utterance, and to equate it with the information given (the message) or the attitude expressed. (128)

> What I am suggesting is that there is no direct relationship between the meaning of a sentence (paragraph, novel, poem) and what its words mean. . . . It is the experience of an utterance—*all* of it and not anything that could be said about it, including anything I could say—that *is* its meaning.(131)

> In the analysis of a reading experience, when does one come to the point?

The answer is, "never." . . . Coming to the point is the goal of a criticism that believes in content, in extractable meaning, in the utterance as a repository. (148)

Perhaps, then, the word meaning should also be discarded, since it carries with it the notion of message or point. The meaning of an utterance, I repeat, is its experience—all of it—and that experience is immediately compromised the moment you say anything about it. It follows then that we shouldn't try to analyze language at all. The human mind, however, seems unable to resist the impulse to investigate its own processes; but the least (and probably the most) we can do is proceed in such a way as to permit as little distortion as possible. (160)

Although these passages do not do full justice to Fish's method—or what used to be his method—they convey some of the essentials of his early approach. Of course, much in that approach is familiar even to critically conservative readers. In many circles it is still generally believed that literary works cannot be restated in other words, that poems *are* and do not *mean*, that reading is a sensuous and not merely an intellectual experience. But Fish's attention to every detail (at least in theory), his minute examinations of each word and phrase for the psychological processes they set off in the reader as he reads, these are part and parcel, despite their theoretical usefulness, of an era of data and of trash art. The rusty pipe that was always on the trash heap but barely noticed is now placed on a pedestal so that the viewer can see the curves and textures that he had never noticed before but which were always "there." In reading a text, everything "works," including one's misapprehensions, and so they must be taken as an egalitarian part of the whole. This complete atomization of experience, this inspecting of the minutiae of creation and finding that it is all good because it all serves an end, is at the heart of the contemporary sanctification of data. What *is* the end that these data are there to serve? Evidently, their end is to be noticed, to be "played" with. The imperative seems to be that one must notice and play with all the data because all the data are there to be noticed and played with. Since in a limited way most people will even agree that everything functions and nothing is empty, what distinguishes so much criticism of this sort is its insistence that everything must be taken into account. All is foreground, nothing background.

This complexity of response (which again, at least in theory, appears to avoid making choices) then becomes the work. At this point, when it is impossible to distinguish between a "public" work and its "private" response, the response becomes as transcendent in value as the imputed work.

Fish's conclusion that "experience is immediately compromised the moment you say anything about it" suggests that all experience is too sacred to be vitiated in any way by even the merest translation or (Why not say it?) even the act of understanding. Experience is like the name of the Lord to the Hebrews: too sacred to be spoken because no speaking can do it justice. Understanding, according to this view, translates experience into another mode of being and thereby perverts it. Thus, despite the positing of an "informed" reader (a concession against chaos that even Fish is willing to make) whose responses can be valued more than sheer ignorance, the data of consciousness are the real repository of value. These data, because of the abandonment of any reusable principles of selectivity (except those imposed by the somewhat arbitrarily "informed" reader), are multiplied into hitherto unparalleled quantities. To the familiar categories of junk mail and junk food must now be added a new concept: junk consciousness, devoid of nutritive value beyond therapeutic play for the player alone. Of course, this subjectivist viewpoint (not fully typified by Fish, however) rejects such a category as "junk" altogether since, for it, everything that is thought is Holy.

In contrast to this philosophy of registration as valuation, it is knowing rather than being that has generally been considered the basis of the humanistic sciences. During most of the history of Western thought, "knowledge" referred to the abstraction of the intelligible from inarticulate personal experience. But during the past few decades a neoromantic trend began to develop whose aim was to redress the balance away from an abstractionism that appeared more and more exclusionary of reality. A number of writers of extraordinary brilliance (such as Paul Goodman, Norman Brown, Herbert Marcuse, and Theodore Roszak) produced a body of works that attempted to demonstrate the ways in which World War II, the Cold War, and capitalist technocracy have gradually shrunk the broad richness of Western man's consciousness into a narrow rivulet of positivist, soul-debunking "enlighten-ment." Marcuse writes against an analytic mode of philosophic dis-course that aims "at a dimension of fact and meaning which elucidates the atomized phrases or words of ordinary discourse 'from without' by showing this 'without' as essential to the understanding of ordinary discourse." Attacking this mechanistic "objectivity," he describes how "the positivist cleaning of the mind brings the mind in line with the re-stricted experience" that it insists is the only real one.[8] Against this, he sets up a view of art sympathetic to Schiller's conception of play: "Art challenges the prevailing principle of reason: in representing the order of sensuousness, it invokes a tabooed logic—the logic of gratification as against that of repression. . . . As aesthetic value, the nonconceptual truth of the senses is sanctioned, and freedom from the reality principle is granted to the 'free play' of creative imagination."[9] In his assault on "The Myth of Objective Consciousness," Theodore Roszak writes: "To a mournfully great extent, the progress of expertise, especially as it seeks to mechanize culture, is a waging of open warfare upon joy. It is a bewilderingly perverse effort to demonstrate that nothing, *absolutely nothing* is particularly special, unique, or marvelous."[10]

These lessons, badly needed in their time, have been very well taught and very well learned, but they have been taken up by literary criticism at a time when they have already worn thin. Some critics would have us believe that *absolutely everything* is "particularly special, unique, or marvelous." Like all ideological movements, the subjectivist move-ment of the sixties has done its work; the pendulum has now swung back. But as some of the humanistic disciplines perversely continue to repudiate knowing in favor of being and abstraction in favor of concre-tion, they are putting themselves out of business. They are undercutting the medium of their very existence. If, in this realization, such critical practitioners were gracefully to bow out of the scene of the sciences of knowing, their valedictory would make good sense as the logical consequence of such a position, but no one appears to be bowing out. Rather, a type of "knowing" that is more and more concrete and ex-clusive, instead of abstract and exclusive, seems to be trying to have it both ways. While the kind of "knowing" advocated by Fish, Norman Holland, and others eschews abstraction while promoting more and more concrete readings that are, unlike knowledge, nontransferable (as technique) to other minds, this kind of "knowing" insists on maintaining the methodology of traditional philosophic discourse, a discourse that makes sense only if the validity of generalization and abstraction still holds good.

There is simply no point in writing an essay if you believe that essays, like texts in general, cannot be understood because they have no determinable meaning. After his lengthy and eloquent essay, Fish reveals that he knows this very well: "It follows then that we shouldn't try to analyze language at all," he observes, adding weakly, "The human mind, however, seems unable to resist the impulse to investigate its own processes." What is there to say to such an observation except, "By all means resist it, because you yourself have pulled out all of the props that might have justified such an analysis."

Having thus undermined the validity of abstraction, how is it possible for Fish to be a literary critic and what is it that he is doing when he examines the texts of seventeenth-century literature, his specialty?[11] Quite simply, he solves the theoretical problems that he poses in an eminently sensible and practical way: he ignores them. Writing traditional historical-interpretive critical essays about older literature, Fish keeps reminding us (lest we too easily forget) that he is showing us *what these works do* and not what they mean, but practically speaking this is a distinction without a difference. Where the old-fashioned critic would baldly tell us that such and such is what Bacon means here, Fish tells us that thus and thus is what the text is *doing to us* here. If what Bacon *does* is to make his readers doubt truisms, then, in ordinary language, we express this agency of the text by means of the expression, "the text says." Of course we realize that texts "speak" to us by means of conventions of reading and that in themselves texts are silent, like the proverbial tree falling in the forest: literary response requires a responding reader. But for a text to *do* things to us, we must have as substantial and determinate a vehicle as we need for a text to *mean* things to us. Fish has resolved no problems.

The case of Norman Holland is much more extreme: after abandoning the excruciating Freudian reductivism of *The Dynamics of Literary Response*, Holland entered a new and even more baroque cul-de-sac.

His variant of "literature in the reader" is "poems in persons." Taking up with several student readers Holland provides us with samples of their readings of poems. On the assumption that all readings are the products of an individual's personal "identity theme" or psychological hobbyhorse, Holland concludes:

> The reader reconstructs, as we have seen, part of his characteristic pattern of adaptive or defensive strategies from the work [from *what* work, if works don't exist except as "readings"?], and this recreation must be rather delicately and exactly made. Once he has done so, however, he can admit through the filter of his particular style some or all of the work [what work, please?], which then becomes the material from which he very freely creates the kind of fantasy that is important to him. . . . In no way can the idea of a poem as a fixed message from poet to reader explain the relationship between different readers' readings or between the poet's conception and any reader's. Interpretation is not decoding. Each reader constructs meaning as part of his own artistic experience." [12]

What sort of things does one student reader have to say to us about her reading? "I liked it very much, right away. Even without saying it out loud, I respond to the sounds, the movement of it. It's got a fairly soft and somewhat, I suppose you'd say, undulating movement. Even the shape of the lines falls into that wave-like pattern. The sound fits in well with what he's saying, which—I'm not exactly sure if I'm holding onto all the ideas, but I like right away the words that he's using and what he seems to be saying. [And she giggled a little]" (70–71).

Most readers, one may assume, would prefer to struggle with the original poem, which can hardly be less existent than this. Holland, however, unlike Fish, does not abandon his theory when it comes time to practice concrete reading. Instead, he allows his students to rattle on, exerting almost superhuman control of his exasperation at their inadequacies. When, in a moment of forgivable self-indulgence, Holland offers us his own self-effacing reading of a poem, reminding us that according to his theory it is no better than anyone else's, we feel almost as anguished as he. How far can a hobbyhorse carry one away?

In methodology like this, the Logos has been discredited while in its place is offered a plenitude of psychological detritus in which all data, like sparrows and hairs, must not only be noticed but must be cherished as well. Since they are not being noticed and cherished by an absent God, they must be noticed and cherished by a seemingly present Man. Formerly, value was derived from presentness in the consciousness of God. Can equally plausible value be derived from mere presentness in the consciousness of Man? Or is it true that when everything is something, nothing is anything? [13]

Reader-response criticism, like deconstruction, is an attempt to purify human experience of the contaminating categories of intellection, of knowledge itself. It is an attempt to restore or provide, in all its incommunicable fullness, the "pleasure of the text." Roland Barthes writes:

> Imagine someone . . . who abolishes within himself all barriers, all classes, all exclusions, not by syncretism but by simple discard of that old spectre: *logical contradiction;* who mixes every language, even those said to be incompatible; who silently accepts every charge of illogicality, of incongruity; who remains passive in the face of Socratic irony (leading the interlocutor to the supreme disgrace: *self-contradiction*) and legal terrorism (how much penal evidence is based on a psychology of consistency!). Such a man would be the mockery of our society: court, school, asylum, polite conversation would cast him out: who endures contradiction without shame? Now this anti-hero exists: he is the reader of the text at the moment he takes his pleasure. [14]

The next step after taking his pleasure (a playful erotic experience without intellection) is clear enough: our man of pleasure must become a reader-response critic and write it all down. "The text of pleasure," adds Barthes, "is a sanctioned Babel." But for whom is all of this Babel to be written? And what would be its purpose? If its aim is merely a solipsistic exercise in expression, the result is of interest only as a case study of the writer. If it is written as ancillary to the understanding of an irretrievable text, who—to return to my original question—can believe that any text is worthy of virtually unlimited elucidations? Especially a text that does not have a determinate or a determinable existence and an elucidation that sheds light only for (or on) its elucidator?

The next step, which is already clear because it has already been taken, is to forget about the original literary texts and to write about the critics of those texts instead, as we find in an essay by Cary Nelson entitled, innocently enough, "Reading Criticism." This essay does indeed provide a "case study" of a number of critics, most tellingly Susan Sontag, the springs of whose utterances have been ingeniously ferreted out, but do we really want a reading of Susan Sontag's "identity theme"? Is it possible that Nelson is impelled to tell us more than we care to know? We sigh with relief as Nelson informs us that "Criticism's dependence on literature can be put into question by the critic's own creative effort, but it can never be wholly eliminated." Nelson concludes:

> If we can forgo the collective professional illusion of objectivity and learn to be somewhat iconoclastic about what we write, the practice and evaluation of criticism will become unashamedly exciting. Both the reading and the writing of criticism will be energized by an inquiry into the dynamics of critical language. For the study of criticism is necessarily also the study of ourselves as critics, just as the study of literature is also the study of ourselves as readers. Those critics who can (or must) risk themselves in their writing not only give us a glimpse of their own inwardness, they also let us see ourselves from a new vantage point. Perhaps that self-reflexiveness, like the self-reflexiveness of this essay, can now be welcomed. I should not wish, at my conclusion, to make a pretense of the very specious objectivity I have questioned throughout. What I have learned about criticism I have learned by moving back and forth between the critics I read and the criticism I have written.[15]

Nelson's point of view is fully clarified in the preface to his own book of critical essays, *The Incarnate Word:* "The resulting book," he advises us, "is theoretical and committed to criticism as a form of literature. The language is metaphorically dense; it mediates between creative writing and exclusively rational discourse."[16] Nelson is by no means alone in treating criticism as if it were literature. Geoffrey Hartman has remarked: "But perhaps, as Lukács argued . . . the very structure of the critical essay is ironic in pretending to be a commentary or a critique of a work of art, rather than a work of art itself. . . . Most works of fiction may be greater than most works of criticism, but both criticism and fictions are institutions of the human mind, and one cannot foretell where the creative spirit may show itself."[17] This is modestly put but perhaps insufficiently so in view of the continental criticism that Hartman has in mind. At any rate, the stumbling block of indeterminability is no less an obstacle to critical than it is to fictional texts.

In "Fear and Trembling at Yale," a wry overview of the critical scene at the end of the seventies, Gerald Graff tried to sum things up:

> . . . it is possible that the true source of the malaise of current criticism is not so much epistemological or ontological as institutional, that it is a reflection of the confusion of the literature department. All the members of the Yale group write self-consciously as critics in an age of critical (and cultural) overproduction—an age in which so many "readings" have collected around even the slighter authors and works that we have begun to lose confidence in our ability to read. Yet even this is to misstate the problem, which is not that there is too much criticism, but that too little of it arises to meet a genuine demand, to answer questions that are really worth asking. . . .
>
> Perhaps we have not really lost our capacity to interpret literary texts with relative correctness, but have simply lost interest in this project. If so, it is not the metaphysical groundlessness of criticism that is at issue, but its pointlessness, at a moment when the humanities do not seem to know what they are trying to do.[18]

This "overproduction" at a "moment when the humanities do not seem to know what they are trying to do" brings us back to the central concern of this investigation. Literary study seems to be caught in a trap of its own setting: like the old puzzle of Achilles and the tortoise, which "logically" demonstrates that Achilles can never get ahead of the tortoise, although we know very well that in reality he will indeed win the race, contemporary criticism is charmed by a logic that shows us that bona fide acts of literary understanding cannot really take place because we can never engage the texts that might afford such an understanding. The school associated with Barthes and Derrida and the school associated with Holland, Bleich, and Fish have arrived at similar consequences via very different routes. The subjectivists (a.k.a. reader-response critics), following Freud, Nietzsche, and psychology, have taken the position that we are locked into our own limited consciousnesses and subliminal yearnings, which convert the raw materials of experience to suit our needs. Cognitions are already converted raw materials, and thus we can never engage anything but ourselves. The structuralists, poststructuralists, and deconstructionists are not so much concerned with our consciousness as with the malleable or indeterminate nature of the raw materials themselves. Thus, the Derridean position, supplanting Saussure's signifier-signified relationship with a signifier-signifier relationship, eliminates referents in a "real" world and replaces them with an endless regress of signifiers that never stand still for longer than a cognition, while the slippery nature of language makes "true" cognitions both a pragmatic and a logical impossibility.[19] In the subjectivist case, we cannot engage texts because we can barely (if at all) engage our own selves. In the Derridean case, we cannot engage the texts because they are literally not there: a cognition, like a single frame of movie film, provides an illusion of fixity, of frozen substance, but corresponds to nothing in the "real" world. With two such views, the engagement of texts is out of the question; instead, an Emersonian "truth for me" (now wildly out of control) requires a new literary critique for each reading of each reader. Yet, as philosophically impressive as these theoretical positions may be, they are not relevant in any *practical* way to the conduct of literary criticism. Reflecting as they do a main problem of philosophy that has been with us at least since Plato, they change nothing in that same real world in which they do not believe and that logically cannot be located by anybody. From Plato's claim that the mundane world is a deceptive echo of a stable world of ideas, to Kant's division of the world into noumena and phenomena whose interrelationship can never be known, there has been no discernible alteration in man's behavior in relation to that illusory "real" world. Today, we can and still do catch busses, produce offspring in accordance with a predictive schedule, and dependably satisfy our hunger by putting things of the right sort into our mouths as though neither Plato nor Kant ever existed. What could be gained by prefacing all of our transactions with "reality" with the talismanic remark, however lucid, "I know this is all pure imposture, pure illusion"? When everything is deception, nothing in particular deceives, and the superstitious casting of epistemological salt over our shoulders before making a practical assertion changes nothing. Soon, we forget the preambular "I know this is an illusion," and in the smugness of our pragmatism illusion again becomes a brilliant imitation of reality. As for the illusory literary texts, if we can engage Derrida and Holland adequately enough to learn that texts cannot be engaged (a feat that they seem to think we are capable of performing[20]), then we can just as adequately engage George Eliot and Wallace Stevens. The infinite regress that exists in literary theory, like the regress in the Achilles conundrum, is logically irrefutable but faultily oriented in relation to empirical reality. Experience teaches us that Achilles wins the race and that readers engage texts with functional comprehension.

Behind the unlimited proliferation of data that accompanies this regressive logic is the wistful desire to arrive at a lost infinity not through the discredited front door of "faith" but through a back door of sheer number. But even if the most advanced system of information storage and retrieval were able to encode every actual and possible thought, every "reading" of reality, the information bank would be a mere simulacrum of the actual world—a chaos of useless and meaningless data. For the Point that was once God was a Point of pure, flexible intelligence, pure knowing, out of which all possible existents could be generated. It was a compact universe, and its "image," the easily portable mind of man, was considered a limited version of that Point, a power of abstractions and universals by means of which a universe of concretions could be grasped and understood. But along with the disappearance of God has also disappeared the value of "knowing" as an abstract enterprise. As abstract intelligibility fades in value, mere registration of concrete multiplicity increases in value. We are surely at a stage where it is plain to see that no amount of plenitude can ever turn into infinity. Without a value-conferring principle, millions of data worthless in themselves add up to worthless conglomerates.[21] The cornucopia of seemingly endless riches generated by "absence" is a cornucopia of drafts on an insolvent bank. That bank cannot be made to reach solvency again merely by writing more and more bad checks in a more and more elaborate and rococo hand.

Criticism's recognition, through arrivals on different paths, that literary texts are part of the same world of illusion as tables and chairs seems to have become a theoretical obsession, but this preoccupation with the ontological status of texts obscures the real predicament in which literary studies find themselves. Their need is not so much for a foolproof ontology of texts as for the establishment of a new universe of discourse and values in which these studies can take place. Since the disappearance of God in the eighteenth century and the adoption of Coleridgean principles of aesthetic value, literary criticism has been coasting along on the doctrine of the transcendence of the imagination. As a metaphorical illumination of the impact of aesthetic activity, that doctrine is an excellent one. But as a philosophic guide for the apportionment and appropriation of our time in the world, a world far removed from that of Coleridge, it is by now highly inadequate. Before the romantic period, when God was still an assured presence, it was possible to see anything and everything as possessing transcendent (i.e., real, absolute) value. As God faded, it was still reasonably possible to see the artist and his works as in some sense transcendent. At present, in a period of "absence," with God beyond the horizon, the very notion of transcendence becomes suspect, if not unintelligible, except as metaphor. Without the assurance of "presence," it can no longer be believed that anything whatever possesses unlimited value, nor do literary texts constitute an exception.

For a subjectivist who consistently practices what he preaches, literary texts and literary criticisms can only be regarded as autoerotic devices, matter for self-play, and like all such aids, none can be expected to have very wide appeal, since *de gustibus non est disputandum.* But those deconstructive and reader-response critics with whose views we are familiar have already revealed that they do not care to practice what they have been preaching and that despite Plato and Kant, despite the absence of referents, and even despite logical contradiction (which Barthes certainly pretended not to mind), they can and will tell us what they mean anyhow. Thus, without transcendence, without presence, and without the nihilism of subjective and deconstructive criticism that might provide a rationale for unlimited private interpretations,[22] very practical questions remain: Though experience shows us that texts are readable, even without presence, what is their value? When particular works of literature are examined over and over again as a matter of unreflective course regardless of one's particular literary metaphysics, or when obscure and questionable works are newly examined, it becomes necessary to ask what macrocosmic values that could justify such attention are available in our own postreligious era? And if mere data and mere play and mere consciousness[23] are not a satisfactory or convincing replacement for God, what claims can be made for the critics themselves in their perpetuation of more responses to literary texts than anyone's metaphysics can possibly warrant?

2

• • • • • •

Literary Professionalism's
Pyrrhic Defense
of Poesy

For some time now the Anglo-American literary establishment has been discomfited by the doctrines of Derrida, Barthes, and their English-speaking disciples. The notoriously brilliant essay, "Structure, Sign, and Play in the Discourse of the Human Sciences,"[1] which Derrida presented at Johns Hopkins University in 1966, seems to have constituted the decisive moment in contemporary literary theory from which no certain recovery has yet been accomplished, even though a wide range of strategies for rescuing literature has been developed by theorists as diverse as Paul de Man, Murray Krieger, and Charles Altieri. Unlike Nietzsche, whose grand presence hovers over this essay but who repudiated nihilism in the interests of a liberating program of self-surpassing for the human race, Derrida has thrown a giant monkey wrench into the venerable machinery of Western thought, a machinery that he nevertheless continues to exploit and to kick, by fits. Like Kafka's country doctor, we cannot but feel abused. "Betrayed! Betrayed! A false alarm on the night bell once answered—it cannot be made good, not ever." The reverberations of this bell continue to sound.

"The absence of the transcendental signified extends the domain and interplay of signification *ad infinitum*." Derrida later develops this key notion from the 1966 essay into the general concept of "deferral" or (to use his coinage) "différance." In brief, every word or sign requires another word or sign to explain its meaning. Since we never arrive at a final or original word or sign that is self-explanatory (except for a few special cases that Derrida would find it inconvenient to acknowledge), meaning is deferred forever. If the meaning of individual words can never be arrived at, then whole works of literature, according to this way of thinking, can never be definitively understood. This conception, with its seemingly plausible logic, has had devastating effects on our entire literary world, as if someone had shown us that in theory it was impossible for human beings to walk, and when they find themselves walking, they explain it away as illusion. Derrida's supposed demolition of the realities of "naive" experience bears a striking resemblance to the paradoxes of Zeno, which sought to demonstrate such absurdities as that motion is impossible or that one runner can never overtake another. As described by Aristotle in his *Physics*, one of Zeno's more familiar paradoxes contends that "in a race the quickest runner can never overtake the slowest, since the pursuer must first reach the point whence the pursued started, so that the slower must always hold a lead." Similarly, "that before any distance can be traversed, half the distance must be traversed, that these half distances are infinite in number, and that it is impossible to traverse distances infinite in number." [2] Although Aristotle rejects these reasonings and shows they are faulty in relation to the realities of existence (a demonstration that hardly requires the powers of an Aristotle), many of the literary theorists who attempt to undo or mitigate the damage done by Derrida to the act of comprehending signs make so many concessions in his favor that they leave us with as many problems as we had before. Meanwhile, writers keep writing and readers reading, and the race is in fact to the swift. The heart of the problem would appear to be to determine who it is that is really hoaxing us: theorists, writers, or readers who are pretending to understand what they read. Like the pupil in Ionesco's *The Lesson* who is unable to perform simple multiplication but who has memorized all the products of all possible numerical combinations, millions of readers seem to have brought off a stunning feat of preestablished harmony with incomprehensible texts.

The devastating effects of literature's plight can be seen not only in the writings of J. Hillis Miller and Paul de Man, who have thoroughly immersed themselves in the destructive element, but in the theorizings of literature's defenders as well. Murray Krieger, for example, who has struggled repeatedly to present himself as a true amphibian capable of living in the divided and distinguished worlds of reason and faith, feels that he is forced to accept the negative theories in the abstract but that he can somehow overcome or outwit them in the actual concrete reading of literary works. As his defenses of readability become more and more nervous and overwrought, he tries to convince us, through a doctrine resembling transubstantiation, that despite the theoretical meaninglessness of texts according to Derrida, we believe in them nevertheless because of the "miraculous" ability of art to speak though dumb, to signify though insignificant. An even greater miracle, however, than Krieger's evangelist fervor will be necessary to convert the unbelieving. To Krieger one must say, Physician, heal thy own dissociation of sensibility.

Meanwhile, a more heroic and positive crusade has been carried on by Charles Altieri, who appears like a young Siegfried laying about him with the Nothung of his own panacea, speech-act theory. Altieri provides us with an instructive lesson in the perils that lie in wait for even literature's stoutest defenders.

Unlike de Man, Miller, and Krieger, who more or less accept Derrida's destructive doctrines and try to work with or around them, Altieri comes on, at least initially, as more tough-minded, ready to resist and fight back without making apologies for his continuing ability to take literature seriously. In a series of aggressive attempts to exorcise the shadow cast by Derrida upon literary studies, Altieri demonstrates the ways in which Derrida's universe of endless play has little bearing upon literature and criticism because it is a thought-universe rather than an action-universe, a universe that is *logically* plausible (like Zeno's) but not the same one in which we actually live and have our being. Seeing through the unreality of Derrida's extreme position, he remarks "how his sense of indeterminacy relies on an ideal model of determinate meaning which sounds suspiciously close to positivism. He makes determinate meaning depend on logical simples or unique referring names and then uses the inadequacy of that position to justify his own vision of intertextuality."[3] In this same essay, he writes: "We might describe Derrida's theory as deriving from a confusion between an impossible dream that most words can have an ontologically *propre sens* and the likely possibility that they have appropriate senses defined by semantic and pragmatic conventions in specific situations" (84). It is these conventions that make texts interpretable, not autonomous referents that exist independently in a "real" world apart from language. The function of a given literary text is that it serves "as a fixed script to guide performance and as objective evidence by which an audience can assess the qualities of a critical performance. . . . There remains the procedural test of convincing others that a particular way of performing the text articulates the fullest possibilities inherent in the words, situations, and formal patterns" (91).

Fusing together insights from Wittgenstein, speech-act theory, and phenomenology, and regarding words as social conventions agreed upon by groups of culturally interrelated people rather than as signs pointing to a world of primary substances, Altieri sees Derridean theory as destroying a "presence" that never existed and as positing an "absence" that has never posed a problem because it was all we ever had. In his essay on Wittgenstein, he writes:

> Wittgenstein simply accepts the fact so much lamented in Continental thought that we are twice removed from the Christian doctrine of an original Logos. There is no divine word grounding the free play of human words, and there is no way to discover any luminously present object anchoring words to the world. But the alternatives remaining are not just nostalgia and free play, because these themes depend on the absence of what we never had. Instead we can recognize the error so deeply embedded in traditional philosophy and try to restructure philosophy on the grounds of ungrounded but irreducible human actions.[4]

In still another essay, Altieri sees literature as occupying a middle ground between absolutely defined referentiality to an objective outside world and an endless freeplay of textual referentiality: "But a concept like middles allows us to propose another kind of knowledge [i.e., not of the world as fact], one that is less concerned with references to a world that can be tested as propositions or causal hypotheses than it is with dramatizing the ways men respond more or less adequately to specific situations. . . . The authority it appeals to is essentially historical and intersubjective and the relevant norms are those men use to judge one another's behavior rather than one another's propositions, norms of sensitivity, awareness, sympathy, and depth of comprehension."[5]

Using speech-act theory, with hints derived from theorists like Richard Ohmann and Stanley Fish in their developments of Austin and Searle, Altieri attempts to found literary understanding on historically determined conventions of speech as intuitively understood by members of the same cultures. People in each culture and period, he claims, know what speakers of their own language mean even if these meanings do not have reference to an objective reality existing apart from these speakers. Of course, Altieri seems not to realize that the problem remains of how it is possible to understand any word or norms at all, since reference to a shared subjectivity is still, after all, reference, and an understanding, no matter how "intuitive," of "what people mean" when they use given words still leaves unsolved the fact that "what people mean" must be "objective" in order for anyone to understand it. Despite his failure to see that things are still pretty much in the condition supposed by Derrida, Altieri goes on to delimit the areas in which language can validly hope to operate. For him, those areas appear to be the connaturality and sociality of human beings which enable them to intuit a widely shared subjective world of experience. If, according to this view, works of literature are not engaged in making true statements about an objective world but, rather, in exploiting the feelings and values upon which human society is based, then literature can be considered to be both expressive and mimetic at the same time, expressing and representing shared "natural" and social affects.[6]

In attempting to implement such a perspective, Altieri gives his fullest and most concrete account of the required methodology in a later essay, "Presence and Reference in a Literary Text." As he brings together most of the concepts presented in his earlier essays, he reiterates the function of language as action rather than as reference: "Language is not primarily a set of pictures ideally mirroring a world but a possession and an instrument for accomplishing certain tasks. . . .

If words do not copy but produce meanings, then they can be used significantly to focus our attention on the activities of the artist and his
constructed characters as they engage in that process of production." [7]
The vehicle for Altieri's demonstration of literature as act is William
Carlos Williams's poem, "This Is Just to Say," a poem that Altieri uses
to illustrate what he takes to be Williams's own poetics, and which, he
claims, "expresses a logic similar to the one that led Wittgenstein to
develop the definition of meaning as use on which speech-act theory
is founded" (505). The essence of this logic is that "as we learn a language, we develop a grammatical capacity to appreciate utterances as
ways of acting in situations" (505). In examining Williams's poem,
Altieri further attempts to clarify his notion of actions, feelings, qualities, and values as a "middle realm" between the discredited representational function of language and the infinite play of signifiers, a realm
between absolute meaningfulness and utter meaninglessness, two un-
palatable alternatives. Here, unfortunately, a stage is finally reached in
this ongoing philosophical debate at which the act of defense against
the destructiveness of Derridean nihilism threatens to put David into
a camp as repugnant to good sense as that of Goliath. With lyre strings
now overstrained and snapping, the demands being made upon writer,
text, and reader become so overwhelming, the weight that is placed
on language as act becomes so burdensome, that philosophical victory
becomes almost as painful as defeat. In the immortal words of Pogo,
"We have met the enemy and they are us."

Altieri's aim has appeared to be to rescue literary study from the
trivializing doctrine of "infinite play," and whatever measure of success
he achieves in his earlier essays comes about from his ability to underscore the weakness of Derrida's view of language. But as he shifts the
ground upon which literary study is to be seen and judged from speech
as representation to speech as act, something goes profoundly wrong
and a Vietnamization of the humanities begins to take place. The results provide the demoralizing example of how even the kind of critic
who cares about literature-in-the-world can seriously damage the very
thing he has set out to rescue from predatory theorists.

To begin with, Altieri's vehicle—Williams's "This Is Just to Say"—
consists of only two or three sentences (depending on how you read

it) and not very many words, a poem that he himself characterizes as "frail."

> *This Is Just to Say*
>
> I have eaten
> the plums
> that were in
> the icebox
>
> and which
> you were probably
> saving
> for breakfast
>
> Forgive me
> they were delicious
> so sweet
> and so cold

This poem approximates closely the sort of note that one member of a household might fasten to a refrigerator door for the attention of another, perhaps a note from a husband to a wife. Except for the last stanza, which is close to but not quite exactly like the prose of a routine domestic message, the poem could pass for a prosaic note by a person with no special aesthetic interests or intentions. But I do not want to raise the question of whether these words constitute a genuine poem, for I am willing for present purposes to accept the view of theorists like John Ellis and Morse Peckham that literature has no essence and is merely whatever is regarded as literature by the community that has to do with it. Thus, "This Is Just to Say" is to be considered here as a poem.

Alarms begin to sound, however, when Altieri goes on to produce about ten pages of commentary, analysis, and hypothesis about the significance of this frail little piece. Seeing Williams as a poet whose language is not representational (though those plums seem about as representational as you can get) and who, therefore, does not use language to refer to a world "out there," Altieri claims that this poem "asks to be considered primarily as an action and thus invites its readers to attend to the qualities of honesty and concern" that its speaker exhibits.

The words of the poem "may not replace objects or control nature, but they can testify to a realm of potential understandings men have constructed which compensates . . . for their lack of power" (501). If the poem is not to be taken as a report upon reality but as a "purposive act," then we can attempt to understand it "by testing its place in a situation, not by reducing it back into its constitutive formal elements" (504). The "literary actions" that the poem presents "can be described as synthetic images which connect to experience as possible predicates or ways of picturing experiences but do not themselves denote specific states of affairs. These actions refer not to a world but to a grammar for describing actions in the world" (509). Two extended passages from this essay will serve to convey the density and weight of discourse that Altieri seems to feel are required to deal adequately with this little poem, in order to rescue it—and presumably all of literature—from the currently fashionable charge that literature (and language itself) "refers" to a world that has no real existence:

> We must integrate at least three possible meanings of "just to say": "just" is a moral term; a term involving considerations of accuracy; and a term calling attention to the casual, momentary, and minimal properties of the statement. Moreover, the deictic "this" refers to the poem itself as well as to the speaker's note and thus reminds us that we are dealing with two speech acts—one by a character in the poem which is to be assessed dramatically, and one by an implicit poet which invites us to draw parallels between the dramatic situation and general aesthetic considerations. And finally, the content and structure of the dramatic utterance suggest that both these acts are to be understood in relation to the axes of presence and absence, origins and supplementary linguistic structures, and nature and culture—all of which inform the critical issues we have been discussing. (499–500)

> The speaker does not ask for forgiveness because he was especially hungry or because he promises to control his desires better in the future. The justification offered is instead an evocatory memory of the plums' sensuous appeal, an appeal that makes it clear similar transgressions will occur in the future and that threatens to overpower the poem's sense of human relationships. But a profound sense of humanity ultimately prevails precisely because the speaker does not indulge in abstract humanistic plati-

tudes but instead concentrates on his specific situation. The justness of the speaker's note is its recognition of his weakness and its lovely combination of self-understanding with an implicit faith in his wife's capacity to understand and accept his deed and, beyond that, to comprehend his human existence as a balance of weakness, self-knowledge, and concern. (501)

If Williams's poetry happens to lend itself so conveniently to a defense of language as act, a defense that is somewhat fuzzy at best and that at worst tends to support the view of Stanley Fish and Norman Holland that each reader writes his own poem, one wonders what is now supposed to be done with all remaining works of literature, which may actually be so deluded as to think they are dealing with a "real" world instead of with "acts." Will a new machine be set up in the criticism industry to reprocess all existing literature in order to reveal that, contrary to our most naive presuppositions, none of it was ever intended to refer to a world "out there" and that—*mirabile!*—poets were "always already" aware that what they had been trafficking in all along were verbal "acts"? Despite his quarrel with the deconstructionists, even a critic as hostile to Derrida and his followers as Altieri has not only internalized their language but has come to see "reality" in their terms: " 'This Is Just to Say' takes as its theme an appropriately minimal, secular version of the loss of origins Milton dramatized. It literally enacts the process of replacing absent objects with words. [Is there another sort of poetry that carries its objects around for direct presentation?] And like Milton's poem, it does not stop with the metaphysics of loss and the attendant themes of ironic supplementarity but asks the reader to reflect on the qualities of mutual understanding that can be constructed from the speech acts in which we compensate for our fallen condition" (499). Revealing to us—with "origins," "absent objects," "metaphysics of loss" and "ironic supplementarity"—that he is as caught up in the deconstructionist lingo as his enemies, Altieri merely goes on to set their "fallen" world slightly askew, by viewing it in terms of "speech acts" instead of "free play," while crushing us nonetheless with the ponderous machinery of his rescue operations. But to vary the Pogo theme, with friends like this, who needs enemies? Our "fallen state" has been improved at least to this extent: we are now being offered a choice of vehicles for the further descent. If such suffocating methodologies are now required to enable us to read literature without remorse, perhaps the time has come to turn away from these guilty pleasures and look elsewhere for highbrow frolics. For Altieri's ten pages of commentary on Williams's poem would serve as a marvelous demonstration of the position, did Altieri wish to embrace it, that language does indeed consist of an infinite play of signifiers from which anything may be adduced if you can come up with a snappy new code. Admittedly, with a poem so brief and insubstantial one could probably get away with making any claims whatever, since there is so little evidence either for or against any specific interpretation. Such claims, including the sheer totality of those that he actually does make, serve only to undermine the very thesis of determinability that Altieri seems otherwise eager to establish.[8] For who could be expected to arrive at such quirky elaborations without carrying Altieri around as a guide? With our continuing ability to read literature seriously now being made to depend on such a tenuous metaphysic, and with a new corps of literary critics undoubtedly sharpening their mills in preparation for the imminent regrinding of all still-readable literature into "acts," we find ourselves in danger of being treated to a cure that looks to be worse than the disease, as the casuists of a New Scholasticism attempt to decontaminate our vulgar contact with the world.

What is deeply troubling about these grandiose claims for Williams's minor achievement, like similar critical excesses that depend on other reconstitutions of reality, is that they bear so striking a resemblance to the sweeping claims that characterize most inward-looking professionalisms of the present age, against which literature is still being offered nonetheless as an antidote. From the self-perpetuations of the directors of the arms race to the soothing assurances of the custodians of nuclear energy, from the self-involvements of industrial corporations to the parochialisms of lawyers and psychoanalysts, we see the only too familiar aggrandizements of contemporary professionalism. It is far from being the case, however, that when experienced from the inside these professional points of view are implausible or even illogical. On the contrary, their internal logic is often madly impeccable.

The problem, rather, is that for each profession its own limited interests appear to be coextensive with all of life itself. The inner constraints of each professional point of view create a macrocosm that is little more than a projection of a limited and partial microcosm.[9] As the claims become more and more exorbitant, the grounds of credibility for an outside become slimmer and slimmer. In the case of the humanities, at a time when their foundations have been shaken by a society that sometimes supports them but is just as disposed to deserting them, a crisis of believability like the one generated by deconstruction can only be intensified by exaggerated claims, whether by speech-act theorists, deconstructionists, Marxists, reader-response devotees, or anyone else slouching toward Bethlehem. If a particular sort of professionalism can suggest that so much of our being ought to be consecrated to the act of responding to such a modest production as "This Is Just to Say," how much of our being does it suppose should be devoted to richer, more complex, and more rewarding works—not to mention life's myriad other activities? Can a reader really be found, outside the delusions fostered by an inbred professionalism, who is prepared to spend world enough and time to satisfy the professional critics for whom no amount can ever be enough because professionalism by its very nature is insatiable?

A question even more urgent than this is why any reader should be expected to do so. We cannot merely assume that intellectual and aesthetic activities are so privileged as not to require some justification, or so self-validating as to escape the general requirements of all activities in the world that they be seen against a larger background of macrocosmic plausibility, against a rationale of deeper philosophic reflection. When the poets and dramatists of the English Renaissance repeatedly satirized scholastic philosophy, more than an inherited contempt for the Church of Rome was involved: their scorn of "quiddities" was an expression of their sense of the disproportion between a particular kind of act and the larger context of human life. Yet we can perhaps excuse the Schoolmen for what might appear as trivialization when we realize that although they really did not have world enough and time for such activities, they had—or thought they had—all of eternity before them. Those arid explorations of questions that mean little to us today could be seen to function as paving stones in the road to immortality. We, on the other hand, with our increased life expectancies, would on the face of it appear to have world enough and time for a leisurely exploration of "This Is Just to Say," but for the fact that everything has been utterly changed as a result of our loss of eternity. With eternity no longer available for our full self-realization or even as a basis for the validation of our choices, the temporality of our acts seems all the more pressing, all the more in need of constantly being reweighed in the balance—because our acts in time no longer shine resplendent in the glow of a reflected immortality. With the scale now obsolete upon which human preoccupations were judged for so many centuries, there has been a new pressure and urgency directing human choices since the romantic period, in art as well as in life. This pressure, however, is far from generally operative in the academic-humanistic enterprise. Despite the currently overblown reputation of Heidegger in philosophic and literary circles, the study of literature has yet to be seen in the context of its relation to the "Nothing" or in relation to our "Being toward Death." Rather, despite its exploitation of heavy philosophic paraphernalia, contemporary professionalism in the humanities diddles along, oblivious (or seeming so) of the revaluation of *everything* that is required by the loss of God. When inflated claims upon our time and attention are made for any slight artifact, despite the professed aim of rescuing literary studies, not much skepticism is required to draw back in the face of such parochialism and professionalism. For appearances to the contrary not withstanding, the signals from the outside world and from the inside world of our own consciousness—however willfully repressed—seem to be saying that if the Holy Ghost does indeed *not* brood over our bent world with, ah, bright wings, then all is deeply changed for us. Despite the comfortable and uplifting clichés of literary professionalism and its attendant business-as-usual that pays the mortgage by sheathing Ockham's razor, it is no longer self-evident that grandiose and ultimately religious claims upon our finitude can simply continue to be made without challenge or without a new theology to support them.

A description like Altieri's of the requirements that he sees being made upon us by Williams's poem must appear as bizarre as anything

to be found in scholasticism *or* deconstruction. Thus, the problems generated by Derrida have not been made to go away: the trivialization of
literature resulting from deconstruction has reappeared instead from
a different hole in the dike. Since Altieri's excess of meaning is functionally indistinguishable from Derrida's defect of meaning, inflated
claims for literature can end up undermining the whole precarious edifice of literary study as much as the onslaughts of French theorists.
Perhaps these overstated defensive strategies will cause us to question,
as well we ought, the very role that we suppose literary study to be
playing in the context of our total being in time, a being that nowadays
takes place against a background not of eternity but of the Nothing.

3

Public Worlds/Private Muses:

Criticism, Professionalism, and the

Audience for the Arts

When scholars venture to write about subjects that lie outside their own particular areas of specialization, there is often a good deal of nervous sputtering and hostility on the part of specialists in the field that has been invaded. Although some justification for this response can be made in the case of sciences whose demands may even exceed the capacity of scholars in nearby fields, the situation is rather different in the humanities, whose Renaissance motto was: "I'm a man [read "person"]; nothing human is foreign to me." The problem of empire-guarding becomes particularly acute when the arts are involved, because a bundle of perennially abrasive and unanswered questions will invariably arise. For example: Who constitutes the authentic audience for any given art? For whom do poets and novelists write and painters paint? Do works of art display intrinsic qualities such as beauty, truth, or genius, which can bestow permanent value upon them through the ages, a value that is merely waiting to be discovered by anyone with eyes to see? Or is all value adventitious, supplied by cultures and sub-cultures? Anyone who has come upon works of literature or music that created a frenzy in their own time but that are now boring, laughable, or entirely forgotten is forced to think twice not only about the validity of an era's response but about the very nature of "genius" itself.

The dilemma of aesthetic valuation is especially vexing in the case of avant-garde artifacts. Because the range of estimations can run from "garbage" to "transcendent," not only is an audience likely to be baffled but it will also want to know whether underlying any given artwork are real, substantive qualities that are simply *there*. This dilemma becomes even greater in the light of the traditional understanding of "qualities" as nonsubstantive aspects of perception. Are the much-praised qualities of "great" works of art mere phantasms? Or are they purely "political," in the broadest sense, depending, say, on whether you are a feminist or a fascist, a sculptor or a concert impresario? It is easy to sympathize with one of the current hardline positions, namely, that beauty and value are socially determined and that appreciating works of art really means learning to conform one's perceptions and valuations to the models offered by whoever happen to be today's *arbitri elegantiarum*. In literary circles, this position has been strongly taken by Stanley Fish, with his "interpretive communities," and by Frank Kermode, with his Foucault-based notion of "institutional control of interpretation."

A luminary, if unwitting, demonstration of these problems can be seen in the form of an essay that appeared in the *Public Interest* entitled "The Malignant Object: Thoughts on Public Sculpture," by Douglas Stalker and Clark Glymour.[1] It is important to record that Mr. Stalker is a professor of philosophy at the University of Delaware and Mr. Glymour is a professor in the Department of History and Philosophy of Science at the University of Pittsburgh. In venturing to tread amidst the alien corn of public art while neglecting to express even a shred of reverence for the traditional guardians of this field, they have raised more global questions than they ever could have intended about the nature and function of criticism—as well as the role of the arts in society.

Stalker and Glymour begin their argument by pointing out that millions of dollars of public money are spent to put avant-garde sculptures in public spaces even though these sculptures may have nothing to do with their site and no relation to the tastes or lives of the people who will have to live with them every day. They are aware of the common justification that public art is "good for" people but they are made uneasy by the fact that such justification is moral rather than aesthetic. "*Our* view [my italics] is that much public sculpture, and public art generally as it is created nowadays in the United States, provides at best trivial benefits to the public, but does provide substantial and identifiable harm" (4). One of the chief of these harms is the forcing of distasteful objects upon a public that is usually powerless to resist them. The authors feel that this reaction of distaste produces a situation akin to the public presence of pornography, which "intrudes repeatedly into people's normal living routines" (5). Although the authors do not wish to denigrate contemporary art, they do want to censure "certain accounts of the value of that art, specifically those which find in the works of various artists or schools of artists, vital lessons which the public desperately needs to learn" (5).

In the course of their account, they refer to a number of notorious specimens of public sculpture that have been derided—and even vandalized—by an outraged public. One example that can here serve for their many others is alluded to in a letter that appeared in the *Chicago Sun-Times:* "Please tell me how to complain about those unsightly canvas rags that have been wrapped around the pillars of the John C. Luzinski Federal Building. Those rags are a disgrace. While you're at it, what's all that scrap metal doing strewn around? Many blind people go in and out of the building, and it's a wonder no one trips over this garbage." (6) Even though a sizable percentage of the public have been convinced that art is a good thing, Stalker and Glymour feel that few actual avant-garde pieces are enjoyed by the public into whose living spaces they have been so rudely forced. The authors are dispirited by the predictable pattern they see: "Received with joy by a small coterie of aesthetes and with indignation by a sizable element of the community, the sculpture soon becomes an indifferent object, noticed chiefly by visitors. . . . In time the aesthetes move on, no longer interested in a piece that is derrière-garde. But the public must remain" (7).

Since the authors believe that aesthetic value is the only justification for government placement of public sculptures, and since their implicit definition of aesthetic value is quite broad, broad enough to include the pleasure derived from commemoration of historic events through public statuary, they regard as ludicrous many of the justifications that are actually offered by artists, critics, and experts. For example, they quote from an article in *Newsweek* that attempts to extol the virtues of Oldenburg's Chicago "Batcolumn": "Oldenburg's silly subjects state a truth often overlooked: inside those self-important glass boxes [i.e., office buildings], people are really thinking hard about such things as baseball bats or clothes-pins." Their comment is wry: "We have no evidence that this is not the very thought that occurs to people when they see Oldenburg's column—but we doubt it." They conclude that it is "too painful, to examine the range of pretentious, vapid claims made by professional art critics for the intellectual content of contemporary sculpture" (9).

After displaying a host of photographs of avant-garde sculptures, as well as excerpts from both hostile laymen and "superior" experts, Stalker and Glymour move on to their conclusions: iconoclastic and avant-garde works of art fail to "realize and celebrate and exemplify a common tradition and shared political, cultural, and aesthetic heritage. That is what public sculpture is expected to do" (17). They object to special pleadings on behalf of the art community, since public works of art must be endured *by the public.* In fact, they regard the art community as simply another interest group that sells its commodities like any other business. "That industry has captured a piece of the public purse, quite as surely as have the tobacco farmers and dairymen, and thereby has obtained a substantial and diverse subsidy" (20).

Although the authors remark in an addendum that "if the truth be known, one of us actually admires many of the pieces we have discussed (35)," they press to an unexpected coda: "Artists, critics, and art administrators may find this argument to be simply an endorsement of philistinism, but that is a grievous confusion. Philistines are people too, and, whether or not one shares their tastes, the moral point of view requires that their interests be considered" (20).

In the pages following this essay, the *Public Interest* arranged for a number of representative spokesmen from the art world to provide a response. It is hardly worth remarking that most of the response is hostile and that Stalker and Glymour are treated as unregenerable philistines.

Wolf Von Eckardt, architecture and design critic at *Time,* objects that "such intolerant and ignorant generalizations will only widen the unfortunate gap in our society between elitist culture and popular culture, between artists and 'the people.' Besides, intolerant and ignorant catering to the baser, iconoclastic instincts of the common man can only lead to censorship and bad art, such as *völkische Kunst* and socialist realism" (22). He then asks the authors if they would "like to have their classrooms closed because some people did not like or did not understand the philosophy they teach? Art, like philosophy, cannot be judged by a popularity contest. . . . No democracy can function without its experts." Eckardt concedes the possibility that "the shock of the new is getting old, and that the eternal avant-garde is lost in its abstractions," (23) but he finds Stalker and Glymour nonetheless wrong-headed: "Nor can we ask our art selection panels to give us an art that is different from the best our time and its artists produce. We must cure the measles (if indeed we have them) rather than scratch the rash. Stalker and Glymour do not even want to scratch. They do not want *any* (their emphasis) modern sculpture. They want 'swings and slides and trees.' They want to declare the artistic and intellectual bankruptcy of America. That is worse than Know Nothingism. That is a cop-out." (24)

Though three out of the four responses to Stalker and Glymour are attacks, their opponents agree with their major premises, even while appearing to disagree. John Beardsley, for instance, curator of the Corcoran Gallery in Washington, D.C., finds it merely amusing that the authors compare public sculpture to pornography, but his de facto position is not very different from theirs. "We lack universally accepted standards of merit. In a society as pluralistic as ours, this seems inevitable. We have a population that is simply too heterogeneous, too disparate in its moral and social values, and too various in its levels of aesthetic sophistication ever to agree on standards of aesthetic quality" (25).

The final negative respondent, Edward Levine, a professor at the Minneapolis College of Art and Design, takes a similar approach: "In *The Malignant Object* we find a rather casually researched attack, ostensibly against some forms of public sculpture, but tacitly against 'modern art.' It does not seem productive to engage in a refutation of the view set forth in the article. The problems with the article are partly due to ignorance of the discipline" (31). His central argument is that "the freedom for which the artistic activity stands is in tension with the more conservative activities a society must take to protect itself and preserve its stability" (33).

The polarities exhibited in this debate can also be seen almost daily in newspapers, magazines, and highbrow quarterlies. On December 6, 1982, for example, the op-ed page of the *Chicago Tribune* ran an article by Morris Freedman, an English professor at the University of Maryland, entitled "Appreciating Innovative Art." It began: "A large park sculpture in our nation's capitol, not intended to represent anything (but looking startlingly like a tornado funnel in motion), provoked angry letters to the press. One writer wanted to know whether he too could dump his garbage in public." The burden of Freedman's essay is worth quoting:

> Our schools, I submit, ill prepare us to make sober appraisals of experimental sculpture, painting, literature, or architecture in the context of history and on the basis of informed judgment. We have been drilled to express only the most elementary responses. We expect works of art to represent recognizable, dignified places, persons, objects, or events. We immediately understand a general astride a bronze horse but we do not know how to understand parts of a car welded together nonfunctionally.
>
> In short, we have not been encouraged to respond to works in themselves. We immediately compare them with the familiar. . . .
>
> But when a sculptor puts together metal or granite to form an unfamiliar construction, we do not know how to respond to its originality. We are not quite sure even how to take a gigantic public clothes-pin in stainless steel even though we have known hand-sized ones in wood.

Freedman's position seems to be that by means of some instinctual (but unidentified) faculty, we *should* know how to respond to a gigantic public clothes-pin or welded car parts. One can only surmise that had we been "encouraged to respond to works of art in themselves," our clothes-pin-appreciating faculty might have been strong enough to intercept the aesthetic torpor that blunts our responses to what is innovative.

A similar position, but enunciated at a higher temperature, appeared in an article by Samuel Lipman in the inaugural issue of the *New Criterion*. Writing with considerable indignation about a performance of Roger Sessions's opera *Montezuma*, Lipman observes:

> As with the performance of *Four Saints*, a comment on the audience is in order. I attended the last of the opera's three performances, and the Juilliard Theater was full of highly esteemed and decorative characters from the worlds of opera presentation and music publishing. From this audience—at least from the musically trained part of it—one might have expected some comprehension of what Sessions had attempted. Instead, a palpable air of hostility and irritation pervaded the house. Numerous snide comments about the music circulated in the corridors during the intermissions; almost universally the detractors lamented the absence of a richly melodic music. As they described what they wanted, I realized that in fact their heart's desire had already been realized. What they evidently wanted was Puccini. It is to this pass that musical sophistication—even among professionals—now appears to have come.[2]

On the other side, representing a view closer to Stalker's and Glymour's, Joseph Epstein, in a characteristically droll essay, "The Literary Life Today" (from the same issue of the *New Criterion*), complains about the professionalizing and academicizing of the literary arts: "One of the new phenomena in the literary culture of our day is what I think of as the English Department Novel. Written by such writers as Jonathan Baumbach and Ronald Sukenik, and at its higher reaches by John Barth, this is the kind of novel that no one outside an English department would for a moment consider reading."[3] Epstein certainly does not believe that there is some instinctive faculty that would enable us to understand and enjoy these works, if only we would make use of it.

The most celebrated attempts to embarrass avant-gardism are to be found in the writings of Tom Wolfe, who has waged a continuing battle against trendiness in both art and architecture. In *The Painted Word*, his theme is that the art world is controlled by "the antibourgeois singalong of bohemia," which expresses only scorn for the public, if not for their money. The public, he tells us, is never invited, and the prevailing attitude is "épater le bourgeois." After describing some typical cult responses to Abstract Expressionism, he adds: "A man from Mars or

Chester, Pa., incidentally, would have looked at a Morris Louis painting and seen rows of rather watery-looking stripes." As for the avant-
garde's exploitation of the public: "First you do everything possible to
make sure your world is antibourgeois, that it defies bourgeois taste,
that it mystifies the mob, the public, that it outdistances the insen-
sible middle-class multitudes by light years of subtlety and intellect—
and then, having succeeded admirably, you ask with a sense of See-
what-I-mean? outrage: look, they don't even buy our products!"[4] In
From Bauhaus to Our House, Wolfe attacks the worker-housing style
of post–World War II office buildings and the Bauhaus ideology that
produced it. "The client no longer counted for anything except the
funding. If he were cooperative, not too much of a boor, it was acceptable to let him benefit from your new vision." His description of
the application of this style to the notorious Pruitt-Igoe public-housing
blocks in St. Louis—designed by Minoru Yamasaki in the manner of
Le Corbusier—and the slum life they engendered is devastating:

> Respectable folk pulled out, even if it meant living in cracks in the
> sidewalks. Millions of dollars and scores of commission meetings and
> task-force projects were expended in a last-ditch attempt to make Pruitt-
> Igoe hospitable. In 1971, the final task force called a general meeting of
> everyone still living in the project. They asked the residents for their sug-
> gestions. It was a historic moment for two reasons. One, for the first time
> in the fifty year history of worker housing, someone had finally asked the
> client for his two cents' worth. Two, the chant. The chant began immedi-
> ately: "Blow it . . . *up!* Blow it . . . *up!* Blow it . . . *up!* Blow it . . . *up!* Blow
> it . . . *up!*" The next day the task force thought it over. The poor buggers
> were right. It was the only solution. In July of 1972, the city blew up three
> central blocks of Pruitt-Igoe with dynamite.[5]

Although the war between the avant-garde and the traditionalists
rages eternal, there is, however, an element in the Stalker-Glymour
encounter with their critics that is not usually to be found in these skir-
mishes. This time, the people who are in the slot normally reserved
for the philistines happen to be accomplished scholars whose fields
are centrally situated in the humanities. Yet there is something particularly grating to their critics in their rather "ordinary" language as

well as the "ordinary" perspective from which they see the issues. This
ordinariness comes about because they are speaking as extremely well-
educated laymen rather than as the academic specialists they otherwise
are. No one would mistake their essay as an instance of fine-arts writing, for their prose has none of the numinosity we have come to expect
from critics in that line. Though their plain speaking may invite the
charge of Knownothingism—and indeed has actually received it—it
remains highly implausible that professors Stalker and Glymour can
simply be dismissed as philistines. In fact, it would be more appropriate
to describe them as an ideal general audience for the arts. Their disqualifying limitation—according to their opponents—is that they are
not themselves professionals in the arts, but that objection is the very
issue being held up here for scrutiny: is membership in the professional
brotherhood of artists and critics a sine qua non of authenticity in the
audience for the arts?

By throwing a few monkey wrenches into a traditional machinery
that, in any case, has not been running so well, Stalker and Glymour
have caused some minor glitches and have been accused of Luddit-
ism, but the machinery continues to run, more or less, even while the
gears are clashing. The problems have been well described in another
context by Derral Cheatwood as "the paradox of the artist in a public
world." In "Models of Accountability and Modern Art"[6] Cheatwood
charts the evolution of the artist from an anonymous producer of com-
missioned artifacts to the tortured, romantic loner whose self achieves
preeminence over its products. "As art was released from servitude to
systems other than itself . . . it was the producer of art and the process
of production that became primary. It was only through this change
that art became, in a very real sense, a system generating its own internal values" (73). He then traces the curious conflicts that have resulted
when the private "vision" of the artist confronts the public world of
grants, endowments, corporate and government use of artworks, critical evaluations—in a word, when it encounters the universe of discourse (and action) that forms the subject of Stalker's and Glymour's
essay. Cheatwood quotes Frank Lloyd Wright's telling description of
the common man as "the enemy of culture. Culture is made for him—
but in spite of him" (75). Later, speaking for himself, he concludes,

"The product of art has become the artist, moving increasingly away from the physical productions and products which have traditionally provided objects of accountability to the persons or organizations that sponsored them. This divergence of directions [between sponsors and artists] . . . becomes more critical and more pronounced as public involvement in art increases." His final solution is that "there is no solution to this paradox, no pleasant resolution to the confrontation of the public world with the private muse" (82).

Here, in the concept of public world versus private muse, a perennial crux in the discourse of criticism is cast into bold relief. By now, the issues arising from conflicts between philistines and esthetes are only too familiar, more suited to Gilbert and Sullivan than to philosophic scrutiny. What erupts, however, from the Stalker-Glymour contretemps with their respondents is something different: a vivid awareness that the "public world" of this duality may consist not just of an undifferentiated mass of ignoramuses but may very well include almost everyone who is not the artist himself or a representative of one of the professions that feed on the arts.

The fact that three out of four of the essay's respondents assume that they can simply wave the authors out of existence by dismissing them as "philistines" reveals that professional clichés can serve in place of examined principles even for elite and presumably self-conscious professions. Since Stalker and Glymour do not wither up and vanish after these imprecations, we still would like to know who constitutes the authentic audience for the arts. In the atypical instance of public sculpture, the man in the street is indeed a principal, but most of the time the arts do not have such an audience in mind. For a George Eliot, a Eugène Ionesco, a Wallace Stevens, the intended reader is "educated" and delimited in some way. Even for Beethoven, despite television's inept presentations, the audience is not a mass one. When avant-garde works enter the scene, the audience shrinks even further: the only composers residing in university music departments who address an audience other than their peers are those who have recently defected from serialism and begun to produce neo-romantic and neo-impressionistic works. Thus, Joseph Epstein's remark about the "English Department Novel" has some bearing upon audiences for the other arts as well.

If, however, we keep disqualifying more and more constituencies as inauthentic, until we finally dismiss the audience consisting of people like Professors Stalker and Glymour, there will be almost nobody left besides the experts. What this suggests is that once we believe an audience to have some sort of literary or musical competence, they must be part of the bona fide arbiters of taste who establish value. That they are sometimes "wrong" does not get us very far, unless we happen to believe that works of art must be seen and responded to in only one particular way and that they sit—already prized by God—quietly awaiting discovery by the "really" perceptive people. But the "really" perceptive people whom we keep hearing about ex post facto can never be identified a priori: they are, culturally speaking, a tautology. They become "perceptive" only retrospectively because they happen to agree later on with a socially determined valuation.

The abrasive problem raised by "The Malignant Object" controversy, then, is that dismissing the man in the street and dismissing "competent" readers, listeners, and viewers are not similar acts of judgment. Of course, if "competence" is defined as the ability to esteem a particular school, then another set of problems is created by another tautology. If "competence" could be defined so narrowly and cliquishly, the chasm between the private muse and the public world would be virtually unbridgeable and, again, there would be almost no audience besides "the experts." In reality, of course, this is hardly the case.

Avant-garde art provides a particularly embarrassing test for aesthetic judgments. If the value of art is socially determined, the question of its quality cannot be definitively answered, even by "experts." Despite the devotion of professional admirers of Schönberg, Webern, and Berg, for example, only a very small quantity of music by these serialists has entered the operating repertory, and those works tend to be atypical of their composers. It will be interesting to see for how much longer academic critics will champion these composers as part of the real canon. Already, a number of nonacademic critics have given up on them, even as some academic composers have transmogrified themselves into neotraditionalists. One of these, the composer George Rochberg, has recently dealt with some of these issues in a remarkable essay on modernism in *Critical Inquiry*. Describing the post–World War II collapse of American modernism into an "Iron Age," he writes:

> While the modern skyscraper designed by Bauhaus-inspired architects dominated the urban American landscape, and the New York School of abstract expressionism came to prominence—first in the gallery world of the visual arts, later in the museum and corporate worlds—most American poets, novelists, composers, painters, sculptors, and architects took to the university. By doing so—usually for reasons of professional convenience and economic survival—they removed themselves from society-at-large and set up an invisible wall between themselves and their work and the culture that went on outside academia. When modernism went academic in America and divorced itself from society, it lost all capacity to respond to or relate to the world around it, to the pressing needs of a culture which became increasingly empty, bland, and insensitive to the hungers of the human spirit. By sheltering itself in intellectuality, in abstractness, in cold design, it lost its power to interest or move listeners, viewers, readers. . . . Much of what still goes by the name of "music" is either simply sound-generation or soul-less complexity or mindless minimalism.[7]

If the large majority of passionately devoted music listeners who attend concerts and buy records are to be dismissed as philistines because they persistently abstain from attending serialist concerts and buying serialist records, then it is hard to envision an authentic audience for music outside of academia.

As the traditionally shared values springing from religion, nationality, and education have gradually disintegrated, the polyglot qualities of democracy have widened the gap between artist and audience, muse and public. In this Babel-like arena where values in general seem to be up for grabs, what we particularly need to know is how much and what kind of knowledge and experience an audience must have in order to qualify as bona fide. Literary studies can serve well here to illuminate these questions, since the theory that underwrites them, though on the downswing, is still enjoying a flourishing period.

What we find when we look at the literary arts in academia is that the extraordinary expansion of universities since World War II has provided much fiction and poetry with an artificial lease on life. Clearly,

much of it would not survive without the remarkable number of professors and graduate students who need to have something to do. This
pressure for materials to work on has resulted in a good deal of ephemera, both avant-garde and popular, being given life-support systems
that did not exist in the past. As term papers, dissertations, and journal
articles are ground out to justify their writers' existence, large numbers
of experts have arisen who know a good deal of—in this case—literary material backwards and forwards. The fact that so many experts
can discuss so many questionable works so dazzlingly (and sometimes
compose their own) raises uncomfortable questions: What relation, if
any, exists between scholarly expertise and aesthetic judgment? Does
intellectual mastery of a literary artifact confer aesthetic value upon it?
Who are the beneficiaries of such mastery besides the professors who
receive foundation grants and tenure for their efforts?

As literary academics teach and write about poems, plays, and novels
over and over again, their knowledge of the words of texts often reaches
a point approaching memorization, and this holds true for *Paradise
Lost* as well as *The Crying of Lot 49*. Yet extreme intimacy with a text
may hamper rather than enhance the quality of an expert's judgment
by desensitizing him to its peculiar "whatness." For structuralists, of
course, texts are immediately severed from their authors once they are
produced, and the author disappears as a unifying principle behind the
text once he has finished writing it. According to this view, when the
text has been born into the world of free-playing language, it can mean
anything that the current laws of the language allow strings of words
to mean. Thus, the entire notion of an expert or "privileged" reading
is disallowed, since there is nothing outside the text, to use Derrida's
epigram, that could give any particular reading special authority. But it
is not necessary to be a structuralist or deconstructionist to believe that
extreme intimacy with the words of a text does not afford privileged
readings. Literary scholars, whether biblical, Miltonic, or Pynchonist,
know their texts in ways that could never have been possible for their
authors and would not be considered desirable by most readers. Repeated reflection upon a poem's words produces a world of possibilities
that never before existed. After a certain point, the law of diminishing
returns takes over and the powerful experience of a poem as substan-

tive and coherent begins to break up as the mites inhabiting its entrails become more distinct than their host. Since all of the words of a text are not of equal importance (particularly in a long novel), the more these words are reinspected and the "richer" the reading becomes, the further away one moves from the *fiat lux* that gave the poem its initial existence. The overriding affect that animated the production of the author's text can never be recaptured simply from the words or from a knowledge of the historical settings from which they sprang. This affect, like the "soul" that holds corporeality together as life, holds the text together as a unit of "meaning." In the reader, a brilliant intuition of the text's "unity" (I need to put all of these proscribed words into quotation marks) can go much farther in producing a "valid" reading than scholarly expertise, since a cardinal element of a literary work's validity is the emotion it engenders, an emotion that tends to fade away as professionalization of response increases. Of course, various kinds of knowledge are required to read literary texts in the first place, and the act of reading takes place within polarities determined by culture. These polarities establish norms that govern the range of interpretations and keep them tied to a "world" recognizable by others.

On the other hand, scholarly expertise is apt to produce atomized readings consisting of overrich collections of data rescued from the infinite play of the text's words. The resultant reading—excellent for producing critical and scholarly articles—can be too intellectually overwhelming to be persuasive, too conscious, too contrived out of arbitrary selections from infinite possibilities. (In literary study, there is no one more scholarly, more vivaciously intelligent, more fun to read or hear, and more deviously unpersuasive than Stanley Fish.) A case, then, can be made for intuitive graspings of the affective whole that lies behind the written text. This intuition is not a lawless enthusiasm but is subject to the "rules" of culture and history. This is not to suggest that there is one true permanent meaning recoverable behind works of art—but it *is* to suggest that expertise has its own interests and that they sometimes result in philosophers inadvertently walking into volcanoes, carefully scutinizing the perimeters as they fail to take note of the fiery core. In the arts, such expertise is often at little advantage in producing more worthwhile conclusions than the responsive skills of

an educated, intelligent audience with good intuitive faculties and a
capacity for pleasure, a capacity, incidentally, of the greatest importance, since people do not expose themselves to literature and music
as penitential acts. Furthermore, it is this kind of audience that produces the historical judgment that finally decides what works are worth
attending to. Perhaps this procedure comes closest to that of Gadamer's
"fusion of horizons," which finds a mixture of historical knowledge
and present-day intuition to be the most useful tools for interpretation
and evaluation, though I feel uneasy aligning myself with anyone so
Germanically scholarly as Gadamer.

Having said these things, I now need to make a few concessions
in order to redress a possible imbalance of perspective: the historical and critical work of scholars and experts in the arts is something
we could not afford to forego. Attractive as it may be, Dr. Johnson's
faith in the sagacity of the common reader cannot be made to fit the
realities of late twentieth-century Western society. Works of biography,
history, cultural and linguistic analysis, philosophy, and aesthetic criticism have contributed a great deal to the way in which we understand
and experience the arts. Because the gap between the public and the
artist is now so great, help is needed (from the "experts") to enable
the cultivated public to participate in the pleasures and illuminations
of the arts. Furthermore, the arts themselves have been profoundly influenced by academia and by scholarly critics and, as a result, require
greater sophistication in their audiences than they did in Johnson's
day. This means that the fissure between pop culture and high culture
grows wider all the time. Intermediaries, therefore, are needed to guide
educated audiences through the demanding labyrinths of avant-garde
artifacts.

Having made these concessions, however, I must also add that scholarship and academic expertise are themselves a new self-perpetuating
technology that grows as much out of touch with cultural responsibilities as physicists who develop atom bombs and chemists who produce
carcinogenic herbicides and pesticides. The inner logic of fields of expertise propels them onward, irrespective of needs outside their own
closed atmospheres. Experience has shown that humanist scholars do
not have better judgment about their specialties than industrial tech-

nologists have about theirs and, like them, they are always on the lookout for more materials to transform into their own profitable products.
What experts in the arts are especially prone to forget or ignore is that
*the arts do not exist for the sole—or even the ancillary—purpose of keep-
ing them in business.* This proprietary phenomenon is so widespread
that to most academics it is rarely even observable, like the ambient
air, though now and then a keen eye will take it in:

> The assumption that literature belongs to critics sets contemporary
> criticism apart, not only from older criticism (World War II was a water-
> shed), but from all other disciplines with social or cultural practices as
> objects. . . . Nonprofessionals create the culture or the language, and they
> are the ultimate source of all knowledge of it. In an inarticulate way, they
> know all there is to know, and the sole task of the professionals is to make
> this implicit knowledge explicit. . . . But contemporary criticism is more
> like a religion than a discipline, something for a visiting anthropologist
> to study—and a very odd religion at that: *all priests and no communicants*
> [emphasis added].[8]

Despite this priestly takeover, which values formalism, ideology, and
professionalization over the endeavors of art, classical esthetics have
some sap in them yet, though they may require a bit of translation and
adaptation here and there. The alternatives for us are not the choice
between an eternally constant human nature (and all the sentimentality that goes along with such a view) and a human constitution that
changes completely every ten years, as a Skinner or a de Beauvoir
or a Foucault redefines us. Academics, especially those on the make,
display a trendy absolutism that tends to treat passing ideologies like
universal panaceas: everything gets Lacanized or Austinized or Haber-
massed totally (right now it is Walter Benjamin, or is it Bahktin?) as
if nothing about people or culture has remained the same. Just as all
foods and beers suddenly become "lite," this year's academic nostrums
reprocess all of reality into equally unbelievable uniformity and imperatives. Such tidal waves of me-tooism have less to do with love
of "truth" than with academic survival, and by the time they reach
PMLA, they have acquired the character of naturalized academic tics.
The avant-garde, however, always knows where to look for the newest

rough beasts waiting to be born, which are then tamed and killed off by academic overfeeding.

Meanwhile, however evanescent the "human nature" set forth by the Enlightenment (today's whipping boy), people still eat, have sex, reproduce, suffer, hope, enjoy pleasure, hate pain, and finally die. If music ceased to be related to human metabolism and desire, if novels had nothing to say about human life (and only about literary form or the Prufrockian diffidence of the postmodern author), if visual arts had no relation to the satisfactions of our senses and our need for order, who would comprise an audience for such forms of torture? Yet the scholarly treatment of the arts as ends-in-themselves unrelated to human satisfaction, ends that have been created for the purpose of giving work to specialists, collaborates with contemporary cultural forces to drive a bigger and bigger wedge between artists and their audience. If Stalker and Glymour were themselves professionals in the arts, they could be left, without remorse, to fight their own arcane professional battles with their critic-peers. Instead, their scuffle has afforded us a look at an instructive—and somewhat weird—display of victimization by professionalism. In the relatively uncommon role of the professor as layman, both are attacked by insatiable experts for being an inadequate audience for art. But where on earth will these experts ever find an audience worthy enough to meet their demands? The one thing needful that Stalker and Glymour lack is the a priori agreement with all of the aesthetic principles and practical responses required by their critics.

Though written off as philistines despite their excellent credentials and aesthetic concern, Stalker and Glymour can nevertheless take care of themselves. But in a professional atmosphere like this, the sizes of mass and elite audiences can only grow increasingly disproportionate, for at one extreme is the brutalizing cesspool of television and at the other some precious and self-protective critical/artistic fraternities. Though attempts to lure the masses to high culture may be futile, it is senseless to throw out already committed readers, listeners, and lookers by treating the arts as though they existed for themselves and their professional symbiotes alone. A perusal of announcements of new university press books in literature can be a demoralizing experience. For whom are these often bright but pointless books being written? Not

for authentic readers and not for the sake of "scholarship" either, a
frequent but feeble justification. Too many are written to celebrate a
god who is already dead as the books roll off the presses. After reviewing some of their titles, one can begin to appreciate the current
popularity of biography as a literary form: biographies are read because they retain some connection with the human race and when they
are composed with skill, they become high art as well. As a method
of mediation between art and life, biography can perform a healing
function, but on the other side, the empire-building hauteur of some
of the critics quoted above can only be counterproductive. This is not
to say that caviar should be forced down the resisting throats of the
general population, for Beethoven becomes just another variety of pop
culture when presented through television's usual manic techniques.
But critics have an obligation to ask themselves who and what it is they
are really serving by means of their professional skills. If such skills
in fact serve to reduce the audience for the arts to a handful of the
self-chosen who respond only to the right party shibboleths, then these
self-absorbed Laputans with eyes turned inward or upward need to be
recalled from their narcissistic afflatus by periodic Swiftian slaps in
the face.

Part Two

. . . .

Literary Politics

4

. . . . . .

Recycled Lives:
Portraits of the Woolfs
as Sitting Ducks

Every age has its curious and sometimes inhuman games and sports, wrought to satisfy strange and perverse human needs. As society becomes more "mental," however, we turn up our noses at such primitive pastimes as cockfighting and bearbaiting (despite a sizable subculture that still gets its kicks from shooting people) and try to exercise our aggressions in acts from an armchair or a typewriter or simply by watching TV. Among the intelligentsia, political reappropriation is the current mode for attempting to compensate for the loss of socially sanctioned beliefs and aggressions and the power and relief they confer. And it can also be effective in making virtues out of the deficiencies of individual personalities. Thus rewriting history becomes a favored methodology for alienated minorities—and since almost everybody is a member of an alienated minority, lots of rewriting is taking place. Although some of this may periodically be both necessary and justified, much of it is socially destructive and ultimately self-defeating. If every individual were entitled to social recognition of his private or group mythology, there would no longer be a society to protect the individual freedoms derived from this recognition, only a war of all against all. In the world of letters, already suffering from the manifold ills of hyperpoliticization, one of the overriding obsessional vehicles for reappropriation is the lives of Virginia and Leonard Woolf.

Although the use of literary works for private or political ends has been common enough for a long time and is now quite routine, what is novel about the present rapacious interest in the Woolfs is that their lives even more than their writings are being used for political purposes, lives that are taken apart and relived as though their episodes and events were passages in the pages of fiction, texts open for indeterminate reinterpretation.

Whereas novels and poems are created to be responded to, interpreted, and incorporated by the reader into his emotional life, the *living* of one's life—apart from monarchs, presidents, and rock stars—is generally thought to be an end in itself. One lives a life "for itself," as a "subject," and one's words and deeds are the product of the necessities of one's own personality. It is not necessary to inscribe Kant's categorical imperative over the portals to find disturbing and unnerving the freedom with which various political and personal interests rifle through the lives of artists now dead in order to subject them to current standards of value and to find them wanting. If Now were indeed that one far-off divine event toward which all of creation has been moving, a show of plausibility, however thin, might be derived for manipulating and attacking lives of the past, but Now is simply the latest imperfection. Now is only today's bundle of kinks, and some bundles are kinkier than others, as the ensuing examples may reveal.

It is not so hard to suggest why the lives of Virginia and Leonard Woolf should have come to lend themselves so excessively well to contemporary revisionism as lives in need of being relived. As a result of the extraordinary quantity of material that has been published about the Woolfs, including of course their own autobiographical writings and Virginia's letters and diaries, their lives can be seen to have been lived in a milieu that was once associated with a small, creative elite but which, like most social forms, has become more and more the milieu of a large portion of today's democratized masses. In the areas of sexuality, creativity, politics, sexual roles, marital relations, social conventions, feminism, madness and other psychological malaises, Judaism, anti-

Semitism, family life, and whatnot, their lives give a foretaste of things
to come in society at large as the spread of higher education causes
greater numbers of people to break away from traditional social forms.

The Woolfs thus become perfect sitting ducks for an ambiguous kind
of reappropriation and politicization. On the one hand, since they are
seen as having been resistant to many of the conventions of their own
time, they are readily taken up as models of assertive self-definition
in the face of a repressive majority, but on the other hand, since they
did not have the advantage of being postmoderns, that is, of being us,
they can also be seen as having failed to realize to its fullest their will
to power, or more accurately, *our* will to power. In this failure, they
become culpable as betrayers of the Now Revolution. Had they been
purely conventional, they would now repose beneath serious notice,
but having risen above the conventions of their time, they can now be
remarked as special while being put down as not special enough. If
Virginia is sometimes praised as a "patrician" who lived her life as she
pleased without concern for middle-class respectability, she can also be
attacked as an "elitist" who regarded aesthetic quality as the principal
criterion of merit while failing to take sufficiently serious interest in
her more plebian feminist "sisters." If Leonard can be applauded as
a saintly and almost uxorious husband who did not let his own career
hamper the interests of his wife, he can also be criticized as a suffo-
cating custodian who was so solicitous about his wife's health that he
"denied" her the primal experience of having children. In a no-win
game like this, they can be pulled every which way in order to suit the
needs of every party.

One of the earliest salvos to be fired in the burgeoning Bloombury
circus was Cynthia Ozick's "Mrs. Virginia Woolf."[1] Like her earlier
Commentary piece on E. M. Forster, her Woolf essay (occasioned by
the publication of Quentin Bell's biography of Virginia) displays a marvelous prose instrument wielded by a keen critical intelligence. Yet the
politics of appropriation, the aggrandizing self (the terms are apposite), have Ozick in so desperate a grip that the resulting discussion
of the Woolfs and her particularized attack on Leonard Woolf turn

into a violation of the spirit, an invasion of the soul—something out
of a Hawthorne story like "The Birthmark," in which sinister powers
masquerading as science destroy the very ground of human freedom.

What on earth could have caused Ozick to wage so cruel a quarrel
with the Woolfs? What Virgilian fever could have prompted her to heap
ex post facto afflictions upon so excellent a man as Leonard? *Tantaene
animis caelestibus irae?* Can there be such anger in highbrow souls?
The answer seems clear enough: that *for her* Leonard Woolf did not
display sufficient interest in his own Jewish identity. Not content to be
merely a Jew, he wanted to be both an Englishman and a citizen of
the world. For Ozick, whose Jewish self-consciousness has the intensity
that only anachronism can supply, this is the ultimate betrayal. Draw-
ing upon Woolf's autobiography, Ozick quotes his remarks about his
grandfather:

> "No one could have mistaken him for anything but a Jew. Although he
> wore coats and trousers, hats and umbrellas, just like those of all the
> other gentlemen in Addison Gardens, he looked to me as if he might have
> stepped straight out of one of those old pictures of caftaned, bearded Jews
> in a ghetto. . . ." Such Jews, he notes, were equipped with "a fragment
> of spiritual steel, a particle of passive and unconquerable resistance," but
> otherwise the character, and certainly the history, of the Jews do not draw
> him. "My father's father was a Jew," he writes, exempting himself by two
> generations. "I have always felt in my bones and brain and heart English
> and, more narrowly, a Londoner, but with a nostalgic love of the city and
> civilization of ancient Athens." He recognizes that his "genes and chro-
> mosomes" are something else; he is a "descendent" of "the world's official
> fugitives and scapegoats." . . . But a "descendent" is not the same as a
> member. A descendent shares an origin, but not necessarily a destiny. (36)

Thus we get our first major clue to Ozick's exasperation. Aware of
his roots, ultrasensitive to the traditional plight of the Jews, Woolf is
nonetheless uninterested in making a life out of parochial sectarian-
ism. "A descendent shares an origin, but not necessarily a destiny," she
observes, and for Ozick this will not do at all. Her belief is that the
birthmark is the man, especially if the mark happens to be his Jewishness. The rest of her essay is an attempt to destroy the man in order to
rescue the birthmark—*her* birthmark.

Insisting that Woolf lacked the self-knowledge that would have informed him that he, too, and not just his grandfather, looked like a Jew from an old ghetto picture and, characterizing him as resembling "a student at the yeshiva," she asks: "What prompted Leonard Woolf to go into Germany in the very hour Jews were being abused there? Did he expect Nazi street hoodlums to distinguish between an English Jewish face and a German Jewish face?" She does not stop to give a reply, but the odious answer is clear enough: he preferred to be a human being instead of merely a Jew.

Ozick's quarrel with Woolf extends beyond the matter of his "failure" to adopt a Jewish identity; it includes Virginia Stephen as well and, most importantly, the "use" that Leonard made of her (the quotation marks are mine). After citing Quentin Bell's account of Virginia's meeting with Leonard's mother, who seemed even more alien and strange than Leonard himself had seemed, strange because of their Jewishness, Ozick writes:

> This aspect of Virginia Stephen's marriage to Leonard Woolf is usually passed over in silence. I have rehearsed it here at such length not to emphasize it for its own sake—there is nothing novel about upper-class English distaste for Jews—but to make a point about Leonard. He is commonly depicted as, in public, a saintly socialist, and, in private, a saintly husband. He was probably both; but he also knew, like any percipient young man in love with a certain segment of society, how to seize vantage ground. . . . Whether Leonard Woolf fell in love with a young woman of beauty and intellect, or more narrowly with a Stephen of beauty and intellect, will always be a formidable, and a necessary, question. (37)

Formidable to some, perhaps, if they happen to insist on unusual standards of moral purity. But with all the rancor of the above passage and the invidiousness that permeates this entire essay, one is very apt to question the purity of the motives behind such standards. For what, after all, was Leonard Woolf's moral flaw according to Ozick? To put it bluntly, that he chased goyim; one, to be exact. What is worse, she was upper-class English. Instead of looking into the mirror to discover and acknowledge his ineradicable Jewishness, his mark of Cain, instead of seeing his Jewishness as the alpha and omega of his existence and his destiny as the art of capitalizing on the persona of an eternal scapegoat, he chose to inhabit a larger universe; indeed, to be a mensch. For this, Ozick cannot forgive him.

> What Leonard needed in Virginia was not so much her genius as her madness. It made possible for him the exercise of one thing Bloomsbury had no use for: uxoriousness. It allowed him the totality of his serious-ness unchecked. It *used* this seriousness, it gave it legitimate occupation, it made it both necessary and awesome. And it made *her* serious. With-out the omnipresent threat of disintegration, freed from the oppression of continuous vigil against breakdown, what might Virginia's life have been? The flirtation with Clive [Bell] hints at it: she might have lived, at least outwardly, like Vanessa [Bell]. It was his wife's insanity, in short, which made tenable the permanent—the secure presence in Bloomsbury of Leonard himself. Her madness fed his genius for responsibility; it be-came for him a corridor of access to her genius. The spirit of Bloomsbury was not Leonard's, his temperament was against it—Bloomsbury could have done without him. So could a sane Virginia. (38–39)

As if this were not already the Unpardonable Sin, as if seriousness and responsibility were human interests to be disparaged, Leonard adjusted only too quickly, says Ozick, to the disappointments engendered by his wife's various afflictions: "A wife who is seen to be frigid as well as mad is simply taken for that much sicker [as opposed to being perfectly healthy?]. But too ready a reconcilement to bad news is also a kind of abandonment, and Leonard seems very early to have relinquished, or allowed Virginia to relinquish, the sexual gratifications of marriage" (39). As for his reputed "saintliness" in nursing his wife so that she could continue to write novels, Ozick asks: "A saint who successfully secures acquiescence in frigidity, childlessness, dependency? Perhaps; probably; of course" (41).

Of course, too, without Leonard, as we are reminded, there would have been no Woolf novels and (one ought to add) probably no Virginia to write them. His vice was to devote his life to preserving her being as well as her sanity. Why did he not just let her sink into madness?

> Why did he not? . . . Because she was his wife; because she was the beloved one to whom he had written during the courtship, "You don't know what

a wave of happiness comes over me when I see you smile. . .."; because his conscience obliged him to; because she suffered; because—this before much else—it was in his nature to succor suffering. And also: because of her gift; because of her genius; for the sake of literature; because she was unique. And because she had been a Miss Stephen; because she was Thoby Stephen's sister; because she was, like Leonard's vision of Cambridge itself, "compounded of . . . the atmosphere of long years of history and great traditions and famous names [and] a profoundly civilized life"; because she was Bloomsbury; because she was England. . . . In her he had married a kind of escutcheon; she represented the finest grain of the finest stratum in England. *What he shored up against disintegration was the life he had gained—a birthright he paid for by wheedling porridge between Virginia Woolf's resisting lips* [emphasis added]. (41–42)

After such a display of indecency as this passage, one is driven to ask yet again, what is that Unpardonable Sin capable of reducing all of Leonard's remarkable virtues to nothing but grounds for execration and loathing? Nothing more than that he forgot—or failed to care— that no matter what his aspirations or achievements, in the final analysis he was only and always a yeshiva boy "wheedling porridge" into the mouth of an Anglo-shiksa instead of comfortably relaxing into the superior role of a stigmatized ghetto waif.

Ozick's assault on Leonard Woolf, more demeaning to herself than to him, with its savage bigotry and rage at anything that resists the notion of Jewish supremacy (cf., "white supremacy"), exhibits the all-too-familiar way in which political positions develop as emanations of private psychological needs that then are projected as binding morality to be "wheedled" down the throats of a resisting outside world. This becomes all the more easy to do in the last quarter of the twentieth century, when biographical materials are more available than they have ever been before in human history. With letters, journals, diaries, biographies, autobiographies, and memoirs pouring off the presses, there is a vivid illusion that the lives of other people now dead are really there, laid out before our eyes as accessible texts that can be examined and reexamined for unlimited interpretation and use, like *Finnegans Wake*. Combined with the legacy of psychoanalysis, itself questionable, but further cheapened by the amateur psychopolitics of litterateurs, these

masses of biographical data lend themselves quite easily to revisionist appropriation by intellectual special-interest groups, the way that
other kinds of interest groups bomb railway stations in Bologna, set up
temples in Guyana, or abduct famous people for ransom and murder.
As for Ozick, a sophisticated intellectual who has taken up the primitive rituals of a sort of fundamentalist Judaism and who finds herself in
the inevitably defensive position of intellectuals who adopt archaic or
reactionary ideologies that they nevertheless insist on throwing in the
faces of their incredulous contemporaries, she can only be incensed by
the cool skepticism of a fellow Jew like Leonard Woolf, whose religious
commitment to Judaism was minimal even though he had an obsessive
awareness of the perennial sufferings of the Jewish people. Like T. S.
Eliot, who ludicrously proclaimed his allegiance to Anglicanism, royal-
ism, and classicism and who found it necessary to attack "freethinking
Jews" in his notorious *After Strange Gods,* Ozick finds that she must
attack Woolf's disdain of primitive religiosity in order to strengthen
the plausibility of her own recidivism. For to Ozick as to Eliot, *freethinking* Jews constitute an omnipresent threat to an orthodoxy that is
always vulnerable to ridicule. The last thing in the world required by an
emperor's new clothes is a tailor, especially when the fantasized clothes
are actually in tatters, having been acquired centuries too late from an
ideological resale shop.

When we turn to Elaine Showalter's *A Literature of Their Own,*[2] we
find ourselves in a more familiar world of discourse. Despite its wealth
of information and its attempts to structure or restructure the history
of women's writing since the eighteenth century, the book has been
produced principally to set forth a feminist program. This turns out,
unfortunately, to be its most serious weakness, for its combination of
literary history, revisionist critical readings, and feminist politics results in a scattershot assault that finally seems to have led nowhere.
Though Showalter is clearly polemical, it is never fully clear what she
is really attacking.

Dividing the literary history of women into three major phases, she
sees the earliest as a period of "feminine" writing, in which women
fiction writers mostly remained in their historically and socially as-

signed gender roles in relation to men, while complaining about or quietly undermining the established structure. In the second or "feminist" phase, a more consciously belligerent and political movement arises in which women writers are openly antagonistic to the prevailing male social structure. Although the reader is led to expect that the third phase, that of twentieth-century "female" literature, will move very close to a point of womanly self-realization, this does not appear to be the case. There are no "female" writers who satisfactorily play their roles for Showalter, not even those she treats at the end of her book and who at first look most promising, Doris Lessing and Margaret Drabble. Both of them fall short of unabashed "femaleness" by either finally accepting what is merely traditional or by going off into otherworldly fantasy. We are left with a sense that Showalter has been writing about a race of beings who have not yet begun to have any actual existence. For when all the stages of women's writing are judged to be inadequate and when all of these women writers have failed to live their lives in a way that is satisfactory to Showalter (whatever that may be), we feel that she has been engaged in a quasi-religious exercise in which the actual world of daily existence, like that of traditional Christianity, is only an empty show, with *real being* scheduled to take place as some far-off divine event, when this corruptible must put on incorruption and this mortal, immortality.

Amidst such a scenario, Virginia Woolf appears as just another one of those "female" writers who have shirked their true vocation, in this case by taking off on a "flight into androgyny." Showalter's chapter on Woolf, like her passim references to her throughout the book, invariably levels charges of "evasion." Although Woolf falls into the period of the "female" novelist, Showalter finds her writing suffused with the failure of nerve that characterizes the merely "feminine." Thus, "the delicacy and verbal fastidiousness of Virginia Woolf is an extension of this feminized language" (27). This paralyzing refinement "forced women to find innovative and covert ways to dramatize the inner life, and led to a fiction that was intense, compact, symbolic, and profound" (27–28).

Paradoxically, the more female this literature became in the formal and theoretical sense, the farther it moved from exploring the physical experi-

ence of women. Sexuality hovers on the fringes of the aestheticists' novels
and stories, disguised, veiled, and denied. Androgyny, the sexual ethic of
Bloomsbury and an important concept of the period, provided an escape
from the confrontation with the body. Erotically charged and drenched
with sexual symbolism, female aestheticism is nonetheless oddly sexless
in its content. Again, "a room of one's own," with its insistence on artistic
autonomy and its implied disengagement from social and sexual involvement, was a favorite image. (34)

A good deal of this discontent with virtually all of her women writers
stems from the fact that Showalter is much less interested in their art
than in their lives. Although writers first come to the public's attention
because of their art, and although their art is the basis for a continued
claim to such attention, politicians like Showalter are mainly concerned
with lives, as if it were their lives that made them famous. Art, on the
other hand, is seen as little more than a screen for vulgar substitute
gratification. Thus, after her curious reading of a Dorothy Richardson who seems mostly unrecognizable, and as a prelude to a reading
of Woolf that will seem equally unrecognizable, Showalter observes,
"The female aesthetic was meant for survival, and one cannot deny
that Richardson was able to produce an enormous novel, or that Virginia Woolf wrote several, under its shelter. But ultimately, how much
better it would have been if they could have forgiven themselves, if they
could have faced the anger instead of denying it, could have translated
the consciousness of their own darkness into confrontation instead of
struggling to transcend it. For when the books were finished, the darkness was still with them, as dangerous and inviting as it had always
been, and they were helpless to fight it" (262). A translation of these
remarks into less portentous language betrays the essentially plebian
ethos of Showalter's operations: writing novels helped these women to
bear up under the stress of being females in a male-dominated society. But how much better off they would have been if they could have
faced reality directly, not wasted their time fiddling with literature; if
they could have told men to "chuck it" and crashed through the iron
gates of life by exchanging the trivialities of art for the more serious
business of the world. In other words, scrape away the neuroses of the
artist and underneath you will find the real self, which turns out to

be nothing other than the archetypal contemporary Western human being: a sexed-up bourgeois. In offering this as a model for the liberated woman's psychic health, Showalter has raised *bovarisme* to new heights. Little wonder that creative people are scared to death of humdrum psychoanalysts, whose ultimate therapeutic goal is apt to be little more than a good screw. Freud and Kris, at least, were not so eager to cure artists of their art.

Inexplicably seeing Woolf's life as a tragedy, Showalter observes that "her adoption of a female aesthetic . . . ultimately proved inadequate to her purposes and stifling to her development" (264). Yet it is hard to find any basis for such an outlook. Woolf's life in this universal vale of tears constituting mortality was filled with as much gratification as anyone has a right to expect—she had just about everything!—and as far as her writing was concerned, there was little in her life or art to hamper her successful development. No doubt her "female aesthetic" made it impossible to write *The Sun Also Rises* or *Ulysses*, but by the same token neither Hemingway nor Joyce was able to produce *To the Lighthouse* or *Between the Acts*. The essential question is why Showalter thinks that both women's art and women's lives should be built so closely upon the model established by men. Although the theoretical burden of her book is to reject such a model, she protests too much. The practical consequence of her dismissal of women writers' lives and works (by seeing them as taken over by substitute gratifications) is that men become the criterion for both life and art. This stance lurks behind such a remark as "Woolf is the architect of female space, a space that is both sanctuary and prison. Through their windows, her women observe a more violent masculine world in which their own anger, rebellion, and sexuality can be articulated at a safe remove" (264). The apparent lesson to be learned is that women should abandon their evasive cloisters and behave like men.

Like Ozick, Showalter attacks Leonard Woolf for his protectiveness, his practice of consulting doctors who forced a "rest cure" upon his wife, his insistence upon childlessness. But had Leonard turned Virginia into a sow, would Showalter have complained about that too? Perhaps instead of living a quiet life writing books, Virginia should have produced children who could be dropped off at a day-care center (the sine qua non of contemporary emancipation) while she went off to IBM to become an executive capable of tossing her male underlings into bed for a jolly tumble. In place of such profound self-realization, "she sought a serene androgynous 'oneness,' an embrace of eternity that was inevitably an embrace of death. In recognizing that the quest for androgyny was Woolf's solution to her existential dilemma, we should not confuse flight with liberation" (280).

In the light of the failure of all of Showalter's women to achieve "liberation," and to the extent that their literary productions were hampered and misshaped by their "repressed" life roles, the reader of her book becomes witness to another variant of the Utopian-Christian-Marxist vision in which all of actual life is dismissed as phantasm, as preparation for the *real* life that is yet to take place. Art is just another form of seeing through a glass darkly, until face to face becomes possible. And for Showalter, face to face may mean little more than a romanticized version of uninhibited routine sex. Men, as usual, are the lucky ones, since their lives and values, however disgusting, are the only real ones. Thus, unless Showalter's vision of the gratified life is based upon intimations of a species yet to be evolved, the moral is clear: Utopia arrives when women become like men.

Showalter's assault on Virginia Woolf ends, however, with a few backhanded concessions. "Yet," she writes, "there is a kind of power in Woolf's fiction that comes from the occasional intense emotion that resists digestion by the lyric prose" (296). True, this is only another way of saying that Woolf succeeds only when her intense emotions resist being transformed into art, but Showalter is not ultimately interested in art. "For Mrs. Ramsay, death is a mode of self-assertion. Refined to its essences, abstracted from its physicality and anger, denied any action, Woolf's vision of womanhood is as deadly as it is disembodied. The ultimate room of one's own is the grave" (297). It hardly seems worth adding that it is a room awaiting everyone, however liberated. Showalter's equation of art with death makes us wonder why she bothers to take notice of women *writers* in the first place when her real interest is political. But politics, like "death," is just another mode of "self-assertion," and triumph over "death" through politics is just another mode of self-deception.

When we turn to Exhibit C, we may find ourselves almost grateful for Ozick's and Showalter's familiar universe of discourse. For in what purported to be a review of the final volume of Virginia Woolf's letters for the *Times Literary Supplement,*[3] Phyllis Grosskurth produced a series of virtually inconsecutive paragraphs that only extreme generosity could characterize as an essay. Indeed, only extreme generosity could enable a reader to suppose that Grosskurth was quite all right when she produced this wild and incoherent outpouring, so one is forced to assume that the subject of the Woolfs has once again liberated demons.

Grosskurth's review-essay, like all incoherence, resists summary, but a distillation, however unsatisfactory, is nonetheless required. It appears that despite all the evidence to the contrary, Grosskurth regards the marriage of the Woolfs as anything but harmonious. (This is not to suggest that the Woolfs had no differences, but a relationship of total harmony is hard to conceive.) Much of the "evidence" for this opinion seems to come from Virginia's three suicide notes, all of which praise Leonard for his goodness and express a desire to spare him from any further suffering from having to nurse a mentally ill wife. (Books by Roger Poole and Stephen Trombley resist the notion that Virginia was mentally ill, but it is not possible to consider here such gross reconstitutions of reality.)[4] Grosskurth takes all of Virginia's praise of Leonard as merely the surface protestations of a very deep hostility. As if this account were not problematical enough, she also sees Virginia as a relentlessly bitchy anti-Semite who lost few opportunities to fling mud at Jews, not excluding her own husband. As a counterpart to this surmise and quite contrary to Ozick (the Woolfs are as inexhaustible as the cosmos, as fecund as prime matter), Grosskurth regards Leonard as obsessed almost to derangement with the history and fate of the Jews, so much so in fact that as a subject of contemplation his wife offered very little competition against it for a hold upon his mind. The final chink in this quivering edifice is filled by means of a series of dark innuendoes to the effect that far from being taken unawares by his wife's death by drowning, Leonard may at the least have been an abettor and at the most a devious engineer in this painful denouement of her life!

Though some of Grosskurth's assertions are not entirely without foundation (e.g., Virginia did seem ambivalent about Jews, but on the other hand, she married one, hardly out of desperation; Virginia *was* hostile to being locked up, as it were, during her periods of madness), the implications of her thickly woven plot take one's breath away, and the tone of her narrative and her salient observations suffer from an ambiguity that grows increasingly incomprehensible:

> The cult that has grown around Virginia Woolf would be slightly comic were it not for her suicide. She is no longer a fallible woman, but a complex image constructed of woman, writer, suicide—an objectified symbol of our death instinct. The quality of her work has been confused with a deeply neurotic, rather frightening human being. Throughout these volumes we have witnessed the spectacle of an ego held in precarious balance between eros and thanatos, a spectacle which appeals to morbid voyeurism. That final act might have been cathartic were it not for some grave problems raised by Nigel Nicolson in the appendix to the last volume.

The meaning of each sentence here, like most of the other sentences in the essay, poses a problem: Why does Woolf's suicide change the character of her cult? Why has suicide exempted her from fallible womanhood? How does she objectify "our death instinct"? What does it mean to confuse *her work* with a deeply neurotic and frightening *human being?* If she is neurotic and frightening, why is she no longer fallible? What exactly was this balance between eros and thanatos? Is not Grosskurth herself a morbid voyeur? Why would Woolf's suicide have been "cathartic" and for whom? And why do Nigel Nicolson's editorial remarks about Woolf's suicide notes prevent her death from being cathartic to whomever?

Grosskurth makes much of an interesting essay by Susan M. Kenney (*University of Toronto Quarterly*, 1975) on the relationship between Woolf's suicide and her last novel, *Between the Acts*, incorporating Kenney's essay into the larger fantasia of her own psychofictions. Putting on the mantle of divine judgment (by now a bit threadbare after heavy wear by Ozick and Showalter), Grosskurth finds that Leonard was insufficiently apprehensive when Virginia returned from a walk soaking wet about ten days before her drowning. According to Grosskurth, he "merely makes a single terse entry in his diary that she seems 'unwell.'" (Grosskurth seems to subscribe to that peculiar school of biography that assumes the subject's total life has been written into diaries and letters, with nothing going on in the life between jottings.) If Leonard could only have suspected all the harpies lying in wait for the swoopdown years later, he would surely have written more acceptable journals for their benefit. When Virginia finally drowns herself, Grosskurth presents the following scenario:

> He searched for some time, he says, and then informed the police. In the official search, how thoroughly was the river dragged? If it was thought that the body had been washed out to sea, where did the draggers commence the search? At whose direction? The Ouse is a tidal river, but not fast flowing. How could her body have been wedged in some underwater debris? It would surely have required some very heavy rocks to have held it down, until it was found three weeks later *floating* like a decomposed Ophelia. Further: if Leonard was such a beloved figure in the village of Rodmell as he implies in that curious, tortuous account, "Virginia's Death," why would anyone even suspect that he had done away with his wife as Kenney states they did? In fact, how does she know there was such gossip? A statement like that is irresponsible if not backed up with solid evidence. Kenney's suspicions seem to have been aroused mainly because she finds the ending of the posthumously published *Between the Acts* so positive that she does not believe Virginia could actually have intended suicide. What she does not consider is Leonard's brief mention of Virginia's death amid pages devoted to the persecution of the Jews and nostalgic memories of Cambridge friends, nor the questionable choice of photographs, not one of which is of Virginia Woolf. Above all, there is the curious section about his own intense compassion when forced to drown some day-old puppies when he was a boy:
>
> > I put one of them in a bucket of water, and instantly an extraordinary, a terrible thing happened. This blind, amorphous thing began to fight desperately for its life, struggling, beating the water with its paws.
>
> Leonard does not see any connection between this incident and his wife's tragedy; yet he manages to relate it to what generations of Gentiles have done to Jews.

Adequate comment on such a discourse seems impossible. The shifting timbres, tones, and viewpoints of this prose are more alarming,

more terrifying, than anything Grosskurth can cite about the Woolfs.
Although at first she appears to be suggesting that Susan Kenney's report about the villagers' suspicions of Leonard is unfounded, she then
immediately goes on to suggest that there really *is* good evidence of
Leonard's crime—namely, that he failed to include a photo of Virginia within the pages dealing with her death in the final volume of
his autobiography. And what is the connection that Leonard fails to
see between his horror at drowning the puppies and his wife's death?
Presumably its occult revelation to the world that he has murdered
his wife!

One last reference to Grosskurth's essay must suffice (since mankind
cannot bear much more unreality): quoting at length a passage from
The Years in which Sara bitterly alludes to sharing a bathroom with
a Jew who leaves hairs in the bathtub, Grosskurth refers to Quentin
Bell's account of Virginia's nervousness when Leonard was reading the
galleys of that novel (he had not read the manuscript). Then she remarks: "The scene of Virginia watching Leonard as he read the passage
about the Jew could be a tableau from Strindberg. No wonder she was
frightened. How could he ever forgive her for this most devastating
of humiliations? How would he retaliate?" Not only does Grosskurth
seem to think that no life was taking place for the Woolfs in the in-
terstices between these texts, but this quite specific scene is wholly an
invention of her own, extrapolated from Bell's account of Virginia's nervousness while Leonard was reading *The Years*, parts of which he read
in her presence. "How would he retaliate?" Grosskurth asks, or makes
Virginia ask. Again the answer is presumably obvious: by murdering
his wife.

The series of letters to the *Times Literary Supplement* that followed
Grosskurth's shocking performance was surprisingly muted. John Lehmann, who had had a long relationship with the Woolfs stemming from
their Hogarth Press days, replied first.[5] "I feel," Lehmann writes, "I
must protest vehemently against the innuendoes about Leonard Woolf
which run right through Phyllis Grosskurth's review." Commenting on
the scene in which Leonard supposedly reads about the Jew in front of
Virginia, he continues: "This is absurd, and worse, because Leonard
was not reading only the particular passage she refers to, but the whole
long book in its page proofs."

A week later, Grosskurth replies to Lehmann: "The burden of my review was an attempt to question the widespread belief that Leonard was a devoted husband. Indeed, I go further: is it possible, I have suggested, that Leonard Woolf's treatment of Virginia could actually have hastened her death?" (Grosskurth seems to have quickly forgotten that the "treatment" was murder.) Two weeks later, Quentin Bell enters the fray: "On the whole the charges that Professor Grosskurth makes seem to reveal a degree of silliness which I must say shocks me in so eminent a writer." (Nothing can quite equal British reserve.) He then goes on to question her use of Virginia's novels to bolster her arguments and to point out inaccuracies in Susan Kenney's article.

A few weeks later, Susan Kenney writes a curious letter of her own. Thanking Grosskurth for making her essay famous, she then objects to the charge that she did not document her claim about village rumors that Leonard had done his wife in. She defends herself by alluding to unpublished letters at Sissinghurst Castle which she was permitted by Nigel Nicolson to inspect.

The whole affair finally comes to an end when Nigel Nicolson objects to Kenney's shaky support of her remark about the villagers. "She must be remembering a letter which I showed her from Vanessa Bell to my mother, Vita Sackville-West," in which Vanessa wrote that "Leonard had one anonymous letter saying 'The Coroner has been very kind to you.'" Vita's reply to Vanessa was, "Isn't it incredible?"

"This," says Nicolson, "is the only 'solid evidence' for Susan Kenney's allegation that the village gossip took the extreme form that Leonard had murdered Virginia."

To try to decode Grosskurth's meaning and intent would be difficult: her essay engages in a series of reversals that mirror her own confused motivations. To discover what festering wound could have been soothed by such an all-out attack on the Woolfs is impossible. What does remain for public consideration, however, after examining this essay along with those of Ozick and Showalter is the nature of these astonishing appropriations of other people's writings and—more seriously—other people's lives as screens upon which to project dissatisfactions with society and (more covertly) self. These projections can generally be distinguished from bona fide biographical work, whether historical or critical in character. Neither Ellmann's *James Joyce* nor

Haight's *George Eliot*, powerful as they are, seem to be telling us more
about the biographer's desires and frustrations than the lives of their
subjects. Their success stems from the fact that the biographers, despite
their own psychological needs, are principally concerned with grasp-
ing the lives of their subjects (however ideal such a goal), not merely
using these lives as vehicles for acting out personal, religious, or political obsessions. Even Crocker's life of Rousseau, for all its hackneyed
psychologizing and limited conception of normality, gives us a Rousseau who is far from being just an advertisement for the kinks of its
author. Phyllis Rose's *Virginia Woolf, Woman of Letters* is open and
clear enough about its feminist point of view and its theory of the relation between art and life so that we can be impressed with the justness
of most of its insights even if we reject the operating principles as too
facile.

The visions and revisions of the Woolfs examined here, however,
inhabit a different psychological world. Intellectually, they are specimens of the familiar maimed outlook of post-Nietzschean culture in
which the loss of a widespread transcendent ideology induces small
groups and individuals to create their own homespun substitutes. After
the death of God, the deity's scattered members take root as numerous pretenders briefly occupying the scene, each requiring passionate,
fanatic, and arbitrary devotion. Unfortunately, if it is no longer possible
to embrace one vast universal system of epistemology and morals, it is
even less possible to accept other people's private revelations and the
systems they generate. When these private revelations are built upon
quirky valuations of arbitrary data—in this case what Leonard did or
did not feed Virginia when she was or was not mad, whether Virginia
really wanted children or just thought she did, why Leonard did not
include Virginia's photograph on such and such a page of his autobiography—the black comedy of contemporary unbelief becomes all
the more palpable. For in place of the inexhaustibility of the Infinite
we are offered the inexhaustibility of the Infinitesimal. Arbitrary bits of
data become makeweights in private ethical and metaphysical systems.
People are committed to hell for not wholeheartedly committing themselves to this year's political shibboleths. The tyranny of the Universal
is replaced by the tyranny of the Inconsequential.

Beyond the intellectual character of these revaluations of the Woolfs is the problem of their emotional and ethical character, and emotionally they function as a form of pornographic titillation for a middleclass intelligentsia who are too refined, perhaps, to be seen at adult bookstores and peep shows but who have passions of their own that need to be satisfied. If cheesecake and beefcake and X-rated movies can be accused of using other people's bodies as meat for gratification (a familiar cry of feminists), one can just as well charge these literary analysts with something even more harmful and degrading: a pornography of the soul. If it can be said that cheesecake and beefcake provide, after all, a healthful stimulation of the body's juices, which have got to come out in one way or another anyhow, then perhaps a similar justification will have to be made for soulcake, a more complex and insidious phenomenon, a form of gossip elevated to metaphysical heights promising a transcendent payoff. Pornography, at least, is relatively direct and unpretentious, whereas Ozick, Showalter, and Grosskurth speak as if they were operating on a decidedly more celestial plane. But what exactly is that plane and why should psychological sport be a higher thing than physical?

In the present instances the lives of two extraordinary people have been separated from their writings in order to be used in some sort of iconic, totemic fashion, like Jesus and Mary, who are no longer mere "people" but who indeed have had thrust upon them all the sins of the world. Have the Woolfs become the Linda Lovelaces[6] of the intelligentsia? Should not their trivial nits—so voraciously picked—be put in proper perspective alongside the major gifts they have left us? Is it not time to realize that, unlike their art, intended for public judgment, their lives—though open to examination—have been fully lived out "for themselves" and are not really up for grabs?

Is it not time to say, Enough already? Time to say, *Dona eis requiem?*

5

. . . .

Leonard Woolf
and His Virgins

If Leonard Woolf could be said to have a motto, it was not the "Thoroughly" imprinted under his father's emblem of a wolf's head; rather more appropriately it would be the reiterated theme of his autobiography: "Nothing Matters." "In the end," he would say again and again, "nothing matters."[1] This apparent insouciance, however, was the mask of a pessimism and fatalism that permeated not only his life but his writings as well. Of the Sinhalese natives among whom he lived during most of his seven years in Ceylon, he wrote, "When you get to know them, you find beneath the surface in almost everyone a profound melancholy and fatalism which I find beautiful and sympathetic—just as something like it permeates the scenery and characters of a Hardy novel."[2] Both of his own novels, *The Village in the Jungle* and *The Wise Virgins*, are amplifications of this bleak purview: they show helpless but gifted protagonists self-deluded by an appearance of free will and control which, in fact, leads to disaster.

Woolf's apparent stoicism, as reflected by the refrain that nothing matters, was the product of a sensibility that cared too much, not too little. Early in his autobiography, he writes: "When I look into the depths of my own mind (or should one say soul?) one of the characteristics which seems to me deepest and most persistent is a kind of fatalistic and half-amused resignation. I never worry, because I am saved by the feeling that in the end nothing matters, and I can watch with amusement and detachment the cruel, often undeserved but expected, blows which fate rains upon me" (*Sowing* 23–24). But he also observes: "The moment at which officially I emerged from non-existence was the early morning of November 25th, 1880. . . . In the interval between 1880 and today I have lived my life on the assumption that sooner or later I shall pass by annihilation into the same state of non-existence from which I suddenly emerged that winter morning in West Cromwell Road, Kensington, so many years ago. This passage from non-existence to non-existence seems to me a strange and, on the whole, an enjoyable experience" (*Sowing* 11). To a man who was capable of enjoying life amidst a universe honed for annihilation, the claim that nothing mattered was a form of whistling in the dark, an anodyne in the face of man's uncontrollable destiny. This psychological condition is adroitly characterized by Leon Edel in his *Bloomsbury: A House of Lions:* "Behind Leonard's will to live lay a love not only of life, but of the despair of life: an eternal melancholy—as of the wailing at the sacred wall in Jerusalem for the perishable things of this earth."[5] Yet Woolf's life, as opposed to his umbrageous philosophy, seems to have provided very little ground for such premonition of disaster. Like Milton's, every stage of it was good, its beginning, its middle, and its end. To measure a life against a purely putative yardstick of perfection is common but senseless, for a life can usefully be measured only against other actual lives, against human possibility, not against the fantasies of heart's desire. And when a realistic measure is used to gauge Woolf's life, every part of it can be seen to have been superior.

Born into a well-off middle-class family with high standards and values; inheriting splendid genes; winning scholarships to England's best schools; obsessed by the handicaps of Jewishness while enjoying only the advantages; experiencing a remarkably successful career as a young civil servant in Ceylon; returning to England to marry Virginia Stephen and to have as his friends some of the most distinguished of British intelligentsia; having a marriage that was far happier than most people can reasonably expect in a postreligious age when, cosmically speaking, nothing really does matter; enjoying a productive life through both his wife's and his own substantial accomplishments; and

living to an old age filled with the gratifications that come from retaining one's powers to the very end and making the most of them (his
autobiography, written in his eighties, is already regarded as one of
the masterpieces of British life-writing)—having, doing, and enjoying
these things, he was sorely misled by a fatalism that may have applied to
the rest of the world but that certainly did not apply to him. Everything
finally mattered and everything was good.

That his wife had bouts of madness, that he was afflicted with a tre-
mens, that he endured two great wars, that his wife ended her own
life—in the context of human actuality these represented no unprecedented bad luck. All these things were the inscription of mortality, and
most of mankind has seen much worse. Against the dark possibilities of
ordinary human existence, Woolf's life shows up as an extraordinary
success, an esthetic and moral triumph over the gods who may be dead
but whose capacity for unleashing horror continues unabated.

Indeed, if there are any problems with Woolf's life, they would appear to be merely posthumous. Cynthia Ozick complains that he was
insufficiently Jewish and that he dominated his wife; Elaine Showalter
finds that Virginia was not womanly enough to suit her program and
that Leonard has to share some of the blame; Roger Poole and Stephen
Trombley believe that Virginia was not even mad and that Leonard's
patriarchal Victorianism was responsible for his shipping her off to brutal doctors who were invested in the madness business; Phyllis Grosskurth darkly hints that Leonard had a hand in Virginia's death by
drowning. Leonard, it seems, has become archvillain in a Foucaultian
Power/Knowledge operetta, but his life was even better than he could
have known, since he did not live to see it taken apart and put back
together again by people claiming to know how to live it better than
he did.

Woolf's fatalism and its by-product, the protestation that nothing
matters, are demonstrated with relentless and depressing intensity in
his novels. Biographically speaking, this poses no problems with regard to *The Village in the Jungle*. The contrast, however, between the
despairing conclusion of *The Wise Virgins* and his own life, upon which
the novel draws to a considerable extent, has been a puzzle for many
readers. Why, they would like to know, does the protagonist Harry

Davis (the Leonard character) fail so dismally in his attempt to marry Camilla (the Virginia Stephen character) when Leonard was so brilliantly successful in achieving this coup in real life? It is a question, one must add, whose answer is central to the impact that can be produced by the sort of reading of *The Wise Virgins* that is willing to range beyond biography into literary terrain.

Woolf began to write *The Village in the Jungle*[4] late in 1911, shortly after returning to London from several years in Ceylon as a major administrator for British colonialism, and the novel made its appearance in 1913. Although it is regarded as a classic in a number of specialized literary circles, it is hard to understand why such a compact masterpiece has not attained wider currency. The tale is extremely well drawn, the narrative voice masterfully controlled, the philosophical point of view provides a focus without authorial interference in the narration, and the drama is magnetically conducted to its fated catastrophe, which is really the fate of human life itself. Although the early pages insist on the cruelty and evil of the jungle, to an extent this characterization is belied by the narrative that ensues. The jungle and its creatures are presented both with sympathy and with a perception of their ecological beauty, and the human actors and the rigid, blind conventions that direct them are, in the final accounting, the real sources of evil and horror. For though the animals necessarily live in accord with their full capacities, man in society is a creature always capable, in potential if not in fact, of being other and better than he is. So we feel less disgust at animals that kill for food than we feel at men who kill for money, sex, or power.

The village of the tale consists of only ten houses set off in a jungle clearing, with a small population of whom the principals are the hunter-farmer Silindu and his wife, their two daughters, and a recently acquired son-in-law (in role if not strictly in law). Their individualist behavior sets them apart from a collection of villagers who regard their eccentricities as the cause of miscellaneous public calamities, although this assumption has no factual basis. In social life, however, perceptions and beliefs are as good as facts, since they become facts and have the same consequences. Thus, the daughters are seen as threats because they have learned to hunt by accompanying their father on his outings;

and the unofficial "marriage" between the village headman's brother-in-law, Babun, and Silindu's older daughter involves a caste difference that the villagers find unsavory. As for the younger daughter, they look upon her as positively unnatural when, having been forced into a marriage with the village doctor, she leaves him after their child is born and, to make matters worse, nurtures, even suckles, a young fawn that she finds in the jungle, as if she had produced *two* children. In one of the novel's most shocking scenes, the villagers stone the fawn to death and the daughter perishes soon after, having lost her will to live.

Silindu's older daughter is the next victim in a plot set into motion by a sleazy creditor named Fernando who craves sex as well as cash. When she rejects his advances he contrives with the help of the village headman to have both her husband and her father accused of theft. Babun, the husband, goes to jail and Silindu is acquitted, only to murder the false accusers in a rage of impotence and despair and a desire to protect his daughter from Fernando. When Silindu and his family have been picked off one by one as a consequence of the imperatives of their history—their fate, in other words—the novel draws to a close in a scene almost surreal in which Punchi Menika, Babun's loyal wife, is the family's sole survivor. In a collapsing house being pressed upon by the surrounding jungle, she realizes that she is about to be destroyed by a hungry animal ready to pounce.

The overriding emotion of this tale is the resigned helplessness of impoverished peasants in the face of uncontrollable forces. These forces, however, are products of social life rather than rays from the determining cosmos. The superstition of the villagers is hard to distinguish from socialization itself: it consists of an uncritical acceptance of social mores, a narrowly self-interested irrationality, a distrust of unconventionality. It has little to do with a jungle or with primitive society. Added to this are the insatiable desires for money, sex, and power which direct the behavior of the petty bureaucracy of local and regional chiefs. The cumulative force of all these lusts (the word's particular multivalence is exactly right here) produces the real operating fate that determines their sordid human destinies. The occasional introspective, questioning, or self-determining person who arises in this milieu—the very milieu of social life—is hardly in a position to thwart such irresistible powers, and more often than not his or her special gifts precipitate the catastrophe. If this network of forces is socially determined rather than god-begotten, we should not be surprised by the effects produced when we witness its action in Western suburbia, in Putney outside London, to be exact. The result is a somewhat more elaborately orchestrated re-play called *The Wise Virgins*,[5] as the genre shifts from sophisticated folk tale to tragicomic novel of manners in the suburban marriage market circa 1912.

Leonard Woolf's own family home in Putney is the model for the Richstead of *The Wise Virgins*. Although his father's early death had precipitated a move from their more affluent Kensington home in London proper, the novel presents us with a Davis family consisting of both mother and father, a son Harry, and a daughter Hetty. Harry and Hetty are certainly derived from Leonard and his sister Bella, but to claim that they *are* those very two would be even more inaccurate than to claim that Stephen Dedalus *is* James Joyce. While it is true that Leonard's mother was greatly offended at what she took to be a por-trait of herself, and while George Spater and Ian Parsons report, in *A Marriage of True Minds*, that "Leonard's mother and his sister Bella are treated roughly,"[6] it seems more accurate to say that the novel's counterparts are not simulacra of the originals, which may be the reason that his relatives were so offended: they took the portraits to be more literal than they actually are. Spater and Parsons add, moreover, that "Leonard treats himself equally harshly."

The novel tells the story of the newly arrived Davis family, who are Jews, and the growing friendship with their neighbors, the Garlands, who are suburban Anglicans. We witness a short period in the life of the intellectual and rebellious Harry, who yearns to leave the suffo-cating philistinism of Richstead society and become a member of the Bloomsbury circle of Camilla Lawrence, derived, of course, from the family and friends of Leslie Stephen. As he falls more and more deeply in love with Camilla, he is increasingly frustrated by her lack of sexual interest in him. At the same time, he is carrying on an ambiguous guru-student relationship with young Gwen Garland, who is dazzled by his penetrating criticisms of her mundane suburban existence. As their relationship becomes increasingly eroticized, they are driven to each other for sexual gratification, as a consequence of which Harry finds himself forced into a loveless marriage and the loss of Camilla Lawrence.

Surrounding *The Wise Virgins* are a host of problems and mysteries. Though one can only speculate about why Leonard Woolf began to write such a novel within a few months of his marriage to Virginia Stephen in 1912, the question is worth considering in view of the surprising fact that unlike their real life counterparts, Harry and Camilla do not get married at the end. That he wrote another novel at this time may well be accounted for by his economic circumstances after resigning from the Ceylonese civil service in 1911 with the hope of marrying Virginia. But the psychological atmosphere that induced Leonard to write about his marriage at almost the same time it was taking place, and in such altered terms, has remained unclear. His failure to discuss *The Wise Virgins* in his autobiography, apart from a passing reference, suggests that the conflict it created with his family left a bitter taste in his mouth. He did not allow it to be reprinted after its 1914 appearance, nor was it published in America until 1979.

Thus, only a small body of critical response now exists, and most of it is unfavorable, though "platitudinous" might be a better word, since those who bother to attend to the novel at all keep making the same unsophisticated use of it as biographical source material. Spater and Parsons reflect the prevailing tone when they say, "Its interest today is in its portrayal of character, since the principal actors are Leonard and Virginia" (81). (Though when Parsons writes by himself in his 1979 introduction to the novel, he is more enthusiastic.) Leon Edel treats it similarly in his book on Bloomsbury, while in an essay on *The Wise Virgins*, he dismisses the novel as "trivial" in a disappointingly inattentive reading of it as fiction.[7] Even Selma Meyerowitz, in her full-length account of Woolf and his writings for Twayne, uses it mainly as biographical material, while grudgingly assenting to its "compelling development of the three main characters—Harry, Camilla, and Gwen—and some strikingly poetic description."[8]

As biographical source, however, the novel is unreliable for the very reason that it is fiction. Harry, for example, is so aggressive, cynical, and moody, so much at odds with the received assessment of Leonard, that the attempt to reconcile the two either falsifies his character in life or tears the novel to shreds. The task of the critic, however, is to explain why the characters and events of the novel differ from their sources in real life—not to explain these differences away or, even worse, explain why they really are accurate representations of their sources when in fact they are not. A demonstration case of the absurdities that follow from these latter courses can be seen in Roger Poole's programmatic book on Virginia Woolf, in which he prefers not to discuss aspects of the novel that might undermine his political interest in throwing mud pies at Leonard.

When *The Wise Virgins* is examined as a novel, however, a new entity altogether confronts us. Instead of the bits and pieces of biography that heretofore dominated the scene, we become aware of a theme and point of view that hold all of this material together as fiction, despite its undeniable flaws. Leon Edel threatened to open things up when he finally asked but did not correctly answer the question: Who *are* the wise virgins? To answer that question correctly would go a long way toward revealing the thematic glue that makes this work a coherent—and sometimes powerful—philosophic novel of manners, a compact and quite remarkable bildungsroman that would grip the ordinary reader and positively stun today's cultural and Marxist critics. After all, its contemporary relatives are Joyce's *A Portrait of the Artist as a Young Man* and Lawrence's *Sons and Lovers*. No busts of the gods would crash to the ground if Woolf's novel were acknowledged as their cousin.

Right from the first page of *The Wise Virgins* analogies are made between the jungle life that Woolf had recently left and the civilized suburbia to which he returned, setting the tone for a view of life as predetermined by powerful and irrational forces beyond individual control. That Richstead seems unmenacing only serves to underscore the forces behind the unwitting traps that human beings set for themselves via culture internalized as vague desires.

The Garland family—a widowed mother and her four "virgin" daughters—are getting to know their new neighbors, the Davises, who are just settling in. Harry is an artist, whose visits to art school serve the author as a pretext for acquainting him with Camilla Lawrence and

her father, sister, and friends, who distill much of the character and
circumstances of Leslie, Virginia, and Vanessa Stephen and their circle
of Bloomsbury intellectuals. Harry, like a Proserpine commuting back
and forth between the worlds of light and darkness, gradually makes
his way into this Parnassian circle, the goal of his quest. But the task of
the novel is to show how and why Richstead ordinariness—which he
desperately hates—claims him in the end.

Although three of the Garland daughters seem merely peripheral,
all four of them are indispensable to the working out of the novel's
surprising web. Each exists in relation to the institution of marriage,
Ethel and Janet as spinsters, May and Gwen as incarnations of nubility.
Ethel, at thirty-seven, is universally regarded as a cheerful, pathetic,
and identity-less old maid, suited only to tea parties and volunteer
work, now that life—in the form of a husband—has passed her by. Even
to Harry's ruminating intelligence, Ethel is a puzzle. "What's she at?
What does she think or feel? Is she satisfied with life, to go on like that
year after year until she dies? She seems somehow to be cut off from all
reality" (70). On the other hand, when the two families dine together
at a hotel, Harry is baffled "to notice that at dinner the only one to be
really natural and comfortable was Ethel. She was not more talkative
nor more silent than usual; always ready with her gentle smile . . . in
a silence infinitely more easy and reassuring than the rattle of Hetty's
conversation. Her eyes never wandered, horribly fascinated by the forty
eyes at the other tables; they never had to drop hastily or turn away
flurried only to catch and drop before another pair of strange eyes; they
were fixed in quiet abstraction upon—what?" (185). On still another
occasion when only Ethel appeared calm and natural, Harry thought
to himself, "A foolish virgin" (239). Ethel, it seems, is a dilemma.

Janet, somewhat younger, is both more and less of a puzzle:

> She was one of those female "sports" born into so many families in
> the 'eighties. . . . She played golf perpetually, tried to drop her g's, and
> dressed in pleasant, rough grey tweeds. Hanging like Mohammed's cof-
> fin between the nineteenth and the twentieth centuries, between the soft,
> subservient femininity of Victorian women and the new woman not yet
> fully born, she compromised with life by finding it only in the open air
> and on the golf links. Life in return had made her singularly pleasant to

look at; [sports] had hardened her muscles so that even under the rough
jacket and rough skirt, which always looked as if it might at any moment
change into trousers, one realised that there were human limbs; her face
was startlingly and provocatively sexless; the feminine sex of the hair and
the delicate texture of the skin cancelled out the male sex of the shape
and expression, which were those of a boy of eighteen. (11)

After Harry meets her, he remarks to Gwen, "Janet? she's a dear. . . .
One doesn't pity Janet, she's a *lusus naturae*, she's happy. She's ancient
Greece, Hermaphrodite, the soul of a young man of twenty in a woman
of thirty" (71).

Although May is important for the novel, she is herself of little interest beyond her personification of middle-class nubility. Destined to
marry a boring and fatuous clergyman (who is perfectly in tune with
the suburban environment scorned by Harry), she and her tiresome
husband will doubtless be popular residents of Richstead, reflecting as
they do the respectabilities of bourgeois society. For Harry, May and
her marital longings represent the culturally determined ordinariness
that he cannot abide and from which it is his principal occupation to
escape, preferably to the society of the Lawrences in Bloomsbury.

Gwen, the last of the daughters, suffers from the self-dramatized immortal longings of late adolescence and finds in Harry's dour, cantan-
kerous, and antisocial posturings the answer to her romantic prayers.
She devours his knowing comments about their world, reads with perplexity the Dostoyevsky and Ibsen that he recommends, and begins to
see her bourgeois family life as commonplace and boring, but underneath it all, she is a realist whose motivation is ultimately to succeed
in a conventional suburban environment. For all her flirting with "liberation" and Harry's exotic program for life, the music to which she is
dancing is the same Richstead serenade as her sister May's. Sex and
marriage, not Ibsenist new womanhood, heads the hidden agenda—
and it is not very hidden.

Harry is a surprisingly moody, brash, and even boorish young intellectual whose soul feeds on continental literature, with Ibsen providing
the seriocomic obligato against which the plot is played out. Harry's
alternations between stubborn silence and noisy fulmination against
philistines, anti-Semites, and suburban morality strike a sharp con-

trast with the Leonard Woolf of the autobiography, by then of course
a venerable sage. Even Leonard's youthful letters to Lytton Strachey
from Ceylon, among others, present us with a personality whose resemblance to Harry's is only *in potentia*. Leonard indeed had elements
of character that *could have* transformed him into a Harry under other
circumstances, perhaps, but which erupted in force only on special
occasions. Leonard's sister Bella confirms this view in Spater's and Parsons's report that "she saw in Harry Davis all Leonard's 'less pleasant
characteristics magnified to the nth power.'" She added (to Leonard),
"If you had made—or would make—Harry really yourself you would
make a fine thing of him" (81). This assessment is particularly helpful in dealing with the problematic relation of Leonard to Harry—and
autobiography to fiction—when reading *The Wise Virgins*.

Harry's obtrusive Jewishness, which is brandished at every inopper-
tune moment, has been an insuperable stumbling block for many readers. Duncan Wilson, in his book on Woolf's political career, is one of
the few who are calm enough about it to note that there is little sign
of this Jewish unease in the autobiography, though Spater and Parsons
do point out that Judaism had little real weight in his life.[9] Although
Woolf is always conscious of his Jewish roots and refers to them with
an ambiguous satisfaction in the autobiography, he had little patience
with religion in general or with folk sentimentality in particular. He
connects the best qualities of his intellectual sensibility with Jewish
tradition but at the same time he refuses to wear any mark of Cain, a
specialty that he bestows on Harry instead.

Thus, Harry's obsession is all the more enigmatic. His constant an-
ticipation of being treated as a scapegoat causes him to exhibit the very
sort of baiting behavior most likely to elicit anti-Semitic retaliation.
Even after such repeated ravings as "I'm a Jew, I tell you—I'm a Jew"
(52), or "We [Jews] wait hunched up, always ready and alert, for the
moment to spring on what is worthwhile" (110), he is consistently well-
received by the friends he cares about the most. Woolf's delineation
of Harry, far from being a self-portrait, makes a certain kind of Jew
look bad. In this, his purpose seems at one with that of Philip Roth: to
castigate, from an insider's privileged position, the moral deficiencies
of his own people.

Although some readers' attempts to equate Leonard with Harry in this regard are grossly defective, there is another area in which such an equation can be fully supported: the novel's sexual intensity. Neither the autobiography, nor *The Village in the Jungle*, nor Quentin Bell's recollections of Leonard in his biography of Virginia Woolf offers anything to contradict this impression of Leonard as a highly sexualized being. Harry's libidinous restlessness, often reminding us of Stephen Dedalus, provides a pervasive tattoo throughout *The Wise Virgins*. When Harry calls to mind the ambiance of Camilla's presence we almost feel that we are somewhere in Joyce's *Portrait:* "He liked to recall the purity of her face and her voice; the remoteness of a virgin, he said to himself. When one knows the coarseness and tortuousness of one's own mind, the foulness and ignobleness of one's own thoughts, he used to think to himself, such purity of beauty is almost frightening. One longs to be intimate with it, but is there any point of contact?" (36–37).

This contrast between the sensuality of Harry and the "purity" of Camilla is at first a serious obstacle in the way of Harry's otherwise intense pleasure from Camilla's wonderful imagination and intelligence. In conversation with Arthur Woodhouse, another member of the Bloomsbury circle (modeled after Clive Bell), Harry responds most feelingly to Arthur's frustration at Camilla's coldness. Arthur's outcry, "They don't realize that we've got bodies" (96), perfectly expresses Harry's own suffering, a suffering that eventually leads him into his disastrous liaison with Gwen Garland. Camilla's letter of response to Harry, after his expression of love and proposal of marriage (a letter bearing more than a casual resemblance to Virginia's well-known reply to Leonard's marriage proposal), sets forth the polarities as she experienced them: "I want love, too, and I want freedom. I want children even. But I can't give myself; passion leaves me cold. . . . And then there's so much in marriage from which I recoil. It seems to shut women up and out. I won't be tied by the pettiness and the conventionalities of life. There must be some way out" (231). Although Harry is not yet aware of it, this is also his own view of marriage—a sexual trap—and his love for Camilla springs from an unconscious awareness that the core of their relationship would not burn out with the inevitable satiety of sexual desire. Marriage for sex frightens both of them, though sex in itself also frightens Camilla.

Given Harry's superior sense of security from the vulgar fates, it

becomes the novel's central irony that something as commonplace
as sexual desire should propel him into his involvement with Gwen
Garland. This central irony is doubly ironic, for Woolf's stand at the end
of the Edwardian era was against sexual repression and hypocritical
Victorian prudery. Both his narrator and his protagonist clearly speak
for the author when they express, as frankly as conventions will allow,
Harry's sexual needs. As Harry sees things, what "the male wants [is]
a certain fierceness of love, mental and bodily" (41). He notices the
sensual leer on the face of the Vicar, Mr. Macausland, when he is examining his fiancee's appearance, and he knows that for all his celestiality,
underneath, the Vicar is "mere man." When the two try to settle on an
appropriate place to hold the Garland-Davis picnic, the Vicar objects
to one possibility (amusingly, named Maidenhead) because it is notorious for lovers behaving passionately in their rowboats. Inevitably, when
the picnic does take place, Harry and Gwen behold in a passing boat a
young man who "had his arm around the girl's neck, and her arm was
around his. He was kissing her on the lips." Harry's comment to Gwen,
"That's one of the things worth doing" (74–75), becomes a portentous
refrain. His ability to express such a thought reveals a frank acknowledgment of sensuality that was only then beginning to be seen again
in English literature, after a long moratorium. Throughout *The Wise
Virgins* this frankness prevails, first in Harry and then in Gwen's de-
cision to flout middle-class convention by giving her virginity for love.
Nor are these sexual needs suffused with Shelleyan mists but treated,
rather, as everyday animal promptings. Once they are seen as physical itches devoid of "romance," Harry's powerful love for Camilla can
also be seen for what *it* is: a profound devotion to her very being, not
dependent on sex for its validation.

The late twentieth-century reader is apt to understand this frank
sexuality so well that he will end up misunderstanding how it actually
operates in *The Wise Virgins*. For though Harry's sensual outlook, like
that of Stephen Dedalus, is meant to be taken as social criticism of a
still repressive era, that is not its ultimate purpose. Frank sensuality
may be an admirable quality in the protagonist as Ibsenist rebel and in
the author as candid Modern, but in the context of the novel, Harry's
insouciance as a rebel against philistine culture blinds him to an even

more important consideration: Can a gifted person achieve a superior life if everything is sacrificed for the scratching of a plebian itch? What is the ultimate cost of satisfied desire?

Harry is so fired up with his own bravado in telling Gwen about the Master Builder and other Ibsen originals that he fails to observe her fancying *herself* to be one of them. As she grows more desperate for love and attention, as her fears of being an old maid like Ethel increase, she determines to flout bourgeois convention by sacrificing everything for love, one of Harry's "things worth doing." Taking his ironical chatter most literally, she admits that she too feels "different." "But what can one do?" she asks:

> "Do?" he said violently. "Anything. What the devil does it matter what one does? Nothing matters, that's the first thing to remember in life, Gwen, except about two things."
>
> "But what are they, Harry?" Gwen asked almost timidly.
>
> Harry laughed. "You'd be shocked if I told you."
>
> Gwen flushed. "Don't say that. You know I wouldn't be. Do talk to me as you would to—to anyone [she means "to Camilla"].
>
> Harry looked up at her. "Do you mean that?" he asked slowly.
>
> Gwen was hot with excitement. (178)

Trouble is already in the making, however, and an esthetic point of view like "Nothing matters!" can only increase it when the Parcae have spun their thread. Harry's subsequent suggestion that Ethel would have been better off bearing an illegitimate child is overwhelming, because Gwen is unable to intuit the avuncular, half-jocular tone with which he expresses his ambivalent, playful consciousness. As her feelings are stirred to fever pitch, she blurts out that Harry was right all along, that love *is* the most important thing, and that nothing else really does matter. She will leave her family, go away with him if he will take her, and if he will not, she will behave like an Ibsen heroine in any case.

Harry is caught unawares by the seriousness with which Gwen has absorbed his lessons. It has not occurred to him until now that there is an immense chasm between an intellectual and an ordinary person: for the former, it is perfectly clear what belongs to the world of thought and what belongs to the world of real life; for the latter, there is only one world: everyday reality. "Harry covered his face with his hands; everything seemed to be whirling round him. He could think of nothing to say. One sentence only kept on absurdly coming again and again into his head: "People don't *do* those sorts of things." Ibsen, of course—Hedda Gabler. People don't *do* those sorts of things. Could he say that to Gwen—now? Wouldn't it, after the last week, sound too contemptible, too mean?—people don't *do* those sorts of things" (208–9).

As a metaphysical gesture, Nothing matters! is not without merit; as a guide to daily life in conventional society, even Harry now recognizes its limitations. But things have gone too far for him to resist Gwen's erotic advances, especially when they are offered as a gift of one of those "things worth doing." After a night of lovemaking, followed by a day of euphoric exuberance from sexual release, Harry, like his counterpart, Stephen Dedalus, falls into an abyss of panic and despair. Gwen's deep bond with her family overrides Ibsenist yearnings, turning her toward her mother in fear of what she has done. Harry, who is really a decent sort when the crunch arrives, responds to the pressures of both families by offering to marry her.

What we now witness is the crushing weight, the sweeping tide of social convention. The reader will not easily forget Camilla's earlier response to Richstead suburbia when Harry had invited her for a visit: "Imagine those poor Miss Garlands waiting, waiting for those abominable young men in straw hats and that disgusting clergyman to come up and ask them to marry them" (136). A nausea of tragic waste comes upon us as the wedding plans of May and Macausland are now revised to include a second couple, Harry and Gwen. It is the novel's cutting irony that Harry's most salient characteristics, his wide-ranging intelligence and his aversion to the commonplace, have amounted to little more than a piquant aphrodisiac for arousing the passion of Gwen. Sometimes the implacable Fates require grandiose machinery for crushing their helpless victims. The mountains labor to produce a mouse.

> So ended dreams and the romance of life [thinks Harry]. The brave, wild
> words, the revolt of youth, the splendour of love; the fringe of what he had

seen and touched for a few hours, what he still saw fading away now into another world in Camilla; hopes and desires and dreams and words. False hopes and vain desires and absurd dreams and empty words, how they crumbled before the first touch of this world! How he despised himself, one of the millions of ridiculous little souls, enmeshed, struggling feebly, stuck fast in the intricate sordidness of life.

He sat there brooding over Gwen. Already she was the woman, his wife, trusting, timid, submissive, unseeing, loving. He watched her coldly, saw her already *his*, his chattel, his wife, his dog. He did not hate her; he hated himself. (226–27)

Why did Leonard Woolf choose to portray Harry as aggressively Jewish when he was not that way himself? Why did he not permit Harry to marry Camilla when he himself had married Virginia? Who are the wise virgins? And what do they know? These are the questions that require to be answered.

The wise virgins are a subject that the novel never discusses. Various of its young women are referred to as virgins and Ethel, as we have seen, has already been described by Harry as a foolish virgin. But the wise virgins per se are never brought on stage to do their thing. Still, we know who they are. They are Camilla, Ethel, and Janet. Camilla's claim is beyond dispute, since she is treated throughout as a virtual goddess. But Ethel? Janet?

As the story draws to its close at the Garland-Davis wedding, Harry meets Ethel once more:

> "Wish me luck," he said to her.
>
> "I do, Harry."
>
> They shook hands.
>
> "No oil in your lamp, Ethel. But who knows which is wise and which is foolish?" She did not understand what he meant, but she smiled at him, because he said such funny things. He shook hands with her again.

Then he meets Janet.

> "I wish you luck," she said reticently, but not unkindly.
>
> "I wish I knew what you really think about."
>
> "Golf." There was a trace of contempt for him in her voice. It roused him.

"You despise me. I expect you're right."

She laughed. "My good fellow, don't let's get sentimental. I think: 'Poor Gwen,' if you want to know."

And then she goes on to add:

"You're a jolly sight too clever, Harry, that's what's wrong with you. . . . You think I've never thought about anything but golf. Oh, yes, you do. But I have. When I was eighteen I thought a jolly good deal too much about myself and what people thought of me. Then I suddenly found I was twenty-six and I thought an awful lot about what was going to happen to me. I'd rather be out of doors than in this"—she looked quietly round the drawing-room—"anyway. And to tell you the honest truth, I had rather be playin' golf this time next year than nursin' babies. I can't exactly explain what I mean, but you're so jolly clever I dare say you'll twig it." (242–44)

Now Harry collides with Ethel one last time. " 'Good-bye, Ethel, good-bye.' Harry kissed Ethel, to her astonishment. 'You've been very nice to me,' he went on in a low voice, 'and you're wise' " (245).

In this remarkably oblique scene, major thematic strands have suddenly been gathered together. Only now is it apparent that both Ethel and Janet have resisted, each in her own way, the most powerful pressures of society upon its members in general and upon women in particular. The pressures of *their* class have been much harsher than those of Camilla's, where eccentricity is more easily tolerated. In resisting the sexual and marital constrictions of their milieux, all three have chosen their own courses of life instead of caving in to the first "disgusting" young man to toss them a marriage bone. By the common standards of Richstead, Ethel may seem a vacant nonperson, but Harry perceives her early on as contented and "natural," though still a foolish virgin. Not until the wedding reception does it strike him fully that she is more genuinely liberated than he is. Unlike Ethel, Janet and Camilla know what they are about and are able to explain it. But none of them will be thrown upon the scrapheap once they have done their procreative bit, for the wise virgins have rejected conventional sexual determinations, still very constricting for both women and men. Thumbing their noses at the gods, they continue to exist as individuals.

Leonard Woolf himself, always impatient with irrationality, sentimentality, and religiosity, followed up his marriage to Virginia Stephen by producing *The Wise Virgins* as a gesture of thanksgiving. Sensing the most dangerous currents of his personality, he projected their terrifying fulfillment upon his protagonist alter ego, Harry Davis. Virginia's sexual coldness had rescued him from the bitter fruits of a quest for sensual gratification that posed a dangerous threat. In its place she offered him a lifetime of intellectual pleasure. Leonard's feelings about sex were in any case highly ambivalent: as a passionate man he believed in sexual satisfaction and openness and rejected Victorian prudery and prurience. In his autobiography, he relates with distaste the smarmy atmosphere of one of his boyhood schools and describes how he and his brother cleaned the place up when they attained seniority. Leon Edel remarks in his Bloomsbury book, "Whatever Leonard's participation in the free Eastern sexual life of the towns [when in Ceylon], he returned to his sense of reality. . . . As he wrote to Lytton, 'I am beginning to think it is always degrad[ing] being in love; after all ninety-nine one hundredths of it is always the desire to copulate.' "[10] In the *Growing* volume of his autobiography, Woolf recalls how a couple he knew in Ceylon had been changed by marriage: "They reminded me of those pairs of insects—some are spiders or worms—in which a very small male is attached to a very large female—fitting ignominiously and neatly into her gigantic body—I sometimes think that this must be the ideal life for a male—and, after performing his male functions, is killed and eaten by her or just dies" (*Growing*, 72). Harry's fate was indeed like this one, not because Gwen was a monster, but because the lesson he taught her did not result in the liberation he fancied; rather it entrained and trammelled him in a net of social conventions that Leonard could never have tolerated. Virginia prevented any of this from happening.

Harry's perfervid Jewishness represents a kind of parochial ingrowth for which Woolf felt a powerful disgust but which had not been outside the realm of possibility. Though his own family had not been bad for him, without resistance they might have been much worse. In his escape to Virginia and Bloomsbury, Leonard was able to become the more tolerant man of the world that his better self had always yearned to be. Harry Davis, seen in this light, is a brilliant creative act of antipathetic magic in which the most alarming and undesirable of the author's potentialities are sloughed off onto an effigy for sacrificial purification. Leonard had had stroke after stroke of good luck—and would continue to do so—but he knew that the universe could not be trusted and that is why he had to believe that nothing mattered. Had a hair been different, had an electron vibrated once too often, his endowments might have turned him into a Harry Davis. But even with all of Virginia's afflictions, Leonard was able to recognize his privileged existence. After writing *The Wise Virgins* and examining what he had wrought, he could look at Harry Davis and think without hubris: There but for the grace of the implacable Fates go I.

6

. . . . . .

The Lives and Deaths
of Charlotte Brontë:
A Case of Literary Politics

Although the Ego, the Self, the Author, and even the Book have—in some circles—been disposed of as fictions in the aftermath of Derrida, Barthes, and Foucault, a reading of *Jane Eyre* and *Villette* could easily convince us that there is still a lot of life in those hastily dismissed concepts. For if anything can be said to hold these novels together to produce their strange, unique power, it is the mesmerizing force of Charlotte Brontë's literary Self, a world-creating Word straight out of Coleridge's romantically infinite I Am. Charlotte Brontë's twentieth-century next-of-kin can only be D. H. Lawrence, another moral-erotic dynamo who taxed the dams of conventional respectability.

Brontë's power is indeed manifold, for she has survived the many uses to which she has been put for more than a century. Regarded as impious, "coarse," and risqué by some of her contemporaries, venerated by Mrs. Gaskell as a model of filial piety and Christian self-sacrifice, treated as neurotic by some post-Freudian psychological critics, kicked up and down the Liberation Mountains by various schools of feminists, and subjected to Marxist readings by armchair revolutionaries, she still can overwhelm us as the "genius" that some have claimed her to be. Even *The Professor* emits sparks and *Shirley*, whatever its problems, displays a virtuosity that can still inspire awe, and for some readers *Villette* is the great masterpiece, a bold ancestor of the psychological novel.

When Elizabeth Gaskell, however, began to write the first biography of Charlotte at Mr. Brontë's request in 1855, her disposition was to stay far away from Eros and to treat Charlotte as a saintly exemplar of Christian devotion to duty and virtue. Mrs. Gaskell, who had come to be a good friend of Charlotte during the last few years of her life, was too close to the Brontë circle to be able to consider Charlotte principally as a famous novelist. Her own emotional ties and her own religious temperament caused her to focus on the terrible ordeal of the serial deaths of the Brontë children and Charlotte's role as survivor. Furthermore, both Charlotte's husband of less than a year, Arthur Bell Nicholls, and her father, Patrick Brontë, had sensibilities that required protection and this reined in Mrs. Gaskell's treatment of a number of delicate subjects. In addition, Mrs. Gaskell's knowledge of Charlotte's intense erotic attachment to her Brussels schoolmaster, M. Heger, was much greater than she was willing to indicate nor were the complete texts of Charlotte's revelatory letters to him to become public until the early twentieth century. Although a very great deal has been made of these letters, perhaps the strongest conclusion yet to be reached was announced by Tom Winnifrith in 1983, on the basis of a poem he discovered at the Berg Collection: "Charlotte Brontë probably on the evidence of the Berg manuscript contemplated adultery."[1]

Of Mrs. Gaskell's dilemmas in facing such intimations, Alan Shelston remarked that "she is forced, in this period of Charlotte's life, to positive manipulation of the evidence surrounding other issues—notably Branwell's decline—to provide an explanation of Charlotte's psychological state."[2] Also, Mrs. Gaskell did not see fit to say very much about Mr. Brontë's handsome and personable young curate, William Weightman, who for a while, at any rate, exerted some charm over all the Brontë sisters. The contrast between him and another Brontë curate—Arthur Bell Nicholls—did not lend itself to expansive treatment.

What seems curious, however, to the twentieth-century reader of Charlotte's letters and the more recent biographies is that she had in reality very little of the conventional religiosity that Mrs. Gaskell so

esteemed. As a clergyman's daughter, of course, she had been sur-
rounded by a world of religious "discourse formations." She knew the
Bible backwards and forwards (and turned it to forceful literary use)
and she had mastered all the accepted religious sentiments. But she
is rarely convincing when she utters them, either in her fiction or in
her life. Writing to her best friend, Ellen Nussey, about her poor health
in London during one of her infrequent escapes from the isolation of
Haworth and the demands of her father, she remarks: "Sometimes I
have . . . been tempted to murmur at fate which condemns me to comparative silence and solitude for eleven months in the year—and in
the twelfth while offering social enjoyment takes away the vigour and
cheerfulness which should turn it to account. But circumstances are
ordered for us, and we must submit." This is a very characteristic religious obeisance, but in her novels religion is almost never chosen in
preference to passion. When it *is* chosen, it is apt to be a vehicle for
passion, as in the famous scene in *Villette* in which the Protestant Lucy
Snowe confesses to a Catholic priest—in sheer desperation. (Indeed,
Winifred Gérin makes a good case for this confession—which actually
took place while Charlotte was in Brussels—to have been an explicit
admission of guilt for her love for M. Heger.) Or it is apt to have an air
of inauthenticity, as when the concluding sentiments of *Jane Eyre* are
devoted to the repellent and narcissistic evangelist, St. John Rivers, as
though Charlotte felt it were her duty to appear to support him although
she personally preferred the world. Even with these gestures, however,
many of her contemporary readers felt her to be "irreligious." Gérin
reports of Charlotte's benefactor, Mrs. Atkinson, who paid for much of
the cost of her education at Roe Head: "In later years when she came
to read *Jane Eyre* she was appalled at the secular nature of the work
and the scant respect paid to the Cloth, and severed all connexion with
the author."[3] In an ironic way these readers were right after all. For
as a late romantic, Brontë was more concerned to harness her affective energies to the interests of the self rather than the interests of that
lily-livered old Victorian God.

  Well over a hundred years passed before Mrs. Gaskell's life of Charlotte Brontë was followed by another major biography, one which, oddly
enough, did not herald a revolution but rather consolidated the find-

ings of a century and brought that era to a close. In a decade that had
already become highly politicized after an extended period of relative
stability, Winifred Gérin's magisterial achievement of 1967, though
criticized for its own omissions and attenuations, exhibited what can
only now be seen as an extraordinary neutrality. As a result of the publication of the Heger letters, of Fanny Ratchford's books on the Brontë
juvenilia, the preoccupation with psychoanalysis in post–World War II
literary circles, and the subterraneous rumblings of the feminist and
neo-Marxist movements, what had solidified for so long into The Life
was soon to break up into the lives, most of them serving as vehicles for
one or another ideological mission. Though it reflects one individual's
personality and point of view, Gérin's biography can hardly be accused
of pushing a cause. Rather, Gérin saw her task as using twentieth-
century discoveries in order to put an end to the perpetuation of old
myths, especially since she regarded Mrs. Gaskell as unreliable and
as someone who "would never wholly be able to conquer her novelist's
tendency to romance about ordinary things" (416). Instead of myths,
Gérin provides substantial quantities of new or previously unintegrated
materials. Thus, she has a great deal to add about the Brontës' juvenilia
and their bearing upon the mature works; the influence of various artists and writers on Charlotte's fiction; the backgrounds of Charlotte's
friends and employers, like the Nusseys, the Taylors, the Sidgewicks;
the pensionnat in Brussels where Charlotte spent much of two years;
the characters of M. and Mme. Heger and Charlotte's obsession with
him. (More than a hundred pages are spent on this subject alone, a
subject almost completely avoided by Mrs. Gaskell.) Perhaps Gérin's
most remarkable achievement is her keen use of the novels to illustrate her treatment of the life, a biographical technique that more often
than not breeds distrust. Because her knowledge and use of the texts,
however, inspire such confidence, when she informs us that William
Crimsworth's remark about erotic triangles in *The Professor* derives
from Charlotte's recollection of her brother's debauchery and drug-
induced death, it is hard to doubt her. "Limited as had yet been my
experience of life," Crimsworth notes, "I had once had the opportunity
of contemplating, near at hand, an example of the results produced
by a course of interesting and romantic domestic treachery. No golden

halo of fiction was about this example, I saw it bare and real, and it was very loathesome. I saw a mind degraded by the practice of mean subterfuge, by the habit of perfidious deception, and a body depraved by the infectious influence of the vice-polluted soul" (297).

Gérin, like virtually everyone else who has written on the Brontës, is harshly criticized for factual unreliability by Tom Winnifrith. In *The Brontës and Their Background*, Winnifrith writes, "Miss Gerin's most damaging fault is her reliance on untrustworthy printed evidence,"[4] such as the Shakespeare Head edition of Charlotte's letters. This might be a worthwhile criticism but for the fact that Winnifrith is the sort of scholar who regards almost everything as questionable, waiting for all the data to be corrected and all the facts to be in before he can begin to read in earnest, rather like Kierkegaard's would-be believer who is awaiting final factual verifications while on his deathbed. Twenty pages later, however, in a lucid moment he remarks: "Though it is easy to show that a complete and reliable edition of Charlotte Brontë's letters is a necessary preliminary to any scholarly study of the Brontës, it is much harder to suggest what should be done in the absence of such an edition" (25). Winnifrith's immensely useful book provides indispensable materials on the Brontës' religion, reputation, social class, publishing history, critical response; indeed, he is probably today's leading Brontë scholar, but in his quest for absolute accuracy, he says and unsays everything, seriatim. After more than one lengthy harangue about the crimes of T. J. Wise, one of Charlotte Brontë's shadier editors, who altered editions to make them seem firsts, misused manuscripts, attempted to pass off the juvenilia of one Brontë for that of another, Winnifrith concludes of the Brontë juvenilia that "it does not matter a great deal who wrote what" (17). Or "It is a mistake to look for parallels between Charlotte's life and her novels. . . . But it would not be too fanciful to conjecture that it was from Henry Nussey, who after all did think of becoming a missionary, that Charlotte derived her Calvinistic fears in the same way that Jane Eyre heard Calvinistic doctrines from St John Rivers" (21). One's head aches after two hundred pages of this sort of thing.[5] And it is one of those crowning ironies of academic absurdity that after count- less remarks like "Mrs. Gaskell was not a professional scholar, trained to give an accurate transcription of documents" (1), Winnifrith's re-editing of the standard Shakespeare Head edition of Charlotte's poems (1984) should be accused of vast numbers of inaccuracies and mistranscriptions by a correspondent to the *Times Literary Supplement* in the issue of August 23, 1985.

Despite his criticism of Gérin, Winnifrith's own work belongs to the same truth-finding tradition as hers, while Margot Peters's *Unquiet Soul*, which appeared in 1975, came into being in the midst of a feminist revolution. If Gérin saw Charlotte from the outside looking in, Peters presents Charlotte from the heart of her own feminine subjectivity. Thus, her narrative is passionately intense, a psychological or phenomenological account rather than a "documentation." Peters also makes different use of the letters and the novels, seeing (with much justification) more feminist material than Gérin, comprehensive as she was, could even begin to hint at. But Peters is not so involved with her subject as to slight historical and psychological complexities. Reacting to Charlotte's indignant reply to Harriet Martineau's censure of *Villette* for its obsession with love, she writes:

> Charlotte's violent reaction to Martineau's criticism was typical of the curious double-thinking of her age. While many writers challenged convention on one or two fronts, virulent Victorian piety and prudery forced them at the same time to shore up their defenses higher on others. Thus Mrs. Gaskell found nothing wrong in writing about an unwed mother in *Ruth*—a novel that was greeted with cries of outrage—but believed in her heart that Charlotte wrote coarse novels. Charlotte could see nothing indelicate in her own novels but was repelled by Harriet Martineau's atheism. Harriet Martineau took her atheism as a matter of course but was disgusted by the love emphasis in Charlotte's novels, and, later, unreasonably vicious over George Eliot's liaison with George Henry Lewes. Elizabeth Barrett Browning cried out against woman's role in *Aurora Leigh* yet condemned *Jane Eyre* as savage and free-thinking.[6]

What finally impresses us about these three biographies is the necessity of reading all of them to get a comprehensive picture.

In 1976, only a year after Peters, Helene Moglen's *Charlotte Brontë: The Self Conceived* appeared as if to italicize the rapidly evolving feminist-psychological Zeitgeist. Moglen's book opens up the novels by means of penetrating readings that relate the qualities of the fiction to

Brontë's personal development, even convincing us that the novels we regard as the masterpieces achieve their success because of the author's superior self-awareness in weaving their complex web. The faults of *The Professor* and *Shirley* can indeed seem to derive from the author's own irresolution and evasion in facing the problem of selfhood as a dependent woman in a patriarchal society, although it is perhaps an unfair accusation against someone as sensitive to these anachronistic priorities as Brontë herself.

Moglen's book, however, is otherwise sadly crippled by the over-wrought psychoanalytic clichés of its programmatic analysis. Addicted, for instance, to reifications of psychoanalytic metaphors, Moglen compares the relationship of Charlotte and Branwell with the incestuous one of Byron and his sister Augusta, but in the case of the Brontës, "Theirs was not an incest of body but of mind: an incest of the imagination" (39). This sort of wild swinging that takes images for things can only undermine the reader's confidence. What, after all, is an "incest" of the imagination and what has it to do with physical incest? Such metaphoric license hurtles the book toward its self-parodying finale: "Nine months after her marriage, Charlotte Brontë conceived a child and fell ill of the conception: sickened, apparently by fear. It was the last of her neurotic illnesses; the last of her masochistic denials. Love had come too late. . . . On March 31, 1855, at thirty-eight years of age, in the early months of pregnancy, Charlotte Brontë died. She could not bring to birth the self she had conceived."[7]

Moglen's programmatics herald an era in which "culture criticism" and "death of literature" polemics start to flood the literary scene (literature becomes inseparable from culture as a whole). A good specimen of this phenomenon is Terry Eagleton's *Myths of Power: A Marxist Study of the Brontës.* In his polemical introduction, he remarks: "I read Charlotte's novels as 'myths' which work towards a balance or fusion of blunt bourgeois rationality and flamboyant Romanticism, brash initiative and genteel cultivation, passionate rebellion and cautious conformity; and those interchanges embody a complex structure of convergence and antagonism between the landed and industrial sectors of the contemporary ruling class."[8] Eagleton applies to the novels the well-known antinomies of Charlotte's character and fiction—domi-

nance and submission, attacks on the aristocracy combined with a respect for their gentility, defense of middle-class radicalism tempered
with criticism of *parvenu* presumption—in the way that Moglen applies criteria of self-realization, and he arrives, not very surprisingly,
at a similar ranking of their merits. What is of the most interest about
Eagleton's handling of Charlotte Brontë is that, despite the elaborate
Marxist mugging and twitching that mar his work in general, the least
new or illuminating in this criticism are those very ideas that he insists
on as Marxist-generated. Since it is not necessary to subscribe to his
ideology in order to come to most of Eagleton's conclusions, his Marxist obligato often seems merely puerile, whether in this book on the
Brontës or in his brilliant *Literary Theory: An Introduction.* Indeed, before any of his Brontë writing appeared in print, Tom Winnifrith had
already dealt with most of these tensions in Brontë's novels: "We shall
find a similar dichotomy in Charlotte's social philosophy; she does not
believe in existing rigid class divisions, but does believe that good birth
is important," and so on.[9]

What makes Eagleton's work so notable, however, both here and
elsewhere, is his astuteness as reader and critic. One can almost be
tempted to believe again that there really is such a thing as "literary
merit." For despite his emphasis on class struggles, he does not lose
sight of the command of literary form and conventions that produces
masterpieces. Like an orthodox Christian compelled to attribute all his
talents to God, Eagleton (though not a modest type) ascribes all his insights to Marxism, but such quaint modesty is just a pro forma feint, a
party-line afflatus, since no methodology will turn a dim-witted critic
into a bright one. Summing up the prevailing structure of all the Brontë
novels as a struggle between romance and realism, Eagleton rightly
concludes:

> 'Romance', I am aware, is a crudely inadequate term; but I mean by it
> merely the passionate self's free, eloquent expression, in contrast to that
> calculative rationalism which I designate as 'realism'—the analytic ade-
> quation of means to ends in the name of worldly progress. All the 'higher'
> characters are Romantic in this sense: they manifest a rich fluency of
> selfhood, a flair, *brio* and flamboyance which in its overriding of ratio-
> nalist meanness wins the heroine's envying wonder. The heroine admires

this life-style because she lives it also—but lives it as a guilty secret, as submerged, unspeakable fantasy. (75–76)

We tolerate Eagleton's programmatic self-delusions because we realize that it is intelligence, not doctrine, that makes him so enjoyable to read. Capitalism is getting good value for its subsidy of his writings. And now that he has become an establishment literary presence, his neoconservative phase cannot be far off in any case.

Eagleton's polemics seem merely nugatory, however, when placed alongside those of Sandra Gilbert and Susan Gubar in their 1979 magnum opus, *The Madwoman in the Attic: The Woman Writer and the Nineteenth-Century Imagination.* Here, Charlotte Brontë is given the most extensive treatment of any of their writers—more than 125 pages as well as numerous passim references. The reader who is not already a member of their party must feel both overawed by their scholarship and flattened by their resistless polemical steamroller. Rarely have brilliance and bombast been so forcefully combined.

Their accounts of women writers present, moreover, an unresolved epistemological dilemma: the authors are addicted to wordplay and punning (particularly Sandra Gilbert) in the mode of Derridean deconstruction. Indeed, they *are* attempting to deconstruct certain conventional responses, mostly nineteenth century, to women writers. "The roots of 'authority' tell us, after all, that if woman is man's property then he must have authored her, just as surely as they tell us that if he authored her she must be his property. As a creation 'penned' by man, moreover, woman has been 'penned up' or 'penned in.' As a sort of 'sentence' man has spoken, she has herself been 'sentenced': fated, jailed, for he has both 'indited' her and 'indicted' her. As a thought he has 'framed,' she has been both 'framed' (enclosed) in his texts, glyphs, graphics, and 'framed up' (found guilty, found wanting) in his cosmologies." [10] Unfortunately, this quaintly animistic writing, with its throwback to Adam naming the animals, seems to confuse essences with words while at the same time presuming to be at the cutting edge of postmodern self-consciousness. Whereas Derrida, for whom there is nothing outside the text, can afford to play around with words because for him there *is not* anything else (i.e., reality is a "text," a system of signs, subject to interpretation), Gilbert and Gubar are trying to convince us that there is indeed a great deal outside the text: for example, history, social conventions, and the effect of both upon women's roles. This uncontrollable and antithetical wordplay, however, tends to undercut the authors' apparent aims, to reduce much of their treatment of the past and of literary texts to a trivial esthetic game. Whereas their real epistemology and their real ontology are presumably entirely serious, their rhetorical strategies are misappropriated from the decadence of academic deconstruction, which pretends not to believe in "truth" or "reality," as *they* surely seem to do. This opposition between serious substance and frivolous style leaves the reader uncertain as to whether they are ultimately aiming at feminist reform in the world or whether they are only, after all, contemporary incarnations of ivory tower academicism—trendy, playful, but in the long run, inconsequential.

Perhaps their most successful treatments of Brontë's novels are Sandra Gilbert's account of *The Professor* and Susan Gubar's of *Shirley*. Although much insight and careful reading lie behind these, there are the inevitable feminist reductions: "Though Brontë may not have consciously admitted this to herself, through the medium of Crimsworth she suggests that a female is a servile and 'mentally depraved' creature, more slave than angel, more animal than flower. And—the book implies, even if Crimsworth/Brontë does not—she is like this because it is her task in a patriarchal society to be such a creature" (322).

From *Jane Eyre*, which is more or less the keystone of their book, the authors derive their title, *The Madwoman in the Attic. Jane Eyre* tells a "distinctively female story of enclosure and escape, with a 'morbidly vivid' escape dream acted out by an apparently 'gothic' lunatic who functions as the more sedate heroine's double" (314). This notion of a "double" is one of the book's half-dozen pervasive ideas.

> As we explore nineteenth-century literature, we will find that this madwoman emerges over and over again from the mirrors women writers hold up both to their own natures and to their own visions of nature. Even the most apparently conservative and decorous women writers obsessively create fierce and independent characters who seek to destroy all the patriarchal structures which both their authors and their authors' submissive heroines seem to accept as inevitable. . . . The madwoman in literature by women is not merely, as she might be in male literature, an antagonist

or foil to the heroine. Rather, she is usually in some sense the *author's* double, an image of her own anxiety and rage. (77–78)

It is ironic, however, that Gilbert's powerful reading of *Jane Eyre* should dissipate force rather than concentrate it by its insistence on Bertha Rochester as Jane's double, a role that most readers will simply not *feel* as they read the novel. "What Bertha now *does*, for instance, is what Jane wants to do. Disliking the 'vapoury veil' of Jane Rochester, Jane Eyre secretly wants to tear the garments up. Bertha does it for her. Fearing the inexorable 'bridal day,' Jane would like to put it off. Bertha does that for her too" (359). Yet these equations are less than convincing because Gilbert overlooks the differences in quality and motivation behind such outward similarities. It is this willingness to overlook disparities in order to support a program that ultimately does so much damage to the credibility of Gilbert's and Gubar's accounts.

Though even Susan Gubar's enlightening description of *Shirley* is harmed by this disposition, it is her treatment of *Villette* that causes the reader particularly to question the rationale of their whole enterprise. Dense with scholarship and allusion, Gubar's reading of *Villette* makes every word of the literary text portentous, bowed by the weight of centuries of palimpsestic cultural accretions, until it seems the very articles and expletives are sodden—in this case with feminist significance. The nun in the attic, Mme. Walravens, the actress Vashti—everything becomes a smothering apparatus of equal importance. One is hard pressed to believe that this is a novel by Charlotte Brontë rather than by James Joyce.

As an androgynous "barbarian queen" possessing demonic powers associated with Eastern enchantment, Madame Walravens resembles Vashti, for she too is an artist, the creator of crafty plots which result in the death of her characters. Her malevolent plotting, however, only solidifies the connection between witchcraft and female artistry, since the source of the witch's power is her image magic, her *buried representations* that cause weakness, disease, and finally death for the represented victim. With all her egotism and energy, Madame Walravens seems to be a black parody of the artist, perhaps of the author herself, because her three-foot height recalls Brontë's own small stature (four feet, nine inches). At the same time, with her silver beard and masculine voice, she is certainly a sort of

male manqué, and having attained power by becoming an essential part
of patriarchal culture, she uses her arts to further enslave women. (432)

This is heavy going indeed, carrying the reader past incredulity to
the brink of despair. One cannot but feel that a critic who says things
like this is prepared to say absolutely anything, if it will serve her
interests, even indulging such depths of absurdity as the remark about
Brontë's height. This is not so much an interpretation as a dismember-
ing, another sort of violation of both text and history. With feminists like
this, who needs a patriarchy to bash women? But Gilbert and Gubar,
for all their scholarship, their insight, their often powerful reading of
texts, are driven not so much by "truth" as by a congeries of precious
academic critical conventions that depend upon on a tissue of loosely
strung conceits, played with, reiterated, litanized to hypnotic effect and
too often mistaken for reality. As we turn the pages of *The Madwoman
in the Attic*, this tissue disintegrates, falls apart, and one remembers the
conceits as if they were striking images retrieved from dreams rather
than as coherent guides to real or esthetic experience.

With the last item in this twenty-year Brontë retrospective, we take
an engaging detour from polemics. John Maynard's *Charlotte Brontë
and Sexuality* explicitly distances itself from Moglen, Eagleton, Gilbert
and Gubar, and other programmatics, making free use of whatever insights they have to offer, while rejecting their dogma. In this regard
we benefit from the best of several worlds without the need to accept
the orthodoxies of a true believer. Starting from Brontë's juvenilia,
especially the novelettes, Maynard sees the writings as suffused with
eroticism and sexuality, indeed, sees these as their most salient defining qualities. In *Jane Eyre* he shows us how the Reed sisters, Bertha,
Rochester, St. John, as well as Jane herself, constitute a spectrum of
diverse modes of sexuality, and in *Villette*, Madames Beck and Walravens, de Hamal, Ginevra, Vashti, Graham, Paulina, M. Paul, the
painting of Cleopatra. At almost every turn we are presented with distinctive erotic sap. Maynard acutely reveals how the restrictions of
the era and the accusations of coarseness after *Jane Eyre* reinforced
Brontë's already strong tendency to use coded metaphors to stand for
sexual qualities. "Whereas D. H. Lawrence felt able to begin to use
images of genital organs directly to speak about differences in sexu-

ality, Brontë could only expand the intrinsically sexual aspects of other parts of the body until they stood for sexuality as a whole. The heart, especially, always associated with love and feeling, becomes in *Villette* a kind of sexual organ, a measure of the potency and warmth of the entire person."[11] Indeed, in her own characteristic way, she is seen by Maynard as offering "the fullest and most sophisticated discussion of sexual issues of any major Victorian writer before Hardy" (viii). In the juvenilia, "Writing truly for private publication, for that unblushing audience of three sibling fellow authors, Brontë could and did write with freedom on issues of sex and scandal that she, and far more her fellow respectable authors, dared not exercise in published works" (40). The "world below" of the Angrian fantasies "was a world called up almost in scorn of the world of girls' schools, country isolation, and restriction in which Brontë lived" (41).

The pervasive theme of Brontë's fiction, as Maynard sees it, is sexual awakening, a theme that in some respects has much in common with the discovery of the self that is emphasized by Moglen and Peters, but Maynard sees this self as so highly sexualized that the "awakening" and the "discovery" become hard to distinguish. His rich reading of the four mature novels builds upon while transcending almost all the earlier accounts described above, another way of saying that his "sexual" approach is neither constricting nor monomaniacal.

Maynard's Rochester, far from being Exploitive Patriarchal Society, is an embodiment of male sexual needs—a precursor of Lawrence's Mellors—that counterpoints similar needs in Jane. "Like Lawrence . . . Brontë looks for an Adam of mature passion. Rochester is clearly associated with this resuscitated Adam and as clearly contrasted to the distorted, civilized St John" (114). Bertha, instead of being Jane's double, represents for Maynard "the dangers of madly uncontrolled sexual feeling" (126). Nor are Rochester and Bertha used by Brontë to express her own rage against men: "Brontë herself seems . . . a bad candidate for an extreme hidden anger against males: like Jane, she could accept men she liked with warmth and she could be clear and direct in her criticisms of men who were bullying or authoritarian." (250) For all her worship of Thackeray, one could add, she had very little trouble telling him off when he incensed her.

Maynard's tour of the novels reaches its high point in his impassioned

account of the richness of *Villette*. Incredulous at one critic's claim that
Lucy Snowe "rid herself of her libido in making love to Dr. John's letters" so she could "pursue her real nature as a frigid woman" (254),
Maynard shows us how the novel allows M. Paul and Lucy to express
their complex love in a chapter that "celebrates a kind of marriage":

> M. Paul takes Lucy into a small house. There is, pointedly, no servant,
> nobody but them-selves—something not generally allowed in Victorian
> fiction. . . . The house recalls some of the idyllic places of love of the early
> tales. It is filled with plants and flowers. French windows are "kissed" by
> green leaves of climbing vines and open onto gardens and fields. Upstairs
> Lucy even has a bold look at "two pretty cabinets of sleeping rooms." . . .
> The emphasis is on loving and giving, not seduction and lust. But the scene
> and place nonetheless provide the magic of an initiation into a mature
> relationship for the two lovers. (208)

Maynard's Brontë, in sum, is neither a neurotic nor a twentieth-
century feminist, but a pioneer of expressive sexuality whom one could
easily be induced to regard as pretty healthy, but nowadays, when it
has become politic to see everything as just politics, perhaps proclama-
tions of neurosis or health will be seen as one more political act. Why
not say, then, that, for Maynard, Brontë comes off looking better than
most. Whom shall we offer as a paragon if *she* is merely a basket case:
Yeats, Eliot, Hemingway, Pound?

As an important bonus, Maynard provides as addendum a new version of his earlier essay on the possible causes of Charlotte Brontë's
death. Although Mrs. Gaskell had treated the marriage and death
very briefly, she did convey implications of a pregnancy, but her very
terse description of the death also suggests a debilitating weakness and
delirium, possibly stemming from a bad cold that Charlotte had con-
tracted somewhat earlier. The Brontë family doctor ascribed the death
to "phthisis," which Maynard characterizes as "a general term for a
tubercular wasting disease." In 1920, Lucile Dooley in "Psychoanalysis of Charlotte Brontë, as a Type of the Woman of Genius" attributed
her death "to neurosis over marriage and motherhood," according to
Maynard. This was the beginning of a strain of psychosomatic explanations that was later on encouraged by Dr. Phillip Rhodes, an M.D.,

who explained her death as hyperemesis gravidarum, a kind of severe morning sickness and vomiting that can lead to death in very neurotic women.[12] Rhodes also spoke of "unconscious rejection of the baby" and "failure to achieve satisfactory psychological relationships with most others." Parts of this explanation have been accepted by Peters, Moglen, and others and we have already noted above how Moglen's use of this material characterizes the preposterous quality of much psychoanalytic post-mortem. Maynard remarks that "because this view of Brontë as a crippled neurotic has often been used to support a view of her work as artistically naive (written by her neurosis) and intellectually limited (written from compulsion, not understanding) the issue of Brontë's death even bears upon one's ultimate assessment of the nature and importance of her work" (218–19). For variety's sake, it is worth mentioning here the view of Rosamond Langbridge, in her wild 1929 *Charlotte Brontë*,[13] that Charlotte's death was the final consequence of her obnoxious husband's habit of coercing his wife's innate dutifulness—here the duty to be a mother!

Maynard, with the assistance of Dr. Gerson Weiss of the New York University Medical Center, reviews these various hypotheses of Charlotte's death. Examining every known reference to Charlotte's health near the time of her death, they reach their own conclusions:

> Perhaps the most important point that emerges is how little can be surely known about the causes of Brontë's death. Dr Weiss's reasoning calls into strong question even the assumption that she was pregnant. His conclusions about her illness lend most weight to the traditional view that she died of some kind of rampant wasting disease such as the tubercular disease given in the original death certificate. What seems clear is that there is no ground for using the facts of her death to establish a psychological illness. It should be noted indeed that Brontë's mental health seems good in the records we have of her life before and after her marriage. She may not have found marriage at thirty-eight easy or Nicholls the ideal or romantic ideal of a husband. But she enjoyed her honeymoon trip to Ireland, took to her new life with energy, and testified to her continued affection for her husband. Dr Rhodes's account is not a careful look at the evidence concerning Brontë's death but another attempt to read her life (and her sisters' lives) according to a pattern of neurosis. . . . The evidence

and reasoning about the evidence presented here . . . provides no support
for the view that she was neurotic. Far less can we justify romantic notions
that her death was caused by her psychological revulsion from motherhood or marriage, whatever we may think of the suitability of a woman of
genius for either role in the nineteenth century. (224)

Although the fiercest literary politicians insist that nothing is apolitical and that what *looks* apolitical is always only naturalized establishment politics, this position exists mostly to flatter their own immoderacies, which are themselves just attempts at violent naturalization.
Everything is a rape anyhow, they appear to be saying, so when I violate
you, just lie back and enjoy it, but when we review the positions taken in
these various books about Charlotte Brontë, her life as well as her death,
we must reject such facile blurring of distinctions. Moglen, Eagleton,
Gilbert, and Gubar, at their most ruthlessly polemical, attempt to force
mouthfuls of bristling hay down the throats of their resisting readers.
Eagleton's Marxism comes so close to entr'act buffoonery that it is
easily separable from his valuable contributions, though it is harder
to make this separation with some of the other writers. Even though
Mrs. Gaskell and, once or twice, Winifred Gérin, exhibit some religious
tendentiousness with which we may not sympathize, we do not feel exploited and abused. Unlike postmodern writers, Mrs. Gaskell had very
few philosophic options. When Eagleton, Gilbert, and Gubar sit down
to compose, it is with a consciousness of the whole overturned philosophic tradition, going back to Plato through Nietzsche, Derrida, Foucault, and Richard Rorty. In place of Reason with a capital "R," there
are now "reasons" and "paradigms." Reality is now seen not as the
will of God but as Language, Metaphor, Textuality, Socialization. In
the atmosphere of today's antifoundationalism, which calls into question epistemology and distrusts all accounts of the relationship between
thought and "reality," taking aggressive proselytizing positions is no
longer a matter of naiveté, innocence, or conformity with a divine will,
but a calculating political action. The difference between Mrs. Gaskell
and Mrs. Gilbert is little short of epochal.

Maynard, despite his prevailing theme of sexuality, seems the least
programmatic and as a result he is notably persuasive. On the subject
of Charlotte's death his conclusions are the coolest and most plau-

sible of any. Yet even Peters, who looks at Brontë's life from a feminist point of view, does not appear to be twisting our arms or manipulating our guilt. Thus, a distinction keeps begging to be made—between what is indeed merely and unabashedly political and what are the unavoidable limitations of individual existence in the world; between the conscious, voluntary, and perhaps "political" choices of our day-to-day behavior (such as writing a certain type of book about Charlotte Brontë) and the unrecognized finitudes of society and personality that provide us all with ineluctable predilections and tics in a world where we must be either fat or thin, kind or cruel, smart or dumb. Since being completely disinterested and without qualities is tantamount to being dead, we all must act from some motivation or other, be one thing rather than another. But to call all motivation and action political because they stem from human interests and finitudes is like calling all behavior selfish because it satisfies human needs. Within the spectrum of human behavior there is a range from selfish to unselfish, from political to unpolitical, and most people can discern the difference. This difference does not depend on disinterest—because there *is* no disinterest— but it does depend on a particular kind of interest. To pretend that no difference exists is not only disingenuous but the most manipulative politics of them all.

7

Emily Brontë
and the Strains of
Modern Criticism

Almost from its day of publication, *Wuthering Heights* has enjoyed a rare critical consensus in the acknowledgment of its anomalous, unprecedented character as a novel, its overwhelming power as an imaginative construct. Even those early critics who found it "coarse" and anti-Christian were nevertheless forced to concede its shocking potency. Today, the consensus about its genius is virtually total and what disagreement remains has more to do with its meaning than its status in English fiction.

Wuthering Heights, in fact, turns out to be one of the most inscrutable works in the standard repertoire, an inscrutability sometimes attributed to its "overdetermination," the coexistence within the novel of various and competing systems of meaning: realism, myth, romance. In providing too much conflicting information as well as too many implications, these irreconcilable systems make it impossible to arrive at any single global interpretation. Although almost every critic is ready to acknowledge this primal and ineluctable inscrutability, such an admission rarely prevents him from forging ahead into an innovatingly unconvincing interpretation of his own.

Added to the already insuperable problem of the novel's meaning is the even more intriguing question of how such a singular masterpiece could have been produced by someone as young, isolated, and indrawn as Emily Brontë. Just where did this novel come from? After all the "influences" have been tallied—Byron, E. T. A. Hoffmann, Scott, as well as obscurer writers whom Emily Brontë read in *Blackwood's* and *Fraser's* magazines—there comes the inevitable admission that when all is said and done *Wuthering Heights* is sui generis. When the lean scraps of Brontë's biographical remnants have been shuffled and re-shuffled—a letter to Ellen Nussey, a "that's right" about religion being a personal matter, and a few other whatnots—the springs of artistic command behind *Wuthering Heights* remain cut off from anything we know about its author.

The liability of most existing criticism of *Wuthering Heights* is its tendency to reduce to more manageable—and more pedestrian—dimensions the same multivalence that engendered the novel's preeminence in the first place. What most of the criticism reveals is not some hidden reconciliatory dimension of Brontë's fiction so much as some hidden programmatic dimension of the critic himself, who is apt to be unsettled by the radicalism of Brontë's invented world. This is not to say that we want or can expect criticism that is the product of no point of view at all, but it seems reasonable to expect criticism to be capable of saying something about its object that is not merely a hidden (or patent) statement about the critic or his desires. Though people are situated in time and place, and shaped by psychobiological configurations they themselves did not choose, not all thought is equally limited by these contingencies, nor is all thinking merely "political," except when "political" is used simply to mean "motivated." (Of course, if all thinking *is* merely political, then so is the idea that everything is political, although people who make this claim invariably believe that what *they* are speaking is the unmediated truth, not politics.) Specimens of relatively unconstricting criticism of this novel are rare, but accounts like those by Mrs. Humphrey Ward, Q. D. Leavis, and Winifred Gérin at least attempt to honor the novel's multivocal counterpoint. Indeed, there is a curious self-contradiction in some of the current condescension toward commentators like these, for in repudiating the idea of transcendent values or perceptions, many present-day vanguard critics attempt to invalidate earlier thinkers by exposing the ways in which they were only mouthpieces for their own ignorant times. When they supplant these older critics with new ones, generally Marxist or feminist, the implication is that these later critics are not merely mouthpieces for *their* times but, rather, that what they speak is simply the truth—in a word, eternal verities. Until the knotty problem of the relation of truth to time and eternity is more carefully worked out by vanguard critics, much of what they have to say will remain precarious.

In looking at a few postmodern treatments of Emily Brontë, I do not wish to suggest that there is some single, ideal way of doing criticism. The skilled practitioner is always free to expand critical methodology, and we cannot know a priori all that criticism is capable of achieving. But we can legitimately feel that some critical performances are positively harmful, that novels and poems are deformed, their power deflected, by reductive misrepresentations, and that readers are alienated from potentially expansive experiences by what amounts to critical blackmail. Students, as captive audiences, are particularly vulnerable—especially to shows of omniscience by dogmatic professors waving political or scholarly banners, who often disparage aesthetic pleasure (and its related enlightenment) as simpleminded. In being subjected to a steady diet of whatever the current critical canon happens to sanctify, students and "ordinary" readers (i.e., nonspecialists) can be easily intimidated into believing that an early romantic novel is *actually about* capitalism rather than its ostensible subject. The charm exerted upon pseudorevolutionaries (whether students or professors) by the one-upmanship of *épater le bourgeois* is hard to exorcise from perverse readings of classic works. Beyond even this, a *credo quia impossibile est* mentality finds considerable self-gratification in the very act of going against presuppositions held by the ordinary, vulgar world.

J. Hillis Miller's two accounts of *Wuthering Heights* can serve as examples of the clerical intimidation characteristic of Miller's work in general. By "clerical," I mean the relentless and obsessional promulgation of stylized, formal, intellectual tropes and patterns irrespective of the interests of a human audience. Perhaps the paradigmatic instance of this is Miller's notorious essay, "The Critic as Host," which aimed to show that it is impossible, given the nature of "intertextuality," to say what one means, a performance whose erudite brilliance is matched by

the radical mendacity of someone engaging in the very practice he pro-
claims impossible.[1] Indeed, in the case of Miller there often seems to be
less regard for truth than for the sheer gratifications of "performance"
itself, for the play of clever, nihilistic ideas. In *The Disappearance of
God*, for example, as a sequence of interesting background information
about *Wuthering Heights* abruptly comes to an end, Miller lets down
a procrustean Murphy bed of theses on which to hack away at the
novel's distinctive multivalence. Speaking of the narrow evangelicalism
of Joseph, Miller remarks that "the central drama of the novel derives
from the children's acceptance of Joseph's judgment of them," itself a
pretty sweeping claim.[2] After this dogmatic assertion, Miller tightens
things up even more: "As is well known, Emily Brontë was influenced
by two forms of Protestantism, the Evangelicalism of her father, who
was an Anglican clergyman, and the Methodism of her Aunt Branwell
and their servant Tabby" (181). The rest of the essay, in Miller's most
offputting clerical mode, is devoted to reducing *Wuthering Heights* to a
monochromatic work that exemplifies these assertions. In the process,
the novel is warped and muddled by obscurantist clarifications.

In his later deconstructive mode, however, Miller repudiates this
earlier view of *Wuthering Heights* in the course of yet another go at the
novel, in *Literature and Repetition*. Beginning with the general thesis
that *Wuthering Heights* is overdetermined by an excess of competing
semiotic systems—certainly a plausible one—he goes on to review its
critical history and the various reductive interpretations that testify
to this overdetermination. Among his list of failures Miller magnani-
mously includes his own previous account of the novel as "a fictional
dramatization of Brontë's religious vision."[3] After this generosity, however, Miller subjects the novel to his new and equally desperate thesis
about fiction and repetition, in which he attempts to explain why this
overdetermined work can never be satisfactorily explained. Running
it through most of the deconstructive techniques that were flourishing
circa 1975, he exhibits an alarming resemblance to television's legend-
ary doubletalker, "Professor" Irwin Corey:

> The trace of such an absence therefore retraces nothing. It can refer only
> to another trace, in that relation of incongruity which leads the reader
> of *Wuthering Heights* from one such emblematic design to another. Each

passage stands for another passage, in the way Branderham's sermon, as I have said, is a commentary on Jesus's words, themselves a commentary on an Old Testament passage, and so on. Such a movement is a constant passage from one place to another without ever finding the original literal text of which the others are all figures. This missing center is the head referent which would still the wandering movement from emblem to emblem, from story to story, from generation to generation, from Catherine to Catherine, from Hareton to Hareton, from narrator to narrator. (67)

And so on, as the deconstructive jukebox plays its worn out old records. Reading this essay only a decade or two after it was written, we can hardly believe that there was ever a time when respected intellectuals could have uttered such drivel with impunity (except for the fact that they are doing it even now). We can take heart, however, from the likelihood that today Miller has probably repudiated this too, as his current thing is "ethics."

When Sandra Gilbert and Susan Gubar produced *The Madwoman in the Attic* in 1979, its effect was so startling that critical response was too overwhelmed to be discriminating. But when Gilbert's essay on *Wuthering Heights* is reread in 1989, it is, once more, hard to believe that it did not always seem a jejune, impressionistic, and tendentious farrago. *Wuthering Heights* in Gilbert's hands is only too scrutable, having the same meaning as most of the other works discussed in *Madwoman*. It could well convince a reader that everything really *is* just politics and that reader-response criticism is correct in claiming that readers only find their own obsessions in the texts they read.

Gilbert sees the novel as another battleground between nature and culture in which nature, as Catherine I, resists the whole patriarchal structure of culture as embodied in Hindley Earnshaw and Edgar Linton, among others, and as internalized even by Ellen Dean. Although Gilbert acknowledges that Milton and his Eve are never alluded to, she interprets all references to heaven, hell, Satan, and God as overturnings of *Paradise Lost* by antinomian Emily, and she does not hesitate to import Charlotte Brontë's passages on Eve and Milton from *Shirley* as if they had been written into *Wuthering Heights* by Emily herself. Whatever value can be derived from the nature/culture opposition, it is rapidly vitiated by Gilbert's monomania regarding patriarchy.

She is enabled to pull patriarchal rabbits from magical hats by means of a technique she uses throughout her criticism, here and elsewhere: without evidence or demonstration she asserts as true those things that she would like to believe are true, and then refers back to them as established facts.

> Given the fact that Brontë never mentions either Milton or *Paradise Lost* in *Wuthering Heights,* any identification of her as Milton's daughter may at first seem eccentric or perverse. Shelley [i.e., Mary], after all, provided an overtly Miltonic framework in *Frankenstein* to reinforce our sense of her literary intentions. *But despite the absence of Miltonic references,* it *eventually becomes plain* that *Wuthering Heights* is also a novel haunted by Milton's bogey. *We may speculate, indeed* that Milton's absence is itself a presence, so painfully does Brontë's story dwell on the places and persons of his imagination [emphasis added].[4]

When absences become presences, the possibilities for critical omnipotence are unlimited. "And indeed, if we look again at the crucial passage in *Shirley* where Charlotte Brontë's Shirley/Emily criticizes Milton, *we find an unmistakable version of Nelly Dean.* 'Milton tried to see the first woman,' says Shirley, 'but, Cary, he saw her not. . . . It was his cook that he saw. . . .' This comment explains a great deal. For *if Nelly Dean is Eve as Milton's cook. . . .* [And then, only a few sentences later:] *As Milton's cook, in fact,* Nelly Dean is patriarchy's paradigmatic housekeeper" (emphasis added, 291). Just a turn of a phrase is all it takes to transform wishes into facts and Nelly Dean into Milton's Eve.

Commenting on the blizzard in the early pages of the novel, Gilbert quotes from *Paradise Lost* in order to establish that Yorkshire and Hell are pretty much the same place, even though the passages from Milton have no resemblance to those from *Wuthering Heights.* Since snow is thereby instantly made into a symbol of "hellish nature" (though elsewhere in this same account, nature is the way for Gilbert to resist culture), we are not surprised that it can also easily be made "female." Or, as Gilbert puts it, "This hellish nature is *somehow female*" (emphasis added). Having said this, it is an easy step to "The femaleness of this 'natural' hell is suggested too. . . . Female nature has risen, it seems, in a storm of protest. . . . *Finally, that the storm is both hellish and female is made clearest of all* by Lockwood's second visionary dream" (emphasis added, 262–3). By incremental reassertion, it appears, new "facts" can be easily generated.

Perhaps the most bizarre moment in all of *Madwoman* is Gilbert's description of the Lintons' dog, Skulker, when he bites Catherine, an example of critical "production" at its most magical:

> . . . when the dog is "throttled off, his huge purple tongue hanging half a foot out of his mouth . . . his pendant lips [are] streaming with bloody slaver." "Look . . . how her foot bleeds," Edgar Linton exclaims, and "She may be lamed for life," his mother anxiously notes (chap. 6). *Obviously* such bleeding has sexual connotations, especially when it occurs in a pubescent girl. Crippling injuries to the feet are equally resonant, moreover, *almost always* signifying symbolic castration, as in the stories of Oedipus, Achilles, and the Fisher King. Additionally, *it hardly needs to be noted* that Skulker's equipment for aggression—his huge purple tongue and pendant lips, for instance—*sounds extraordinarily phallic.* In a Freudian sense, *then,* the imagery of this brief but violent episode hints that Catherine has been simultaneously catapulted into adult female sexuality *and* [emphasis in original] castrated [emphasis added except where noted]. (272)

This passage wins without contest the Bright Sophomore's Literary Symbolism Award. (As every socks-up exam-taker learns early on, when in doubt, say everything you know.) The possibilities of critical freedom seem limitless when bleeding lips become phallic, snows become hellish and female, and Nelly Dean becomes Eve, as Milton's cook. But why not, when the meanings are apparent even before novels are read? Yet Gilbert is not content merely to turn lips into phalluses when it suits her purpose. Only a few pages later, Catherine is referred back to as "seized by Thrushcross Grange and held fast in the jaws of reason, education, decorum" (277). Bulldogs have unlimited potential—even as reason itself—when they become decorous bleeding lips masquerading as phallic symbols.

So global and dogmatic is this account of *Wuthering Heights* in the interests of its rigid feminist program (like most of the other accounts in *Madwoman*) that, despite its "liberating" orientation, it exerts the same repressive force against multiplicity of thinking and freedom of inquiry as we tend to associate with extreme conservatism. Yet it is by no means unique in this regard, for intimately related to this brand of critical absolutism is a shocker like James H. Kavanagh's *Emily Brontë*. Forming part of a Marxist/feminist series from Blackwell's called "Rereading Literature," this examination of *Wuthering Heights* actually precludes discussion, insofar as it rejects with contempt the world of public discourse that might redeem it from its autistic marginality. Kavanagh's universe is an Althusserian-Marxist/Lacanian-Freudian one combined with French feminism, which means that he is concerned with extremely parochial antinomian politics rather than with any sort of general "literary response," though one is willing to grant that in more talented hands something worthwhile could be said from almost any point of view. One reads Kavanagh's book (insofar as one can be said to read it at all) with no recognition of its claim to be examining Emily Brontë's novel. To quote a relatively accessible passage, about the dream in which Lockwood breaks a window to wrestle with the ghostly Cathy's hand as she tries to get back into Wuthering Heights: "Lockwood's ambivalent gestures in this scene—first forcibly penetrating ('knocking my knuckles through the glass') the membrane that separates male adult from girl child, and then literally plugging 'the hole' [really literally?] with words and writing, those marks of culture and the Law—echo the Oedipal father's denial of his own seductive desire."[5] More typical, however, is the slavish Lacanian epigonism— beyond parody—of "Nelly works to pull Cathy out of an Imaginary self-annihilation into the heat of the Father's phallic desire, only to pull her into a Symbolic order whose potentially liberating linguistic power is recuperated for another kind of morbidity and closure under the cold hand of the dead Father's Law" (49). Lastly, Kavanagh relies heavily on Jane Gallop's Lacanian-feminist *The Daughter's Seduction*, from which he quotes passages such as this, which he applies to Heathcliff: "Or, in more pointed language, he is a prick. . . . [T]he prick is 'beyond good and evil', 'beyond the phallus'. Phallocentrism . . . [is] an upright matter. The prick, in some crazy way, is feminine," and so on, in some crazy way (42).

For a book that treats itself as a cutting edge, Kavanagh can be remarkably dull-witted, examining Lockwood's dream, for instance, in neopsychoanalytic terms with no regard for the fact that this "dream" is no dream at all but a conscious construct by Emily Brontë rather than an involuntary operation of someone's unconscious. Emily Brontë would be even more of a genius than we normally allow if she could have achieved conscious mastery of the "laws" of the unconscious well before Freud invented them. But the spuriousness of Kavanagh's messianic rescue of *Wuthering Heights* for Marxist feminism is not my real concern. The most instructive parts of Kavanagh's book for an understanding of contemporary criticism are the preface and the acknowledgments.

Feeling the need to justify his use of arcane language, Kavanagh makes an extraordinary assertion at the start of his preface: "The theoretical framework of my critical practice certainly tends to see 'common sense' as, in large part, a convenient designation for the most firmly established cultural conventions, and 'common sense' language as the *unavoidable jargon* [emphasis added] of the dominant ideology" (xiii). Kavanagh is doubtless correct about common sense being a term for "the most firmly established cultural conventions," but when he goes on to describe common sense language as "the unavoidable jargon of the dominant ideology," we have been granted a rare insight into the mechanisms of contemporary radical antinomian thought that simultaneously repudiates and reestablishes foundations for knowledge.

Social communities and civilization-at-large are made possible by the development of language and conventions that enable communication, which in turn enables the growth of the large institutions of education, medicine, transportation, and food production. The greater the number of people who share a language, the greater the number who are available to further the development of these institutions that nurture human life in society. For along with this relatively universal language, many smaller-scale and specialized languages also coexist, serving the various arts and sciences that contribute to society as a whole. Since the number of people involved in each specialty is quite small, to be of larger use the specialists must also be able to communicate in the universal tongue, which of course they are able to do simply by virtue of their membership in society as a whole. Indeed, it is through this more general participation that their work is able to acquire social value.

When we use the word "jargon," however, we normally intend to describe one of these peculiar, specialized languages. For example, the *Random House Dictionary of the English Language* gives as its most common meaning "the language, esp. the vocabulary, peculiar to a particular trade, profession, or group." To use "jargon," then, to refer to the universal or common language of a civilization is strictly meaningless, since it is the conventionality of the common language that enables any other "language" to be perceived as jargon. When Kavanagh contrasts the general tongue with the specialized tongue of Marxist criticism as the relation of jargon to nonjargon, he engages in quite literally incomprehensible antinomian solipsism. It is not purely arbitrary that the common language is what *it* is and the Marxist critical language is what *it* is. One is a general vehicle for daily life in the world, with relevance for millions of people. The other is an effete mandarin lingo, used by a miniscule portion of society likely to be afflicted with grandiose anachronistic delusions. Far from enhancing or illuminating the daily lives of a large and disadvantaged segment of civilization, Marxist-feminist-critical language is all too often the privileged "jargon" of a small, parasitical, upwardly mobile bourgeois interest group. One questions not only the judgment, but the very sanity of a remark like Kavanagh's about jargon, and once the question is raised, the credentials and social function of a powerful wing of academic professionalism are exposed to scrutiny. For this mentality partakes of the antinomianism we associate with such groups as radical-right neo-Nazis, the Ku Klux Klan, TV evangelists—people of limited culture and education who live in a self-enclosed delusional private world and speak only to each other, or to God—and we may very properly wonder what excuse can be made for privileged educated mandarins who succumb to such mania. The question is not whether the common tongue's assumptions point to transcendent truths. Indeed, the question of truth is not really involved, since "common sense" and its language (whatever they may have been supposed to be in the past) are regarded by contemporary intellectuals as things that make civilization possible, apart from any question of truth. Even the most determined philosophical realist is unlikely to claim that common sense language really *represents* things in the world as they are in themselves. Unfortunately, a number of the fanatic strains in today's radical "oppositionist" disciplines speak as if they believed that their own specialized jargon really does describe some sort of unmediated reality, that (to take a trivial example) Lockwood *really was* (in a functional way) puncturing somebody's hymen by reaching through a window glass, that the Lintons' dog *really was* in some sense "Oedipal." While it is one of criticism's functions to suggest exemplary affinities between literary works and a larger universe, something has gone wildly wrong when more than an affinity is being suggested—when, in fact, the metaphorical terms of the affinity are insisted upon as the real reality and the contractual (as it were) terms of everyday life in the world are regarded as purely phantasmal. In disparaging the common language, however, these critics undermine the very possibility of oppositional or any other criticism, for without a common language widely understood, neither understanding nor subversion is possible.

The alarming character of Kavanagh's remark about jargon is in no way mitigated by the acknowledgments that follow, of which I reproduce two paragraphs:

> There is one acknowledgement that I do not have to make, although its absence should be mentioned, since it is the mark of a significant change in the way intellectual work is produced. There is no patient, untiring typist or clerical assistant to be thanked. This book was composed entirely on a screen, using Waterloo Script running on an IBM 3081, with the final typescript produced on an IBM 6670 Model II laser printer. Those readers who do not know what I am talking about, soon will. Of course, I have ambivalent feelings about the significance of this fact: on the one hand, it marks the beginning of the end of another cottage industry upon which many marginal workers—mostly women, depend; on the other hand, it means that no woman or man—so often an unpaid spouse or companion—wasted a few hundred hours of her or his life being my personal secretary. But my feelings about this matter little, since it is the symptom of a new wave of capitalist rationalization of office work that, now that its effects are felt in the higher spheres of academia, has already become irreversible. I must, however, acknowledge the assistance of the profes-

sional and technical staff of the Princeton University Computer Center, about whom I can have no illusion that they laboured out of love of myself or my project.

My son, Ian, is perhaps the only person who lost something from my writing this book. I cannot give back the time, but I can give him my thanks and love, and hope that one day he will retrieve some value from what I have done. (xviii-xix)

To begin with, why does Kavanagh bring up the whole matter of acknowledging a typist when he has no typist to acknowledge? Presumably, the "patient, untiring typist or clerical assistant" represents certain virtues of devotion connected with an earlier dispensation that are now missing. He supplements this by noting that another "cottage industry" depended upon by marginal workers, mostly women, is coming to an end. In saying that no one "wasted a few hundred hours" of his or her life typing Kavanagh's manuscript, is he directing our attention to a good or a bad thing? If the cottage industry actually "wasted" the life of other people, then it would seem to be a good thing that it is being phased out. On the other hand, Kavanagh sounds sad, if not positively nostalgic, about its demise, which deprives him of a certain worshipful attention as professor. He then goes on to note that the Princeton Computer Center, which has supplanted his typist (whom no one had as yet forced him to abandon, in any case), does not perform its labor out of love, either of Kavanagh or his book. One is inclined to ask, What does this man really want? Just what is it that's bugging him?

Love, recognition, and their deprivation seem to be at the front of his mind. For he now notes that his son is the "only person" who lost something as a result of the time Kavanagh has spent on this book. (The logical connection between this sense of guilt at his son's loss and the preceding remarks about typists is not clear.) It is puzzling that his son is the *only* person to lose from this book, since the implication has been that some marginal typist has also lost, by being supplanted by the Princeton Computer Center. Kavanagh cannot restore to his son the time and attention he diverted to his book. Instead, he thanks his son, though it is not clear for what, since his son was not involved in some voluntary agreement with his father regarding paternal distribution of time. Still, he hopes that some day his son will find this wretched book a compensation for the love that he was denied in order to produce it.

This is already a knockout performance, but there is still more. To have used a mainframe computer before 1985, when this book was published, is to have chosen very early to resist Chartist or Luddite impulses in order to operate at the cutting edge of the computerized academy. Kavanagh, despite his nostalgia for typists and his contribution to the support of a marginal industry (or his participation in an "exploitive" one, if it was his wife who did the typing) not only eagerly embraced a new technology that for most academics was still several years off, he thrusts in our faces all the obscure mainframe and printer model numbers that we associate with yuppies romancing about their BMW's to envious friends. Although he is about to peddle a variety of (admittedly putative) academic Marxism in the form of his book, which aims to subvert the unfounded "jargon" of "common sense" in bourgeois capitalist society with a lexicon of antiphallogocentric epiphanies, he sounds remarkably like a TV pitchman appealing to the attractions of vulgar conspicuous capitalist consumption. He is well pleased with himself to be at this technocratic cutting edge, even though "it is a symptom of a new wave of capitalist rationalization," and even though it involves displacing marginal peasants from their livelihoods. But since there seemed to be something degrading about that livelihood anyhow (i.e., it wasted precious hours in which presumably they could have been operating computers or watching TV commercials about BMW's), Kavanagh's guilt will not prove terminal. It is more than compensated for, in any case, by his sense that he participates in "the higher social spheres of academia."

Although I am unable to offer a precise or deep explanation of all this, what I do see here, as in so much American academic Marxism and avant-gardism, is a powerful drive toward upward mobility, a self-disavowing elitism, a desire for love, approval, and recognition of superiority from others, mixed with *ressentiment* at the insufficiency of what is actually being offered. Finally, there is an air of superiority toward "marginalized" plebes that does not preclude guilt feelings about a failure to give *them* enough love, despite professions of being their supporter against the capitalists whose life-style really seems devastatingly attractive. Indeed, this syndrome is well summed up by John Gray, in a *Times Literary Supplement* review of some academic Marxist scholarship, as the "embarrassing thesis that the radicalization of the intelligentsia is a response to a blockage in their upward social mobility rather than the expression of any commitment to critical reason." Referring to "the American radical intelligentsia" as "preoccupied with the ephemera of the European culture market, whose most grotesque manifestations have enjoyed in American academia a sort of stilted after-life," Gray characterizes it as "an intellectual culture insulated from political experience of radical socialism and an academic class which uses the rhetoric and theorizing of the radical intelligentsia of Europe a decade or a generation ago to legitimate its estrangement from its own culture."[6]

It is this estrangement that seems to me to be the salient quality of work like Kavanagh's, a cultish and blindered criticism that lacks regard either for the literature it examines or the educated audience that might benefit from more serious efforts at mediation between novel and reader. Hillis Miller's arid clericalism can at least lay claim to wide-ranging knowledge and literary skill; few readers will doubt that Gilbert and Gubar are committed to some sort of feminism, even if their critical methods are unreliable and misleading and their writing too facile and fanciful to be persuasive; and Terry Eagleton at his best is a brilliant reader and a master of clear and forceful prose, though not without his own antic disposition.

On the subject of Emily Brontë, however, Winifred Gérin is still preeminent. As the skillful biographer of Charlotte, Emily, Anne, and Branwell, she has produced readings of their works that remain powerfully illuminating. Her use of Emily's poetry to explore both her novel and her life is a model of critical acumen. Years of residence in Haworth, decades of involvement with the entire Brontë family, and incomparable familiarity with their complete oeuvre, as well as the surrounding social and literary culture, yielded a rare lesson in apolitical literary service. (It is worth observing that Gérin was not an academic.) There is a terrible irony in Kavanagh's attempt in his early pages to put her down as a naive precursor of his *sagesse*, and the contrast between their contributions would be comical, were it not embarrassing. Stevie

Davies, in her recent account of Emily Brontë for the "Key Women
Writers" series, is unimpressed with Kavanagh in particular as well as
the general Marxist/feminist program of the past decade: "In James
Kavanagh's *Emily Brontë* we are arrested by the bizarre phenomenon
of a 'feminism' dominated by the bearded patriarchs of literary criticism, Freud and Marx, and claiming to reveal her as 'raped away in the
world of her own creating' by the father's pen/penis. Such phallocentric
'feminism' represents the degeneration of a critical tradition, in which
the quest for insight has become a desecrating voyeurism."[7] Davies
sees Emily Brontë as rebellious as Milton, and with regard to views like
those of Gilbert and Gubar about language as a masculine tool, she
remarks: "It is doubtful whether Emily Brontë could be imagined as
accepting without mockery the proposition which has become axiom-
atic in our own day that language is a universally masculine artifact.
Such a position affronts women by ascribing to them a witless pusilla-
nimity within society. Women have always made language. They have
handed it on from generation to generation, on behalf of our race" (9).

I have chosen these various critical specimens not in order to quarrel with particular moments in their interpretations—and insofar as
they reject a common language, it is not possible to quarrel with them
in any case—but to take issue with their philosophic or programmatic stances, stances of which the critics may not themselves be fully
conscious. Hillis Miller, with his prodigious intellectual gifts, is a rootless professional intelligence whose critical machinations suffer from
insufficiently authentic ethical underpinnings. A mind as unmoored
as his can wander with ease from phenomenology to deconstruction
to "ethics," since his aim is to produce a professional rhetoric rather
than to connect with a reality existing apart from university life. The
particular substance upon which he works is of less importance than
the workings in themselves, and his most recent concern with "ethics"
seems no less deficient than his other literary postures. Yet someone
must speak for "literature," because even though it seems likely that
Wuthering Heights will still matter when Miller's writing is an anti-
quarian's curiosity, it is the case right now that literary works are being
upstaged by their academic critics.

Though the skills of critics like Sandra Gilbert, Susan Gubar, and

Terry Eagleton are not to be denied, much of their effort is misdirected, and they are too ready to assent to gross distortions and equivocations for political ends, even if they do not share the rootlessness of an intellect like Miller's. James Kavanagh's mind, unlike Henry James's, has been only too violated by ideas, so that he is unable to see literary works except as crude political symbols. It was very unfortunate that his book should have been chosen to represent Emily Brontë in a series purporting to "reread" literature, but that it *was* chosen is indicative of present disarray. One squirms uneasily at the thought of being part of *his* captive audience. Unlike students, general readers can at least stop reading, as Cathy and Heathcliff toss Joseph's theological tracts into the fire in *Wuthering Heights.* Crabbed and doctrinaire about the narrow road to salvation, Kavanagh is a Joseph who is not even amusing.

I am content to let someone as currently unfashionable as Q. D. Leavis have the final say:

> I would make a plea, then, for criticism of *Wuthering Heights* to turn its attention to the human core of the novel, to recognize its truly human centrality. How can we fail to see that the novel is based on an interest in, concern for, and knowledge of, real life? We cannot do it justice, establish what the experience of it really is, by making analysis of its lock and window imagery, or by explaining it as being concerned with children of calm and children of storm, or by putting forward such bright ideas as that '*Wuthering Heights* might be viewed at long range as a variant of the demon-lover motif' (*The Gates of Horn*, H. Levin) or that 'Nelly Dean is Evil'—these are the products of an age which conceives literary criticism as either a game or an industry, not as a humane study.[8]

This was written in the hinterlands of 1969, which are beginning to look surprisingly benign. Had she lived a little longer, what would Mrs. Leavis have made of Heathcliff as a prick?

8

The Hegemony of "Hegemony":
Oppositional Criticism's
Flight from Finitude

Unless you have been off to Mars for a few years or are emerging from a Rip Van Winkle retreat, you are likely to know that today's favorite buzzword in literary studies is "politics." "Everything is politics," the slogan goes—and while it is an idea not entirely without merit, a number of sticky problems keep suggesting themselves that are not so easy to dispose of.

To begin with, if *everything* is politics, then objection seems pointless, since nothing could manage to escape inclusion in the only category that exists. Moreover, if there is only one category, there is really *no* category, since categories are delimited by what is outside of them. Presumably, then, some things are *not* politics and the aim of everything else—everything that *is* politics—ought to be (according to such a reckoning) to aspire to the condition of nonpolitics. Whether this is possible, or even intelligible, remains to be investigated.

A neo-Marxist adjunct to this idea—examined by everyone along a spectrum from Herbert Marcuse to Gerald Graff—is that capitalism transforms all that it embraces into a liberal-seeming but actually repressive/conservative politics by permitting and co-opting everything simultaneously. According to this view, the apparently liberal pluralism that exists in the West is mostly a deception, since the multitude of permitted ideas is ultimately self-canceling, resulting in a playpen for intellectuals that quite literally keeps them off the streets (where they might otherwise start throwing Molotov cocktails). Even worse, defused radical ideas are quickly absorbed into the matrix of general culture, where they generate manufactured goods that help to drive the capitalist economy. According to this view, pluralism and diversity are tolerated, even encouraged, by capitalism because they help to feed the planned obsolescence that spurs the economy.

Entwined with the concept of domination is the problem of "complicity." For neo-Marxist critics, the American public is saturated with the dominant capitalist culture, which infiltrates the most unconscious dispositions even of intellectuals, not to mention the uneducated public. Since this domination is not merely economic and consumerist but is enmeshed in the very language that makes thought, public institutions, and daily life possible, evading it would appear to be out of the question. Yet the intellectuals who stress this domination rarely take up the problem of where they themselves fit in: are their yearnings and acts somehow "free" and uncaused, unlike those of the rest of us? Could any society or form of existence in the world be envisioned where human beings are free but harmonious agents, acting autonomously without constraints? And lastly, must we not consider our very incarnations in matter and our existence in time as forms of domination? Our genes, our parents, our education, our age, our health, our hair-color and height, the era and place in which we live—are we not dominated at every turn, and by more than just the iron laws of economics? Indeed, it was this captivity of the flesh that lay behind traditional Christian yearnings for another world in which humankind would be freed from the domination of finitude itself. If all incarnations are "dominated" by one or another set of interests—as it would seem impossible to avoid—is not the very nature of existence an inescapable complicity with finitude, and death its only exoneration?

These and related problems are taken up (or conveniently neglected) by two Marxist-oriented books about the roles and values of humanist intellectuals in the academy. In *The Political Responsibility of the Critic*,[1] Jim Merod's aim is to explode the idea of the disinterested

literary intellectual and to show how even, perhaps especially, some
harmless drudge fiddling away his life in musty archives to produce a
new reading of antique sonnets that nobody in fact reads is ultimately
implicated in human destiny. "Critical writing and critical training in
the United States at present do not envision a social setting for the
critical act, nor do they offer any truly sustained examination of the
critic's political identity and of criticism's political force" (4). Furthermore, "the graduate student enters the career of critic and scholar as
a devoted reader of texts who has very little grasp of the historical and
political complications that speak through texts, complications that sur-
round and in fact situate texts in a world of people and institutions,
a limited and constructed world that at every point in human history
is in the process of being built" (10). Being a critic or theoretician of
criticism in the academy, according to Merod, is a job like any other,
with an employer who provides a living and who rewards or punishes
different sorts of behavior. As free as the academic critic may seem to
be when compared to autoworkers, for instance, his or her situation
is not radically different from that of any other worker, economically
or politically speaking. Thus even a harmless drudge is saying yes to
an established order—an order, according to Merod, that may in fact
be harmful to other people. In consequence, "an examination of the
institutional arrangements binding intellectuals to society as a whole
is necessary," even though literary theorists may appear to be engaged
in a pointless and purely professional activity among themselves; for
this "substitute world" of professional theorizing is actually "situated
squarely in the reproductive heart of Western economic life (the university)" even if it "locates its force elsewhere, in the transcendental
realm of professional competence" (51). The role of intellectuals, then,
is political because it either reinforces or resists the dominant system
of values and rewards; it is never simply nothing at all.

By the end of the book, one comes to feel quite persuaded by Merod's
belief that academics cannot afford to avoid "the social responsibility
and the critical compassion that moves from texts into the world and
from the world into texts with a well-developed understanding of the
human costs of intellectual blindness." His case is strengthened by extremely frank evaluations of some of literary academia's leading radi-

cals, whose reputations do not protect them, in this instance at least, from censure. Few readers will be surprised by Merod's almost total disapproval of Stanley Fish's defense of professionalism and its "insular," "clubby," "clerical" and "rarefied" activities. Like a number of other analysts, Merod finds Richard Rorty's pragmatic interest in the "conversation of mankind" to be too purely aesthetic, conservative, and defensive of the political status quo in contemporary America. For him, Rorty's pluralism is a cornucopia of inconsequence, a pluralism in which ultimately everything is mere talk, divorced from values and self-canceling.

More surprising, however, are Merod's stern conclusions about two critics of society whom he regards as bona fide masters: Fredric Jameson and Michel Foucault. Despite his high praise of Jameson's readings of texts, readings that undermine established views about the autonomy of authors and readers, Merod is drawn to making a sharp distinction between *textual* Marxism and Marxism in the world. Considered in this way, Jameson's brilliance is a purely academic one, "which entices even a writer of his range and ambition to out-theorize other theorists and . . . to entrench himself more deeply in the game of academic rank. . . . The game of professional criticism may generate acute analysis, as it does in Jameson, but unless one finds a more concrete political strategy, that analysis is imposed upon texts and circulates whimsically, if entertainingly, within the commoditization of academic production" (132–33). Not applying its insights to society through action, Jameson's work—like so many others'—is ultimately careerist.

Regarding Foucault, Merod feels that he adds to today's general pessimism and the sense that nothing can be done. "Nothing will really be changed by the logic of Foucault's writing. A few intellectuals will be instructed. Some will be enlivened by a historical and critical effort sympathetic to the oppressed" (165). But in the final analysis, his work "authorizes a disarmingly cool appreciation of domination and institutional control" (167) while remaining "content with an academic authority that it questions systematically" (165).

Only Noam Chomsky and Edward Said receive anything like approbation, and the reason is not far to seek: both are virtuosi who have ventured into the world in various nonacademic capacities—Chomsky to attack the United States war machine, from Vietnam to Nicaragua, and Said sympathetically to present the history and support the aspirations of Arab and non-Western cultures in general. Both go beyond textual analysis and the generalized concern of ordinary academic professionals in order to take polemical action against American "domination." In providing us with such models, even if we are unable to accept them as our own, Merod strengthens his case immeasurably, showing us that work in the world is a genuine possibility for even the most cerebral of intellectuals.

I am not, of course, endorsing everything Merod says, since the fundamental objections I have already raised apply all too well to the Marxist underpinnings of his account, nor do I think he really comes to grips with finitude. He argues, for example, that it is "at the heart of the university's claim to be above and beyond political and economic determinations, [but] that scientific and professional disciplines enforce modes of production that are simultaneously cultural, legal, logical, economic, and ultimately institution-making and institution-breaking—political in essence, derived from the material and ideological fields they inhabit" (37). But when he and other Marxist critics say such things I want to know whether alternate modes of production are possible that could avoid such domination (and I do not mean merely imaginable) or whether this quarrel is ultimately with finitude itself while pretending to be with capitalism. Is this a dispute with the very terms of existence? Could it under any circumstances be reconciled in and with the flesh?

Despite such major uncertainties, however, I have to concede that as an initially resistant reader, I came to be more and more persuaded as I read on. Merod's own admirable character, his eschewing of monomania and extremism, his high moral vision and fellow-feeling for ordinary humanity, his general program (however vague) regarding the responsibility of academics to a larger social world, and his thoroughgoing objections to the ethical evasions of professionalism—all of these exerted considerable power on my *feelings*, and that is what ultimately matters. Though I am inclined to draw back at the suggestion of direct political proselytizing in the classroom, and though an occasional reference to overturning capitalism seems a little risible, in the main I find little to disagree with in Merod's conclusion: "[Criticism] has been an institution, uniquely placed in the culture, more interested in reproducing its own political obedience to the ethic of professional good sense (obedient to a market that does not want cultural and political differences let loose) than in charging itself and its students with the passion to act intelligently, morally, on the evidence of exclusion, intolerance, pacification, and injustice." (193)

Merod's analysis has increased my awareness of the extent of passive complicity and cowardly self-interest by spelling out more concretely than is customary the nature of action (or inaction) that can plausibly be regarded as political. In sum, his argument could be very illuminating to a varied audience of intellectuals.

If this is the case, why, then, must I now make the surprising admission that I think this book is ultimately unsuccessful? The answer to this question requires a discussion of a sort that rarely enters into discussions of academic publications but that is nonetheless badly needed. Merod's book contains 267 numbered pages plus a preface. Of these pages, 195 comprise the main body of text, and 65 consist of discursive notes. This in itself already poses a problem of proportions as well as what perhaps could be called the psychodynamics of reading. But worse, it has taken me almost three weeks to read this text, to work my way through a cotton-wool prose that makes few concessions to a sentient reader-in-the-world. Most readers, however, would very likely have put the book aside as hopeless and unwittingly forfeited what emerges after all as an edifying experience.

One of the main themes of Merod's book is the irresponsibility of specialization, the clubbishness of experts, and the separation of knowledge from the world by professionalism. He speaks of criticism's potential "to make public the antidemocratic habits of expert knowledge" (187) while lamenting "the habit of professional abstraction" and "an academy that additionally resists assessing its own relation to the social whole, a whole that deforms (and constrains) language professionally in order to meet competing commercial or institutional intentions, each self-authorized, self-interested, and self-enclosed." He repeatedly makes such remarks as "Jameson leaves us with a historical vision inexplicably defeated by abstraction and by the subordination of interpretive choice and personal experience to a hermetically textualized world" (136). Yet despite all of these things, Merod's writing is that of a bemused academic whose mental life and writerly instincts have been dominated (if you will) by too much contact with the often stupefying abstractions of *boundary 2, Telos, Cultural Critique, Sub-Stance, Social Text,* and other specialized workshops for leftist academic "critique." That he is not a slavish reader of these sources does not alter the force they have exerted over both his mental life and his prose. Quoting Edward Said, Merod asks, "What disruptive conceptual and institutional force could stimulate largely self-absorbed intellectuals 'to consider that the audience for literacy is not a closed circle of three thousand professional critics but the community of human beings living in society'?" (193) But he seems unable to apply such insights to his own particular case. Though the passages I have already quoted were selected for their relative readability, much more typical specimens from his book look like this:

> Not only the self-disabled technical agility found everywhere that reductive forms of argumentation rout invitations to build collective intellectual arrangements (to enhance both the cognitive and the political grounds of critical work) but the "inability to *disagree*" about the central topics and problems impinging upon scholarly production prolongs the perpetually deferred university-wide debate concerning the social consequences, the human impact, of knowledge. (103)

> More wily, North American critical work, as a collective body of individualizing scholarly or critical projects, as a collection of personal careers, has assimilated greater textual scope in essentially decontextualized modes of knowing that effectively take the place of those without authority to read professionally, legitimately, while also taking the place of those cultural and material territories knowledge depends on in the first and last moments of cognition. (105)

Surely it is especially important to ask of a praxis-oriented theorist (unless "praxis theory" is just another academic specialty, as unrelated to the general world as "theory theory"): Is there not a minimal standard of rhetorical and compositional artistry to be required of anyone who ventures to produce a book, especially one aiming to rescue knowledge from academia and to confer it instead upon the world? Yet what is one to make of sixty-five pages of rambling, discursive notes that often exceed two full pages and sometimes take on the characteristics of *Tristram Shandy?* Are they not a dereliction of the responsibility of an author to create and shape a readable discourse? What could have possessed Cornell University Press to permit such ruinous self-indulgence instead of forcing the author to incorporate this material into his text or abandon it altogether? A book is, after all, a rhetorical performance whose attunements, modulations, and structure either produce—or fail to produce—an altered state of mind. It is a product of art, not of sincerity. Indeed, to think of communicating by means of a book is already to have acquiesced in an artificial enterprise that has been formalized by traditions of persuasion. These traditions can hardly be ignored if one wants to transcend the purely academic and break through to real life. Even the structure of this book seems ill-considered and muddy, a rondo that repeats its theme over and over between interludes that inhibit any real development. The human reader has been forgotten after all, even though it is the interests of such a reader that this book claims to be defending. True, I have admitted to being influenced by Merod, but a reading under duress, as mine certainly was, is a special case. Dr. Johnson's observation is what really applies here: a book thrown away unread is instructive in vain.

In *Politics of Letters,*[2] Richard Ohmann shares Merod's point of view as well as his aims, although he thinks that any aspirations to overturn capitalism are unrealistic. He has written a blurb for the dust jacket of *The Political Responsibility of the Critic* besides quoting, in his own book, a passage from Merod's (which was then still unpublished). Merod in turn expresses "heartfelt appreciation" for Ohmann's help, but the character of Ohmann's *Politics of Letters*, despite its similar theme of capitalist hegemony over verbal culture (to borrow terms from its preface) and the Marxist sympathies between authors, is vastly different—and not just because the book is a collection of interrelated essays rather than a continuous discourse.

Ohmann, who has been interested in "prose" for years, as author of *Shaw: The Style and the Man* as well as articles on speech-act theory (not to mention his somewhat notorious *English in America*), writes in what the Victorians might have called a "good clean manly style," though such a characterization would not, of course, be allowable today. Clear, direct, concrete, avoiding convoluted syntax and periodicity as well as jargon and bombastic abstractions, Ohmann seems to have cleaned the Merodian Stables—to have cut the crap, as we might now say. His essays use the first person, eschew omniscience, express their debt to student researchers and helpers, openly confess their author's limitations of knowledge and sometimes programmatically use "she" as a generic pronoun (even when, in one instance, eleven out of the twelve people referred to happen to be men). One has an unusually strong impression of an actual person-in-the-world, of a consciousness-in-process that is all too rare in the scholarly enterprise, where experts pretend to have known everything *ab ovo*. His prose alternates between a somewhat loose sociological style and a close-reading, New-Critical style, using one when he analyzes fiction, the other when he amasses data and tries to make sense of them. Not only are these engaging essays full of interesting materials and insights, they inspire confidence in the integrity of their author as well. Like his classroom manner, which he describes as informal, these essays try to reduce the separation between the academy and daily life.

Ohmann has collected, revised, and augmented twenty essays, most of them previously published in a range of journals embracing *Critical Inquiry, College English*, and his "own" magazine, *The Radical Teacher*. They all hover around the same theme—Gramscian hegemony: i.e., the ways in which capitalism turns everything into a commodity, particularly the cultural (in all its senses) "consciousness" of society. For a collection with such varied provenance, the volume turns out to be a real book, held together by Ohmann's informal voice, his omnipresent major theme, and the reader's confidence in him as a mensch.

The essays are divided into sections on humanism, American literature, mass culture, and "literacy"—all of these in relation to the hegemonic power of capitalism. In the field of education, Ohmann regards the notions of an academic core curriculum and back-to-basics as ways in which the ruling classes, with the help of people like Secretary of Education William Bennett, keep the lower orders in their places by stressing values that make their inferior social positions seem "natural" and moral. Of Bennett he remarks, "His agenda for the humanities is deeply etched with the New Right's design for our future" (16), and depends for its effect on "a spurious common culture handed down from above" (17). He rather pointedly inquires, "And has a good dose of Milton or Goldsmith generally made the farm youth or the Italian immigrant or the recent black arrival in Chicago feel part of a common culture?" (14)

In a chapter on writing and reading, he traces the ways in which a classical education was gradually replaced in America not only by professional training but also by courses in writing and composition, seemingly innocuous though ultimately designed for corporate ends. "The university was gearing itself up to be a supplier and certifier of the professionals and managers" needed by business (32). In a long chapter on "The Shaping of the Canon," he outlines how the *New York Times Book Review* and a small handful of critics, editors, and book-buyers for chain stores determine in large measure the fortunes of the book industry and the contents of the canon. He is at particular pains to illustrate the ways in which the ideal of "individualism" and the theme of psychological illness—i.e., maladjustment to capitalist institutions and their models of success and happiness—are responses to American society that permeate post–World War II fiction because they somehow mediate the contradictions of capitalist society in a way that expresses the needs of the classes that hold the power. In several chapters on mass culture, he shows how popular magazines and advertising developed as interlinked forces to stimulate and satisfy consumerism. Like Merod, he discusses the connection between even so rarefied a pursuit as literary criticism and the class/commodity pressures of capitalist society. (None of Ohmann's accounts, however, has anything like the univocity and dogmatism of my brisk summaries.)

Although a major portion of *Politics of Letters* is devoted to sociology, I find Ohmann's chapters on Salinger and Updike to be the most successful because they exploit so well his great sensitivity as a reader. The long essay by Richard and Carol Ohmann on *The Catcher in the Rye* exerts a strong claim as the best in the book. The Ohmanns' review of Salinger criticism and their commentary upon it are wonderfully thorough and illuminating. The essay's aim is to shed light on the process of canon-formation by establishing the means by which that novel entered the canon. The explanation they offer, a concrete application of the general thesis I have just described, is that illness is a way in which discontented capitalists work out—mostly unconsciously— their dissatisfactions with "the system." In the case of *Catcher*, many of the critics are presented as prototypes of William Bennett, speaking as they do about the "eternal" values inherent in Salinger's novel, values having to do with honesty, the integrity of the self, adolescence and maturity, while ignoring the relation between those values and the institutional needs of the ruling classes. Many of these critics imply or directly state that Holden's

> immaturity calls for growth, for maturing into an acceptance of things as they are, and so does his snobbery. These critics differed as to whether or not Holden is left arrested in his difficulties or moved toward or even through redemption or initiation or acceptance or adjustment. But, in any case, these views of his predicament all imply that the answer, whether realized in the action of the novel or not, lies in some inward movement of the soul or psyche, a kind of resource that might be available to anyone any time, and just as timelessly necessary to saints and sinners as to bewildered young men. (54)

The Ohmanns, however, reject the whole tradition of timeless values, not only moral ones but literary ones as well. They see the attempt of the critics to interiorize, to spiritualize, to personalize Holden's plight as the familiar contemporary ploy—however unwitting—of shifting the failure of the culture at large onto those sensitive protagonists who crumple under its weight. They review the headlines of the *New York Times* on the day that *Catcher* was published to observe how virtually none of the critics of the new novel relates its malaise in any way to the actual problems of the real world of its time. They reveal the method, for example, by which James E. Miller's essay on *Catcher* "takes the novel out of real history and makes it an eternal story of 'death and rebirth.' This critical transformation, evidently, was what it took in the academic American fifties and sixties to claim for a literary work the status of a classic" (56). But the Ohmanns, who have high regard for Salinger, consistently point out examples of Salinger's awareness of class conflict and market mentality, as well as the world of his own day, which his critics ignore. They conclude:

The Catcher in the Rye is among other things a serious critical mimesis of bourgeois life in the eastern United States, 1950—of snobbery, privilege, class injury, culture as a badge of superiority, sexual exploitation, education subordinated to status, warped social feeling, competitiveness, stunted human possibility. The list could go on. Salinger is astute in imaging these hurtful things, though not in explaining them. Connections exist between Holden's ordeal and the events reported on the front page of the *Times,* and we think that these connections are necessary to complete Salinger's understanding of social reality. Iran and Korea and the hard-pressed New York City school system express the dominance of Holden's class, as do Broadway and Pencey and Stradlater. Salinger's novel makes no reference to the economic and military scope of that class's power, but the manners and institutions he renders so meticulously are those of people who take their power for granted, and expect the young to step into it. (64)

In an act of canonizing hegemony, I pronounce this essay a critical classic.

But now I arrive once more at an awkward and surprising juncture where I am forced to say that despite all of the praise I have lavished on this book, despite all of its many admirable qualities, I find it— for the most part—unconvincing. This is not to deny that there are innumerable observations and inferences on Ohmann's part that are very persuasive indeed, as, for example, when he objects to the current hullabaloo about student illiteracy by pointing out that the same objections were raised early in the century when schools were filled with European immigrants, or when he insists that the Great Books are no longer suited as a canon for mass American education. It is, rather, his central thesis that fails to persuade, even though one is willing to agree to it some of the time. It is not even very persuasive in the excellent essays on Salinger and Updike, although it does contribute to an enriched reading of those novels.

To speak as directly as possible, I do not believe for a moment that there is any single "key" that can be used for a totalizing account of anything. Ohmann insists that "hegemony exists in course catalogs, in syllabi, in the conventions of teaching, in the architecture of the classroom, in the institution of college" (129). He complains that Iran, Grenada, the Palestinians are not normally dealt with by TV, and then only when they erupt, so that "we do not see on our screens the long infusion of multinational capital into third world countries, the gradual development of expectations and grievances, the rise of indigenous movements, or the evolution of local politics—nothing that would humanize the mob on the screen and make its actions predictable or comprehensible" (195). He blames this failure of TV to continuously educate its audience in the details of other cultures on the machinery of capitalist hegemony, but when he says things like this (and he is saying them all the time) he is confusing capitalist hegemony with finitude itself, with the fact that to exist in the world at all, things must exist *as* something. If not as X, Y, or Z, then as R, S, and T. Moreover, they must exist as something while renouncing everything else—and once they make this renunciation, their point of view and interests will have one character rather than another. Thus, American TV will usually see the rest of the world from an American centrality and American interests, just as in ordinary life we see other people from the point of view of our own centrality. Surely it is perverse utopianism to regard as "domination" (in this case by capitalism) a viewing of the world from one's own point of view. (At times, however, even TV can rise to semischolarly perspectives by trying to present alien phenomena from their own vantage points, but this is no one's normal mode of perception and no code of ethics could possibly require it to be so.) Thus, if the concept of hegemony cannot be distinguished from "point of view," it would seem to be useless—except for holy wars.

Existent things consist mostly of nonbeing with a little bit of being thrown in. Everything is what it is by virtue of not being the infinite number of other things that it is not. It is fashionable these days to call this exclusion by self-righteous names such as "violence," "domination," and "power." I want to call it "finitude," the limitations of mortality, the "determinations" of being when it incarnates, because it is not possible to *be* otherwise. To exist at all is an act of preemption, and it is no less preemptive to hegemonize as a Marxist than it is to hegemonize as a capitalist. Ohmann's theories about hegemony are plausible enough, as are his accounts of American cultural problems. What is finally implausible is his relentless attachment of these theories to every account of every problem. They amount to little more than a magic key manqué, unable to unlock more than a few moldering doors. "Hegemony" is the dark in which all cats look black as hell. But the crux of the matter is the exclusionary nature of existence itself. To exist at all is to be a predator, to preempt other possibilities.

Still, Ohmann says things worth saying, and his essay "On Teaching Mass Culture" is the most poignantly instructive in the book. Ohmann is now sixty, an age at which the tricks of time can make radicals appear to be conservatives if they too stubbornly adhere to old dogmas. He has apologized a bit (at an MLA session that I happened to attend a few years ago) for some of the immoderacies of his youth (as represented by *English in America*) and his radicalism has sensibly accommodated itself to what might conceivably be brought about in our actual society. As a radical, he is in the embarrassing position—of which he is as keenly aware as anybody else—of being a successful, eminent professor at an elite university attended by mostly well-fixed students. Capitalism, with all its faults, has given him a very good life indeed. Had he lived at any other time in any other place, it is highly unlikely that he would be in anything like his present enviable condition. Now, to add insult to injury and to further confound confusion, some of his students are beginning to regard him as an elitist:

> Radical teaching of any subject in our present context fixes us in an adversary posture toward many of our colleagues, toward the institutions we work in, toward the institutions we teach about.
>
> And yes, toward much that our students believe and feel. This is an especially delicate point for radical teachers of mass culture. Though many students will come into our courses to examine critically their experience of mass entertainments, all of them carry around that experience as an important part of themselves. . . . *Any* criticism can seem a put-down of their own values. *Most disastrously, our criticism can seem indistinguishable from highbrow scorn, grounded in "taste," which usually amounts to either class hatred or the snobbishness of the intellectual* [emphasis added]. (207–8)

As if to rub more salt into his wounds, a "working class" student in one of Ohmann's courses complained: "We're just bending over backwards to find fault, and then being hypocritical about it. Intellectuals put themselves above everyone else and make it seem as though you have the answers." To this, replies Ohmann, "I plead not guilty, but what use is that? What I meant as criticism on behalf of his class came through to him as criticism of his class, or at least of himself and things he enjoys. So offended, I doubt that he learned much from the course" (208).

In pleading "not guilty" (while acknowledging the futility of his plea), Ohmann finds himself in the same everyday world as all the rest of us, radical and conservative alike, whose virtuous intentions are open to infinite reinterpretation by parties with other interests than our own. We are all in the grip of a radical finitude that we cannot outwit through even the most benevolent-seeming and most global of theories. Every tailor's destiny is to be outrageously retailored. Neoconservative is Old Radical writ anew.

Behind these two books lie two others that preceded them in time and that have cast a certain backlight upon them. Although alluded to only in passing, Frank Lentricchia's *Criticism and Social Change*[3] is in fact a strong presence in Merod's book, though whether by coincidence or influence is not discernible. Lentricchia devotes most of his pages to an appropriation of the writings of Kenneth Burke for purposes of social change, but ultimately, as he himself admits, he is mainly involved with his own marxisant, if not strictly "Marxist," program for intellectuals. (Burke, in his postscript to the paperbound edition, is mainly sympathetic to this appropriation.)

Lentricchia's position can perhaps be called Rhetorical Marxism. What he wants to establish is the possibility that intellectuals can do radical work for society *as* intellectuals, not just as activists for causes that take place outside their normal work. Although he finds much to admire in pragmatism and Rorty, he sees them mainly as supporting the status quo of a more or less leisured intellectual class. But though Lentricchia rejects systems of belief in general, agreeing with Rorty's antifoundationalism and deconstruction's infinite deferral ("I do not believe that Marxism or any other philosophy rests on the foundations of reality or history" [12]), he feels that one must entertain *local,* current beliefs, or else nothing can be done, not even crossing the street. He admires Burke, therefore, because he can read him as a thinker who has—to put it my own way—raised speech-act theory into a rhetoric of action-in-the-world. That is, Lentricchia sees speaking and writing as ways of altering the consciousness that changes history. Thus, rhetoric ultimately produces acts of reform in the world.

Since intellectuals constitute—par excellence—the Rhetorical Class, Lentricchia believes they are uniquely capable of *performing* in the world as professional Rhetors. "My presiding contention is that our potentially most powerful political work as university humanists must be carried out in what we do, what we are trained for. . . . We have at our disposal an intimate understanding of the expressive mechanisms of culture" (7). The literary intellectual can reveal the text "as a social text in the teeth of the usual critical lyricism that would deny the social text power and social specificity in the name of 'literature'" (11). Theory, then, for Lentricchia, is really "a type of rhetoric" and his Marxist theory "is a kind of rhetoric whose value may be measured by its persuasive means and by its ultimate goal: the formation of genuine community. Marxism as a kind of rhetoric, a reading of the past and present, invites us to shape a certain future: an invitation to practice, not epistemology. The main work of Marxism, as I see it following Gramsci, is hegemonic" (12–13).

Education, according to this view, is not neutral or disinterested, but a passing on of culturally and personally internalized values that are perpetuated by teachers. The supposedly disinterested intellectual act is in reality a will to power that furthers the interests of a particular class. The canon, then, is an effort "to exclude all but a single, continuing voice of the hegemonic classes" (128), an effort that is achieved through the repression of heterogeneity and through a "dematerialization" (i.e., a concealing) of the actual concrete forces that imbed ideas in culture. "Tradition-making functions precisely to hide class conflict by eliding the text's involvement in social struggle" (131). Each new "reception" (i.e., reading experience) of a traditional text, according to Lentricchia, is a reconstitution of the value-system that endorses that text. Intellectuals, however, are uniquely situated to reinterpret traditional texts in order to supply them with new and reformative social force.

Lentricchia and his book are superior specimens of the urge to reform. Unlike so much that passes for "Marxist" at present—often little more than brainwashed graduate students parroting the dogma of a theoretical academic hegemony whose trendy language promotes about as much resistance to "capitalism" as colorful clothing picked up at The Gap—they have an integrity and plausibility that, at the least, command respect.

Although Lentricchia writes much better than Merod and is more convincing than Ohmann (because he is a more intellectually flexible philosopher, cut loose from incredible party lines), he shares one of the central weaknesses of the Marxist, marxist, "marxist," or marxisant programs: a utopianism that defers real life to a future that never comes and never could come. This is clearly revealed in his discussions of Rorty and of Kantian aesthetics. Rorty's "*edifying* philosophy," thriving on a cultural conversation divorced from any ultimate *systematic* truths, throws Lentricchia into confusion: he cannot understand why "anyone should want, that is *need*, to be edified. Perhaps the needs satisfied by Rorty's cultural conversation are the liberal, personal needs which literary culture has celebrated from Addison to Wordsworth to deconstruction. . . . The words common to Rorty and the literary culture are 'strange,' 'creative,' 'rare,' 'original,' 'different,' 'new,' and 'uncanny.' These words in the literary culture presumably have no social point, but in fact they do" (17). What is their "social" point? They are part of a Great Refusal, much written about by Marcuse and Norman Brown, but started by Kant and Schiller, a refusal that involves a "purposiveness without purpose," that is, a valuing of the aesthetic over the practical that Marcuse—and Lentricchia—see as a resistance to the puritanical shopkeeper values of capitalist culture. Because of this socially useful side to aesthetics and "conversation," Lentricchia can give them qualified approval. But what he cannot approve is the fact that for Rorty and his like, this aestheticism is "*wholly grounded in feeling*" (emphasis added). Rorty's "key value terms are *hedonic;* they refer to the *possible pleasures* of autonomous subjects" (emphasis added) who are abstracted from the materiality of Marxist history (17). Finally (and worse yet), "Rorty's vision of culture is the leisured vision of liberalism: the free pursuit of personal growth anchored in material security" (19), a security that Rorty finds admirably provided for by capitalism. As for Lentricchia's admittedly personal reading of Kantian aesthetics, "The main line of aesthetic theory since Kant develops from its accurate reading of the alienating message of capitalist hegemony. Kantian, symbolist, and aestheticist patterns of thought, all of which father modernist political refusals, originate in gestures of worldly negation that are political through and through" (98).

Here we see the great limitation not only of Lentricchia's often powerful vision but of much oppositional criticism altogether: a rejection of the present sentient life-in-time—in a word, finitude—for a utopian future, and a corresponding inability to grant value to the aesthetic (in its largest and most embracing sense) apart from the political. Their view that everything is political is a wish rather than a reality, for if everything is political, everything can be dealt with politically! Their general failure (except for oddballs like Adorno and Marcuse) ever to deal with music, or immediate pleasure, or even sex, betrays a residual puritanism that can only value experience in terms of what it is capable of buying. Only insofar as the aesthetic Great Refusal pays for a utilitarian future in which "marginalized" or "repressed" people and positions can be absorbed into the center, to that extent feelings, affect, sensuousness, and immersion in the nowness of concrete, actual, finite existence in the world can be tolerated. This view, when all is said and done, is indistinguishable from what I would call "Christian repression," the purgatorial mentality that regards present life as an amassing of brownie points for salvation. Despite all of Lentricchia's antifoundationalism, *this* foundation is clear: feeling and nowness must give way to that one far off divine event that justifieth! And it is never fully clear (though it is partly clear, and I endorse it partly) how one can justify bringing the marginal and the repressed into the mainstream (Lentricchia's avowed goal) when the stream of present life is being systematically devalued. Just what does actual incarnate life have to offer Lentricchia that makes it worth bringing the marginalized and repressed into the enjoyment of it, when enjoyment itself is consistently being disparaged? Are they to be brought in only to enable them to bring in other marginalized and repressed groups, for the sake of enabling them to bring in still more? Why expand the mainstream of "freedom" and "privilege" when activity "freed" from the political is dismissed as undesirable (or nonexistent) and all of life is seen as purely instrumental? Instrumental to what? To more instrumentality? This is grotesquely similar to the hegemonic Christian self-repression

of one's worldly life in order to enjoy eternally the life one basically rejects in its finite dimensions. Why desire infinite amounts of something
that is seen as intrinsically valueless in limited quantities? It is hardly
negligible that music invariably escapes these agendas, since the over-
powering "affect" of music says nothing, promises nothing, and—in
utilitarian terms—does nothing; whereas literature at least offers *ideas*
that can flirt with infinitely deferred utopias. But it is for the musical experience, in its broadest sense (to include all powerful affective
experience, whether aesthetic or physical), that people live their lives.
Even sports—with their pointlessness, uselessness, and frequent imbecility—are variants of this human predilection for a satisfaction in
itself, not justified by instrumentality (though in recent years big-time
sports have been corrupted by capitalism and become as instrumental
as everything else). The profound rift between Lentricchia and Rorty is
a rift involving its own brand of puritanical values: the denigration of
feeling and pleasure (including "edifying" conversation) as "valueless"
and "hedonic." In Lentricchia, the flight from finitude continues apace,
a flight that rejects life in order to "liberate" more and more marginal
people so they too can become alienated from the for-itselfness of the
gratified subject.

My last example of this flight from finitude, the final chapter of
Fredric Jameson's *The Political Unconscious*,[4] deals explicitly with the
problem of instrumentality. Like most of Jameson's writing, it suffers
from problems too great to be dealt with here, but particularly exasper-
ating is Jameson's ipse dixit rhetoric, his tendency to make unsupported
sweeping generalizations and then to refer back to them as truths he
has just demonstrated. When one looks back for these demonstrations,
they can rarely be found, either because they are not in fact there or
because Jameson's prose is so opaque, his rhetorical skills so limited,
that the demonstration is buried.

After an account of the instrumentality of religion and capitalism,
he produces a paragraph that would raise the eyebrows of a sphinx:

> I would argue that the problem of a functional or instrumental con-
> ception of culture is basically transcended and annulled in the Utopian
> perspective which is ours here. In a classless society, Rousseau's concep-
> tion of the festival as the moment in which society celebrates itself and

its own unity, Durkheim's analogous conception of the unifying "function" of religion, and our own view of culture as the expression of a properly Utopian or collective impulse are no longer basely functional or instrumental. . . . This is to say, if one likes, that Durkheim's view of religion (which we have expanded to include cultural activity generally) as a symbolic affirmation of human relationships, along with Heidegger's conception of the work of art as a symbolic enactment of the relationship of human beings to the nonhuman, to Nature and to Being, are in this society false and ideological; but they will know their truth and come into their own at the end of what Marx calls prehistory. At that moment, then, the problem of the opposition of the ideological to the Utopian, or the functional-instrumental to the collective, will become a false one. (293)

One reads passages like this with awe at their self-blinded majesty, their astonishing millennialism, their belief in unique categories of one, of which they are the one. Notions like Marx's "prehistory," with its seeing through a glass darkly until face to face becomes possible, recall Elaine Showalter's handling of the feminist millenium, treated in Chapter 4; and there are black, Third World, White Supremacist, and other millennia as well—the supply is inexhaustible because millennia are the current game. And the idea of *Now* as "prehistory"—is it not the very model of instrumentality? The positing of future states that solve human problems avoids both the sensuous and moral confrontation of the texture of actual daily finite life, while it also makes it easy to avoid coming to grips with the fleshly concreteness of the arts, which can then be reduced to sociology or philosophy.

From these four representative texts, a few generalizations can be made: primal psychological events that are unable to happen right now, can never happen; they are not in the program, and the wires that might enable them to happen are not in any case part of the hardware. They are merely instrumental and utopian fantasies manufactured for rhetorical/political ends, the Big Payoff for self-abnegation. No wonder those hippie-refusenik-crazies of the sixties chanted "Paradise Now!" They were not about to be suckered by the Protestant ethic. But the Protestant ethic is being peddled once more, this time by bourgeois "oppositional" professors—as an avenue to the Realm of Freedom, no less.

Beyond this, the tendency of neo-Marxist thinkers to see every instance of human behavior (except in the ideal future state) as hegemony
is another dimension of their rejection of finitude. In refusing to acknowledge that existence takes place in time and space and is always a
selection from infinite possibilities, that to exist at all is to exist in some
form that rejects every other form, that to have a local habitation and
a name is hegemonic, that hegemony is a condition of life itself, these
thinkers turn Existence into Politics. Thus, in some meaningless sense,
everything *is* political, but such a claim includes no more of truth than
the claim that everything that is simply is—a supreme tautology. Unless the *political* can in some way be differentiated from the *existential*,
politics ceases to be a useful or informative term. Instead, the predicate
"political" becomes itself an act of politics, of hegemony, like claiming
that certain behavior springs from the devil and requires punishment.

The politics of antipolitics is nowhere so flagrant as when Jameson
slips into his magisterial royal mode, a first person plural that sounds
as if it were coming from some Archimedean point unsullied by the
implications of culture, as when he praises the transcendence of "the
Utopian perspective which is ours here." (Scholarly decorum forbids
laughing at such quaint diction, a hegemonic relic from another time,
another place, yet scholarly decorum, they are saying, is part of another
self-serving power structure, so once you endorse a free-for-all against
hegemony, why stop at any particular sacred cow? When "everything
is political," "nothing is sacred.") As usual, Lentricchia is most candid
about this when he says that you have to use capitalist techniques of advertising hype in order to fight capitalism itself. "To attempt to proceed
in purity—to reject the rhetorical strategies of capitalism and Christianity—*as if such strategies were in themselves responsible for human
oppression*—to proceed with the illusion of purity is to situate oneself
on the margin of history. . . . It is to exclude oneself from having any
chance of making a difference for better or worse" (36). Though honest, this observation is problematical, since it becomes questionable to
attack other finitudes for impurity when one is making use of the techniques of impurity to do so, and it reveals yet one more aspect of the
rot and decay in the Marxist arsenal against hegemony. For the millen-
nialist attack against the present, against finitely constituted objects in

the world, against justification Now, is really a Nietzschean struggle for power, and its method is a redefining of good and evil in order to turn the tables. When all is said and done, however, when the texts have been shuffled, the sources cited, the mandarin jargon hurled back and forth—and the author, the book, the self, the subject, the world, have all been annihilated with words—the hidden script of these high-minded fights only boils down to: "It's you or me, you bastard!"

9

. . . . . .

Literary Politics

and Blue-Chip

High-Mindedness

In the fall of 1985, *Critical Inquiry* ran a special issue on the subject of race and colonialism, which they called *"Race," Writing, and Difference*. The idea for such an issue had been suggested to the journal by the well-known black scholar Henry Louis Gates, Jr., who in June of 1983 had published "The 'Blackness of Blackness': A Critique of the Sign and the Signifying Monkey" in *Critical Inquiry*, where he was described as an assistant professor of Afro-American Studies and English at Yale. By the time the "Race" issue appeared, Gates had meteorically risen to professor of English, comparative literature, and African studies at Cornell.

A year after the 1985 "Race" issue had appeared, *Critical Inquiry* published—in the autumn of 1986—two additional essays on "race," as well as seven responses to the 1985 collection and also announced that all of the materials on race from both issues would appear as a book from University of Chicago Press (now available as *"Race," Writing, and Difference*).[1] Five of these responses interlock in a manner that is relevant to my purpose: one by Tzvetan Todorov; another by Houston A. Baker, Jr., a black scholar at the University of Pennsylvania; another by myself; followed by a reply to me by Mary Louise Pratt of

Stanford University; and then a general but detailed response to all of us by Professor Gates.

My own involvement in this affair was the result of extreme irritation on reading the introduction to the Race/85 issue by Professor Gates, an irritation that was in no way soothed by Mary Louise Pratt's essay on European colonialist writings of the nineteenth century. I had immediately braced for trouble when I saw that "race" had been put in quotation marks in the title of the whole enterprise and I was not at all deflected from this anxiety by Professor Gates's remarks on the subject, although they began reasonably enough: "Race, as a meaningful criterion within the biological sciences, has long been recognized to be a fiction. . . . The biological criteria used to determine 'difference' in sex simply do not hold when applied to 'race.' Yet we carelessly use language in such a way as to *will* this sense of *natural* difference into our formulations. To do so is to engage in a pernicious act of language, one which exacerbates the complex problem of cultural or ethnic difference, rather than to assuage or redress it" (4–5). Although "pernicious" seemed a bit extreme, these were sentiments that I was prepared to buy. Gates went on to explain that Race/85 aimed "to deconstruct, if you will, the ideas of difference inscribed in the trope of race, to explicate discourse itself in order to reveal the hidden relations of power and knowledge inherent in popular and academic usages of 'race'" (6).

This "deconstruction" seemed a plausible, if unexcitingly familiar, academic exercise, although by 1985 it had become clear enough to anyone following the rising stock of Foucault in the academic marketplace that—if every act of language was to be a witting or unwitting power ploy—grounds for attacking any particular discourse as vicious would soon evaporate, since what everyone is forced to do by the nature of things could no longer be excoriated as uniquely "pernicious." By the time I had reached the next paragraph, the handwriting on the wall appeared in day-glo fluorescence: "Who has seen a black or red person, a white, yellow or brown? These terms are arbitrary constructs, not reports of reality" (6). Here, I felt, I had indeed been weighed in the balance and found wanting, a balance that perhaps required some recalibration by the Department of Moral Weights and Measures. How was one to interpret such a red flag? I saw only a few possibilities: the

first, that the beings referred to as white, black, etc., had no existence
in the world and were only phantasms produced by sick imaginations.
I was sure, however, that Professor Gates did not believe that. Perhaps
what he did mean was that they should be called X's and Y's or anything
other than white or black, because in literal truth, they are not strictly
speaking those colors, but this seemed too precisian to be plausible. We
speak of short people, tall people, rich and poor, wise and virtuous and
these terms are no more precise than white or black. While enabling
us to identify people in the world, these terms do not suggest to most
users that someone absolutely tall or rich or virtuous exists—only that
in relation to other people, some people look black or white or seem
wise or short. What appears to be tall or black could conceivably vary
from culture to culture, like the number of shades of white reported by
Whorf of the Eskimos, but if white, black, or yellow may be regarded
as constructs, they cannot be said to differ from most other words in
any given society.

An alternate interpretation of Gates's remark, perhaps, was that
there is no essence of blackness or whiteness, that race has no biologi-
cally founded differentia, that nothing corresponding to these essences
can be located in one's body or soul.

Again, this seemed too banal to be worth all the fuss. Words refer
to essences that exist only in thought, not in things, and we point out
existences in the quotidian world by applying as many of these categories or essences as are necessary to yield a positive identification. A
person partakes of blackness, tallness, shortness, leanness, Ohio-ness,
Cleveland-ness until we realize that such a person is Joe Smith of
485 Fifth Street. Thus, I see black people and white people and yellow people every day, even if they are not absolutely or essentially so,
and the differences that enable me to distinguish between them are
no more or less constructed by my language than are the differences
I perceive between professors, handymen, or alcoholics, although language may allow me to make these distinctions in the first place. When
differences are perceived, and when they are enabled by language, for
all practical purposes they can be said to "really" exist, if not for God
at least for us. This makes the use of quotation marks around "race"
seem a case of special pleading, and in my brief, gruff, rhetorical reply

to Professor Gates in Race/86, I asked why "was only the word 'race' in quotation marks? Why not every single word in the entire issue of *Critical Inquiry?*" And I provided my own rhetorical reply: "For to refer, it seems, is to colonize, to take things over for one's own brutal use, to turn everything into a mere Other. There was Gates engaging in the academic's favorite pastime, *épater le bourgeois*, and here was I, a hopeless bourgeois, just asking for a put-down" (396).

In other words, I was making the objection that all language is constructed, all words refer to essences that have no existence, that "race" and "black" and "yellow," far from being special cases, were examples of ordinary and everyday operation of language. If we were to allow Professor Gates's interrogative to set a pattern for future use, why should we not henceforth ask, "Who has ever seen a professor, a university, a theory, a language?" If using language is a form of exploitation, a malappropriation of Others because it fails to enumerate their infinite qualities and thereby reduces them to simplified and exploited objects or counters, then putting quotation marks around one word or every word we use will not make the exploitation go away. Better, then, to leave the quotes off everything. Otherwise we are faced with a choice of keeping permanently silent (in the interests of accuracy and humanity) or engaging in reductive brutality in which we see people and other existents only in terms we ourselves choose and that tender to our own interests. Tzvetan Todorov, in his reply to Professor Gates, put the matter even better: "We are so busy battling stereotypes in the description of Others that we end up refusing these Others any specificity at all. It is true that 'the Orient' is far too broad a category. . . . But does this mean that there is no such thing as Japanese culture or Near Eastern traditions . . . ? Do the past attempts at describing them tell us about *nothing* except the observers' prejudices?" (373–74).

Why should Professor Gates have presented us with so disingenuous a choice, asking us to pretend that the words he chose to enclose in quotes were special or different when in fact they were not? The answer is Politics, and as is so often the case with Politics, it wears a face of outraged virtue. Not content with putting "race" in quotation marks and by implication black, yellow, and every other word in our (or any) language, pressing upon us by one indirection after another the suggestion that all use of language reduces the "for-itselfness" of the human subject to the utilitarian simplicity of the exploited object and is therefore evil, Professor Gates then stuns us with the most surprising body blow of all in the form of a question he raises toward the end of his introduction to Race/85: "Can writing," he asks, "with the very difference it makes and marks, mask the blackness of the black face that addresses the text of Western letters, in a voice that speaks English through an idiom which contains the irreducible element of cultural difference that will always separate the white voice from the black?" (12) We recoil amazed: so whites and blacks have irreducible essences after all? "I once thought it our most important gesture to *master* the canon of [Western, white] criticism, to *imitate* and *apply* it, but now I believe that we must turn to the black tradition itself to develop theories of criticism indigenous to our literatures" (13).

One might acquiesce in such a position if it were to come from a *non-Western* critic defending his own nonwhite tradition from the appropriations of Western critics. But coming as it does from a westernized bourgeois beneficiary of the American academy and all its perquisites, who speaks its language wondrous well, who writes for mainstream journals like *Critical Inquiry*, who is fully at home in the American melting pot (in which he nevertheless pretends to disbelieve), and who has just given us a jeremiad against the imaginary essences of irreducible difference promulgated by language, one is grateful to be able to quote Todorov's comment on such a surprising turn of affairs: "Is this not to say that the content of a thought depends on the color of the thinker's skin—that is, to practice the very racialism one was supposed to be combating?" (376)

When I turned to Mary Louise Pratt's essay, "Scratches on the Face of the Country; or, What Mr. Barrow Saw in the Land of the Bushmen," I realized that I had landed myself in the midst of a flourishing academic industry, as all-pervasive (and one hopes as short-lived) as those of hoola-hoops and cabbage-patch dolls. "Any reader recognizes here," Pratt remarks after quoting a passage from John Barrow's eighteenth-century record of his travels into Africa, "a very familiar, widespread, and stable form of 'othering.' The people to be othered are homogenized into a collective 'they,' which is distilled even further into an iconic 'he' (the standardized adult male specimen). This abstracted 'he'/'they' is the subject of verbs in a timeless present tense, which characterizes anything 'he' is or does, not as a particular historical event but as an instance of a pregiven custom or trait. . . . Through this discourse, encounters with an Other can be textualized or processed as enumerations of such traits" (139). After reading this and the ensuing remark to the effect that such description "could serve as a paradigmatic case of the ways in which ideology normalizes, codifies, and reifies" (140), it seemed to me that in the very act of characterizing colonial characterizing, Pratt was engaged in the same practice as Barrow. When she remarked that "during the so-called opening up of central and southern Africa to European capitalism . . . such explorers were the principal producers of Africa for European imaginations—producers, that is, of ideology in connection with the European expansionist project there" (140–41), I was forced to ask *Critical Inquiry*,

> wasn't she failing to see that in the very act of "producing" her essay she was, like Gates, engaged in the opening up of certain texts to academic capitalism and its own—her own—expansionist project? Was she not ruthlessly reducing a complex world into a simple commodity (without even bothering with quotation marks) for academic consumption, which, when successfully "produced," would lead to promotions, professional recognition, salary increases, establishing of dogma, and the general colonizing of the minds of graduate students eager to cut it with their sahibs? (397–98)

As I read on I became increasingly uneasy and embarrassed by what seemed to be one double entendre after another. "Unheroic, unparticularized, without ego, interest, or desire of its own [Pratt continues, with increasing, but insufficient, irony], it [colonial discourse] seems able to do nothing but gaze from a periphery of its own creation, like the self-effaced, noninterventionist eye that scans the Other's body" (143). "To the extent that it strives to efface itself," this Foucaultian melodrama continues, "the invisible eye/I strives to make those informational orders natural, to find them there uncommanded, rather than assert them as the products/producers of European knowledges or disciplines" (144). Surely, I kept feeling, Pratt could hardly have failed to imagine for a moment the word "academic" in place of "European" in the above and all similar passages. Such sensitivity to the pure passivity of the Other so brutalized and "hegemonized" over by European exploitation could hardly fail also to sense the applicability of these observations to—their interchangeability, in fact, with—her own academic colonization. But no, irony can only go so far.

Speaking of the "reveries" of nineteenth-century writings about exploration, Pratt comments: "They are determined, in part, by highly generalized literary conventions" (145). When I looked over Pratt's own essay, I could see again how well her descriptions of descriptions served to describe her own production. For what are such terms as *discourse, textualized, paradigmatic, seen/scene, site/sight, capitalist mode of production, Other, narration, hegemonic, Bahktinian, gaze* if not the "highly generalized literary conventions" of today's self-aggrandizing, colonizing academic, who tells us we are crude to think there are really such creatures as blacks, whites, whatnots, but who guiltlessly goes right along telling us about sights/sites (as though some essence really underlay the arbitrary sounds of two words and as though this were not just the latest academic sort of fun and games), about "capitalist production" (where do we find it?), and about "textuality."

In the fall of 1986, *Critical Inquiry*'s addenda to its issue on "race" included replies to me from both Professors Pratt and Gates. In a salient passage therefrom, Professor Pratt wrote: "Part of the project of the issue was to destabilize fixed, naturalized meaning systems around race and other lines of hierarchical differentiation. Many of the essays, including mine, sought this end by historicizing such systems, pointing up their constructedness, their means of legitimation, and so on" (401). Unfortunately, my irony had prevented her from seeing that I was engaged in destabilizing *her* fixed, naturalized meaning system, that I was pointing up *its* constructedness and questioning *its* legitimization. Far from exhibiting the cutting edge of innovative and radicalized analysis, her essay seemed to me to be a showcase for some of today's rather shopworn academic orthodoxies and truisms, imitated by every graduate student and ready for a front-page story in *USA Today*. Professor Gates's reply involved a similar lack of reflexivity, but he rightly directed most of his attention to Tzvetan Todorov's more damaging response. Nevertheless, as I see it this entire controversy has raised—however unwittingly—questions of pressing significance for the knowledge professions at large.

To my objection about the use of quotation marks around the word "race," Professor Gates replied: "The editors of *Critical Inquiry* and I decided to bracket the word 'race' in our title after much discussion and debate, and only after an extended correspondence with Tzvetan Todorov. We decided to do so to underscore the fact that 'race' is a metaphor for something else and not an essence or a thing in itself, apart from its creation by an act of language" (402). I had also objected to Gates's question, "Who has seen a black or red person, a white, yellow or brown?" since his implication was that these words too ought to be enclosed in quotes to suggest their special nature. When I then asked why every word in the entire issue of *Critical Inquiry* had not been enclosed in quotes, it was because I did not see any difference between these "special" words and any other words. Professor Pratt, however (and perhaps Professor Gates as well), mistook my purpose and remarked, "Fromm wants a world where words stand still and refer, and don't get changed . . . a world where blacks are blacks, whites are whites" (400–401). This, unfortunately, was the exact opposite of my intent. The observation that I *was* concerned to make was that when Professor Gates suggested to the sophisticated audience of *Critical Inquiry* that words like "race," "yellow," "white," and so forth do not represent essences in the concrete world of experience, he was, in fact, not giving us a lesson in linguistics at all but, rather, a political homily. He was objecting, of course, to any sort of stereotyping or reduction and ultimately, I fear, to knowledge and understanding themselves, for all knowing reduces the open-ended multiplicity of "reality" to manageable units of discourse by eliminating from its purview all those infinite qualities that are not immediately of interest.

The potential qualities of anything are infinite. They could never manage to be named, not only because no one's lifetime is long enough to make such an enumeration, but because the qualities do not even exist as discrete entities until they are perceived as so existing, an endlessly creative process that we now call "interpretation." Engaged as he

was in a political discourse about blacks, Professor Gates objected to
any kind of reductive categorizing—indeed, seemingly to speech itself,
or any speech but his own—yet the logical conclusion of a point of
view like his is to render all knowledge and discourse forms of evil, a
fall, if you will, from the Eden of total Being to the depravity of partial Becoming. The rest is truly silence. It was this that I had in mind
when I remarked, "Here I was, faced with the impossible choice of
keeping permanently quiet or perpetuating ruthless violence" (396).
But it was not in Professor Gates's interest (or Professor Pratt's either)
to appreciate such a remark because in reality he by no means wants
to make it impossible to say anything at all. He wants, rather, to make
it impossible to say *certain* things. This observation was also made by
Tzvetan Todorov. Turning Gates's own words against him, Todorov
wrote: "I cannot help pointing out . . . the insistent allusions [in Gates's
prose] to certain contemporary critical theories ('deconstruct' and 'difference,' 'power' and 'knowledge')—allusions which furnish proof that
the author of these lines possesses a particular *knowledge* and thereby
sets up a particular *power* relationship between himself and the reader"
(371). This power relationship, I am sorry to say, is a kind of moral
blackmail aimed at guilt-ridden liberals, presumably white. They are
being told that they will not be allowed to say certain things without paying the consequences of being scorned as Yahoos by all right-
thinking people. The police, to echo Derrida, are waiting in the wings,
and it is not just the neoconservatives who have them in their employ.

    This brings me back to Mary Louise Pratt's essay, "Scratches on the
Face of the Country; or, What Mr. Barrow Saw in the Land of the
Bushmen." Although Professor Pratt treated my rude hostility toward
her essay with uncommon graciousness, even to the point of accepting
some of my general criticisms about academic colonization, she nonetheless misinterpreted me once again when she wrote: "Harold Fromm
argues that my essay exemplifies a kind of academic colonization, a
form of exploitation in which raw material (in this case travel books)
is processed into prestige, money, and influence" (400). But it was not
"texts" (i.e., "travel books") whose exploitation I was abjuring. I was
objecting to the exploitation of the cultures and consciousnesses that

lie behind these texts. This exploitation often takes the form of pressing one's own ideological hegemony upon another society in the manner that Professor Pratt deplores in the case of colonial travel writers like John Barrow, a pressure that wrests the Other by means of doctrinal violence into a shape most congenial to the academic colonialist. Like his predecessor, he too is "innocently" engaged in applying his own culture's unquestioned truths and techniques of methodology upon a passive victim, in this case what is being represented by a text. My concern was that the kind of exploitation involved in these wry excoriations of colonialism is in the long run harmful. Defending herself from my accusations, Professor Pratt replied: "It was an interventionist project, to be sure; however, the name for such interventions is not colonialism, it is critique" (401).

With the word "critique" we now come to the heart of the matter. The methodology employed by Professor Pratt in analyzing and exposing the mostly unconscious rationalizations of Barrow and her other colonialists derives from the Marx-inspired techniques of the Frankfort School's "critical theory." This method aims to deconstruct the cultural unconscious of any given society in order to reveal the hidden ideological operators that mold and shape the behavior and interests of the society's members. Foucault's accounts of "discourse formations" and Jameson's of the "political unconscious" attempt to perform a similar task. Perhaps, in the case of the Frankfort School, the aim (like that of psychoanalysis) is to unmask the unconscious motivators of behavior in order to free their agents, or subsequent agents, from blind servitude to harmful values. This is certainly an admirable aim, but it raises the traditional concern about Plato: "Who will guard the guardians?"

Although in the present instance the guardians claim to have risen above ideology and are therefore disinterested (since critical theory does not regard itself as an ideology but as a method for unmasking ideology), my profoundly skeptical sensibilities have strong reasons to doubt it. After suggesting to Professor Pratt that she might not be as disinterested as she presumed, I concluded that "Physician, heal thyself" might be the moral that some of the contributors to the "Race" issue needed to consider, but by introducing the notion of "critique," I think that Professor Pratt managed to deflect my point.

The inhabitants of Barrow's society, while they were certainly as
capable of introspection and reflection as people of today, existed before the kind of critical consciousness that has since become meth-
odized by Marxism, Freudianism, Lacanianism, deconstruction, and
similar critical instruments. Now that these methods are widespread, I
believe that a form of noblesse oblige is immanent in the use of them.
There is something very wrong, it therefore seems to me, in the attempt of scholars like Professor Pratt to insist on the ways in which
colonialist explorer-writers reduced and manipulated what we now call
Third World countries—that is, by means of a language that in actuality *used them* (the explorers) as unconscious agents of domination—
there is something very wrong, I am saying, in her doing this without
any sign of awareness of the ways in which *she too* is being used as
an unconscious agent of the domination of currently fashionable academic modes of investigation, modes that are instruments of academic
capitalism. Although this phenomenon of "using" and "being used"
happens to be a condition of mortality and not just an oppression of advanced capitalism, in the present case I feel that the blame that can be
laid upon today's academic agent is far greater than any that Pratt can
legitimately lay upon Barrow. For today's methodologies are posited on
a "critical theory" whose enabling tenet is the nonideological preeminence afforded to critical "consciousness." (Does this not sound much
like "Reason" in the now-despised Enlightenment?) Yet there is no
sign on Professor Pratt's part that she is either critical or conscious of
being herself an unwitting agent of what is, after all, merely currently
fashionable ideology; doing her thing just as naturally, guiltlessly, and
"innocently" as Barrow did his; taking it completely for granted that
the world *really is* constituted by such concepts as "hegemony," "discourse," "textualized," "capitalist mode of production." In a very per-
tinent essay devoted almost entirely to examining this kind of problem, John Carlos Rowe has remarked: "Like Irigaray and Hartman,
[Edward] Said imagines the principal distinction between an immoral
colonial 'will-to-power' and that of the cultural critic to be the degree
of 'honesty' with which the critic confronts this situation and the relative repression of textuality operative in colonialism. Such 'honesty,' I
would argue, would be a very troublesome notion for Nietzsche, who

understands quite well that *every* will-to-power involves a certain and strategic blindness and self-deception."[2]

In a word, I am saying that Professor Pratt (and not she alone), as an exponent of critical consciousness, is insufficiently conscious of her own paradigm-bound agency, which she unreflectively equates with a given, naturalized reality—just like Barrow. Indeed, almost every sentence in her essay applies equally as well to her own inherited methodologies as to Barrow's; and academia stands behind her remarks in the same way that "Europe" stands behind (i.e., empowers) Barrow's. Since her own claim to validity depends on the imputed superiority of a critical theory based on consciousness itself, her culpability is greater because it is a betrayal, an *imposture* of "consciousness," not just ordinary blind self-assurance.

I have no solution to offer to this problem but I am certainly not recommending silence. Professor Pratt's essay is excellently well done in its own terms but seriously defective in mine. The attack I mounted on academic methodologies in *Critical Inquiry*, autumn 1986, stems from moral recoil, and a reference I made to Marxist academics who are hard to distinguish from yuppies was born of this same recoil. It means that when I look at today's deconstructors of unconscious agency, I see consumers, trendies, exploiter-beneficiaries of "capitalism"—in sum I see ordinary people no better or worse than you or I, except for their pretensions. I certainly do not see St. Francis or monks in hair shirts renouncing the evils of the "capitalism" on which they in fact thrive as they race about to conferences in jet planes, enjoy the benefits of computer technology, barter their articles and books for upward mobility in the academy. In all candor, I do not see anything wrong with enjoying computers or jet planes or advancing in the academy, but I do see much to lament in the use of stylized moral jeremiads as coin to obtain yet a bigger share of the very spoils that are being denounced. I lament this as a postmodern betrayal of the clerks, who (to recall Johnson's *Rasselas*) talk like angels but live like men.

If Professor Pratt imperiously pretends to unmask the Western capitalist bourgeois unconscious of her nineteenth-century imperialists without recognizing how much her own confident methodologies resemble capitalist luxury toys for the elite, so Professor Gates in his sardonic attacks on everyone who is not a black reformist seems blinded to the extent to which he himself is actually a Western bourgeois white. Intellectuals who pretend to construct their total identities upon an obsessive minority consciousness easily forget how great a portion of these identities derives from the dominant culture they repudiate but without which their present selves would scarcely even exist.

In the case of Professor Gates, we see a black academic who has chosen to rise in mainstream American university society via Yale and Cornell, and now Duke, where he drives a Mercedes and is a distinguished scholar who does not care to acknowledge the degree to which his constituency is not black. The impression he conveys is that he is not so sure to whom, of whom, and for whom he really speaks. In answering the respondents to the "Race" issue he criticizes Todorov and others by saying, "To discourage us from reading our own texts in ways suggested by those very texts is to encourage new forms of neocolonialism" (406). But when he uses such expressions as "our own texts," "the reader," "contemporary literary theory," and "critic of black literature," he evades answering such sticky questions as: Who are "our"? Who is "the reader"? *What* "contemporary literary theory"? And *what* "critic of black literature"? Are these to be understood as references to black intellectuals from the Third World or are they references to middle-class American academics who are apt to be largely not black? Gates's insistence on a "vernacular" black criticism, which he makes in a very mainstream context—as professor at Cornell, not at a black university; as a writer for *Critical Inquiry*, not for an obscure ethnic journal—certainly invites perplexity. Whom, after all, does he see as his real constituency? As Christopher Miller, who ultimately seems pretty sympathetic to Professor Gates's goals, nevertheless remarks in his own essay in this collection: "The goal of breaking through the nets of Western criticism, of reading African literature [if that is the literature Gates has in mind as well as Afro-American] in a nonethnocentric, nonprojective fashion, will remain both indisputably desirable and ultimately unattainable. No matter how many languages I learn or ethnologies I study, I cannot make myself into an African" (258). And even if Gates (and Houston Baker as well) could manage to create a black "vernacular" criticism, would typical black or nonblack American academics be interested in such a criticism, except as a curiosity? (Even white liberal guilt has its limits.) Gates certainly cares about this traditional audience or he would not be writing and saying the things he does, but "to step out of the discourse of the white masters" or "to escape the neocolonialism of the 'egalitarian criticism' of Todorov and company" could leave him with a very small audience indeed. As acquiescent yes-persons, they might even bore him to death.

Thus, a low spot in this whole debate is reached when Gates writes, "I am sorry that the point I sought to make escaped Todorov. I was engaged in a black cultural game, M. Todorov, one known as 'signifying.' I was *signifying upon* Bate,[3] as my black readers would know from their familiarity with this coded exchange. As Louis Armstrong said, 'If you have to ask . . . !' " (407) But Professor Gates's black readers are simply not enough to sustain a magisterial career, a career so largely made possible by his own semi-white identity. Gates, however, moves in and out of his black and white identities as it suits his polemics of the moment.

In an even more depressing denouement, Gates wraps up his entire reply to the "Race" issues by going off into a huddle with Houston Baker: "No, Houston, there are no vernacular critics collected here; nor did you expect there to be. Todorov's response forces me to realize that the discursive dualism that you criticize is still urgently needed. For we must attack the racism of egalitarianism and universalism in as many languages as we can utter. Todorov can't even hear us, Houston, when we talk *his* academic talk; how he gonna hear us if we 'talk *that* talk,' the talk of the black idiom? Maybe you think we should give up, but I am still an optimist. Things is just gettin' innerestin', as LeRoi says." (409)

This familiar and cozy colloquy is a sad case of talking out of both sides of one's mouth and it cannot sit well with the main body of Gates's readers, for whose approval he writes at the very same time that he disingenuously refuses to acknowledge them. If this is a specimen of "the peculiar timbres of our [black] voices" that Gates is afraid of being "muffled," I do not think a little muffling would do it any harm. For Todorov's "academic talk" is the only possible talk for real as opposed to fantasy discourse, because the other talk, "*that* talk," whether black, Irish, blue-collar, Yiddish, or whatever, cannot be the common talk of mainstream academic discourse, a discourse that both Gates and Baker clearly like very much and that has to a large degree made them the academic stars they are.

For all the compassion (i.e., "suffering with" and not "pity") I feel for Professor Baker's bad experience with New York and Philadelphia taxi drivers who snub minorities, New York cabbies are not yet the measure of all things. Like a million other people, I have had my own harrowing escapades with them, but I have also met some pretty decent ones. (I am tempted to ask here, borrowing a tune from Professor Gates, "Who has ever seen a 'New York cabbie' "?) But Gates's and Baker's introduction of bigoted cabbies, black pug noses, and kinky hair brings this debate perilously close to soap opera and is more than a little dissonant with the abstract postmodern critical language otherwise favored by both of them. All life is a tragic farce, not just the lives of privileged professors torn between critical inquiry and ethnic nostalgia, academic jargon and black signifyin'. If we try to resolve these problems by means of a contest of sufferings and humiliations, we will find that it is a contest no one can win.

In an issue of *Massachusetts Review* featuring essays on "Ethnicity and Literature," Jules Chametzky remarks: "Also we must avoid, I think, an emphasis on unique suffering or grievances. That way madness lies. As Joyce said, history is a nightmare (presumably not just for the Irish) from which he was trying to awaken. Our task, it seems to me, is to honor the past, but not to run mad into that nightmare. To retain our sanity and reason . . . in full consciousness of past brutality and suffering in order to find common ground for humane transformation."[4] If this seems too "egalitarian" and "bourgeois" (though not to me), then perhaps "The Dilemma of the Black Intellectual" by another black scholar, Cornel West, would carry more weight. In this comprehensive overview of problems and solutions similar to those put forth by Professor Gates, West, rejecting the Marxist model, writes: "The 'new regime of truth' to be pioneered by black thinkers is neither a hermetic discourse (or set of discourses), which safeguards mediocre black intellectual production, nor the latest fashion of black writing,

which is often motivated by the desire to parade for the white bourgeois intellectual establishment. . . . The future of the black intellectual lies neither in a deferential disposition toward the Western parent
nor a nostalgic search for the African one."[5] Although Roger Kim-
ball's report of West's extremist performance at Yale's symposium on
"The Humanities and the Public Interest" (in the *New Criterion,* June
1986) is disquieting, West's assessment of these problems, at least in the
present instance, seems more well-considered and promising than that
of Professor Gates, although I may be missing some crucial "signifyin' "
message that would change my outlook.

In sum, what has so badly undermined the arguments of Mary Louise
Pratt and Henry Louis Gates is their failure to recognize their own
complicity in the very same systems whose grossness they are attempting to expose. This sort of contradiction had already been dramati-
cally defined by George Bernard Shaw almost a hundred years ago
in *Widowers' Houses* and *Mrs. Warren's Profession.* The guilty parties
then were more or less ordinary agents of society. But today's academic reformers, with their greater pretensions to omniscience, their
readiness to explode old "discourse formations" with new ones even
though discourse formations are supposed to be part of the problem
itself, their lack of insight into the internecine strife between their frag-
mented selves, and their resistance to the kind of elegant skepticism
represented by Richard Rorty, seem more reprehensible than the well-
intentioned innocents of Shavian comedy.

In *Criticism and Social Change,* Frank Lentricchia expresses admi-
ration for Rorty's skepticism but finally is forced to reject it as politically counterproductive. For him, skepticism is only a form of play that
fails to lead to social reform. Cornel West tries to counter this kind
of potential paralysis by positing an "insurgency model" that "carefully highlights the profound Nietzschean suspicion and the illuminating oppositional descriptions of the Foucaultian model, though it
recognizes the latter's naivety about social conflict, struggle, and insurgency—a naivety primarily caused by the rejection of any form of
utopianism and any positing of a telos."[6] For the intellectual, however,
when this conflict between skeptical quietism and academy-style activ-
ism decides in favor of positing a telos, more often than not it is likely

to lead—as I have been arguing in the cases of professors Gates and Pratt—to a degradation of the intellectual's privileged social position as scholar and sage. (Lentricchia, I think, is a rare exception.)

When thoroughly bourgeois intellectuals affect to wage worldly battle while regarding themselves as revolutionaries, even though the battlefield, the weapons, the language, the attire, the cars they drive, and all the financial underwriting are those of Western bourgeois society (with no risks involved beyond the purely rhetorical), a new and perhaps unanticipated variety of Theater of the Absurd makes itself felt. The reason for this—believe it or not—is that we are *all* bourgeois now. And if we're all bourgeois now, then how can the pot keep calling the kettle black (or antiblack)?

10

. . . . . .

Real Life, Literary Criticism,

and the Perils

of Bourgeoisification

It is hard to doubt that the vast majority of literary works were produced as expressions of passionate involvement with life rather than
as aesthetic objects. The notion of a purely aesthetic artifact intended
to be "art" is, in any case, a relatively recent one in the history of
civilization, and the veneration of the artist as a unique individual
soul—rather than as an agent of transcendence or the state—is a post-
Enlightenment product. Ancient cave drawings, Roman sculpture and
friezes, medieval paintings, early music and literature were practical
artifacts intimately tied up with the aims and qualities of daily life,
more often than not religious or political "speech acts," and later on,
as in the case of Shakespeare and his contemporaries, entertainment
and sources of livelihood. On the other hand, what distinguishes these
products from those we regard as nonaesthetic are the curious supererogatory skills of their producers, skills that seem not to be immediate
agencies in the affairs of birth, copulation, and death—or even money-
grubbing. This extra element of "play," this "purposiveness without
purpose," lifts these works out of the realm of lived life into a more
expansive and pleasure-oriented universe. Atheists can listen to Bach's
Mass in B Minor with as much gratification as the devout, while yuppies

can hang reproductions of cave paintings on their walls even though they have no anxieties about their status with the gods. In a word, even the most practical specimens of what we decide to call "art" are perceived as having an aesthetic dimension that makes them the art we claim them to be. Nor need the artist even have intended to exhibit a skill-in-itself divorced from his practical goal, as long as such a skill seems to shine out from his artifact.

Although there will always be people who become interested in these media in themselves—the languages, methods, or skills whereby lived life undergoes aesthetic transmutation—when intellectual or aesthetic analysis takes place too soon after the artifacts have been expressed as "life" (and a fortiori while they still have currency as "life"), such attention to secondary qualities is apt to seem decadent, Alexandrine, or positively sacrilegious. For the customary pattern has been that analysis of this kind takes place when the artifacts in question have ceased to serve their original ends, after the funeral baked meats have at least had a chance to cool. Although Mrs. Gaskell's novels about the impoverished working class in nineteenth-century Manchester or Dickens's novels about the exploitation of children in factories were of course understood at the time to be "art," examinations of them were usually predicated upon their power to produce life-imitating experiences in their readers. Today, with the problems they dramatized no longer existing in the same forms as before, they are likely to be studied more impersonally and abstractly as aesthetic or historical artifacts divorced from any emotional force they may be capable of providing. As a matter of fact, one of today's greatest pretensions is that works of art can be examined in a purely "scientific" way—as language, psychology, philosophy, completely separated from the interests of any human audience for whom they were produced in the first place. As the academicization of everyday life has speeded up since the eighteenth century, leading eventually to today's "information society," we now find commonplace the turning of "life" into subjects of study while the life is still quiveringly vital. Not only novels and poems of living writers, but the songs of the Beatles, films, TV programs—what we now call popular culture—have become subjects for dissertations, books, biographies, as the search for new materials and "information" becomes more and more desperate.

This rapid appropriation of both life and "expression" as materials for scholarly analysis can seem especially outrageous when the distinctive qualities and aims of the originals have been cast aside in order to pursue entirely other and different aims. If politics, careerism, and the marketplace enter the picture, things can only seem worse.

A particularly concrete and intense enactment of these rather abstract considerations can be seen in the form of a furious debate between three black scholars that took place in the normally sedate forum of *New Literary History*.[1] With politeness thrown to the winds in what was for the principals a battle for survival, the reader becomes a voyeur at a singular exhibit of Hegelian "World History," a drama of *Geistesgeschichte* in action. One can see in this conflict how inevitably and inexorably cultural positions develop, how certain stages of social evolution must necessarily be traversed, how an Emersonian phylogeny lurks behind the apparently "free" adoption of moral and intellectual positions. Not the least remarkable aspect of the initiating essay, "The Black Canon: Reconstructing Black American Literary Criticism," by Joyce A. Joyce, was the fact of its acceptance in the first place. An impassioned piece, written in a voice strikingly different from the canonical ones of *NLH*, its very acceptance became one of the issues in the debate.

Joyce, an English professor at the University of Maryland, expresses her remorse at having been unsympathetic to a student who found an essay by James Baldwin difficult to understand. In defending Baldwin—she later came to feel—she was betraying an aspiring young black student by expressing her own "contradictions and elitism" (335). What Professor Joyce meant by this sense of betrayal (if I may interpret here) was that she had behaved like a rootless, professionalized, upwardly mobile intellectual rather than like a sisterly black, with the implication that such behavior means taking up a white "professional" point of view, a view in which texts, trendy ideas, and academic success take precedence over human obligations, especially to one's "people."

Since she had made use of them as negative examples, two other black academics were invited to enter the picture, Henry Louis Gates, Jr., and Houston A. Baker, Jr., both well-known cultural critics and Afro-American scholars. Contrasting them unfavorably with earlier black critics, Joyce remarked that "the function of the [black] creative writer and the literary scholar [in the past] was to guide, to serve as an intermediary in explaining the relationship between Black people and those forces that attempt to subdue them," whereas now there is a "denial or rejection of this role" (338–39) on the part of scholars like Gates and Baker. As Professor Joyce saw them, instead of acknowledging that black literature is a cry of the oppressed engaged in a practical struggle for survival as human beings, contemporary mainstream academics like Gates and Baker treat black literature simply as another set of "texts" to be processed according to the needs of careerism by means of the currently fashionable "post-structuralist" methodologies.

Speaking of today's reigning theorists, Joyce remarks that "their pseudoscientific language is distant and sterile. These writers evince their powers of ratiocination with an overwhelming denial of most, if not all, the senses." By constantly using such terms as "code," "sign," "signifier," "narratology," and "text," these writers "create the very alienation and estrangement" that they are attempting to undo (339–40).

Although she speaks of them only in passing, Professors Gates and Baker take up the gauntlet with a vengeance, for as a fellow black Joyce has struck sensitive nerves, always primed to be on the defensive. Gates, as professor of English, comparative literature, and African studies at Cornell (followed by moves to Duke and Harvard), is the veritable leader of academic Afro-American critical studies in this country. He has produced so many books and articles in recent years, either as sole author or editor, that it is barely possible to keep track of their titles. He is a gifted, sometimes brilliant intellectual: rhetorical, pugnacious, relentless, engaged in conducting a twenty-ring circus all at once and with considerable skill. He is also a paradigmatic exemplar of what I have come to call "academic capitalism," an enterprise that is complicated in his case by an admixture of self-righteous obsession with race, from which he is nonetheless able to extract every known academic perquisite. His most salient characteristics are his two well-worn metaphysical jumpsuits—one white, the other black—which he is able to zip on and off, sometimes in midsentence, with dizzying bravado as rhetorical needs urge him on. Although as an intellectual he is as white and bourgeois as I, he is nevertheless a virtuoso at exploiting white liberal guilt. Thus, he can play everyone off against everyone else while presuming to emerge with virtue unscathed. His sense of unscathedness, however, is the personal myth that causes his undoing, for in reality he is no more pure than anyone else. It is principally this role as academic capitalist that has irritated Joyce A. Joyce, since as a black agent thereof he has risen like a rocket in the academy by alchemizing the primal metal of black writings into "texts" of gold, subjecting them to the currently fashionable "white" critical methodologies, and living off the academic capital produced therefrom. Furthermore, since "texts" are merely "woven goods" rather than the "expression" associated with "books," the academic textualist resembles a sewing-machine operator processing yards of cloth, each as sewable as any other. Fancy stitches are what make for distinction, promotion, and bourgeoisification, yet while bourgeoisification is invariably part of even the most avant-garde academic's hidden agenda, radical good form requires that it always be furiously denied.

Houston Baker, though treated by Gates with the deference of a disciple, is in reality less of a master and more of a disciple than Gates. His earlier book, *The Journey Back: Issues in Black Literature and Criticism*, published in 1980, is a traditionally conceived work written in a clear and accomplished prose, but already dominated by a prior conversion to linguistic and rhetorical concepts that superimpose a grid of gratuitous complexities upon black writings. Concepts like "foregrounding" and "Sinnfeld" contribute about as much to an enhanced understanding of these works as Monsieur Jourdain's awareness that he is talking "prose." Baker's later book, *Blues, Ideology, and Afro-American Literature*, is an astounding but mostly unreadable mixture of earlier writing in his lucid mode and newer essays in the clotted, derivative, obfuscated jargon he has produced since his almost instantaneous— but much too late—conversion to Continental epigonism, which he describes in his introduction as if it were some radiant epiphany that transformed his life. Thus—to quote a passage at random—"Episte-mological cataclysms in historical discourse bring to view dimensions of experience excluded from extant accounts. And in the reordering effected by such ruptures (i.e., their constitution of revised models), one discovers not only new historical terms but also the variant his-toricity of the statements and terms of a traditional discourse. In *The Archaeology of Knowledge*, Foucault explains. . . ."[2] Like Johnson's woman preacher, Baker is a marvel not so much because he has man-aged to do this well as because he has managed to do it at all in the course of an overnight transformation. Indeed, Baker's own Achilles heel is his excessive receptivity to the influence of gurus altogether, an influence, incidentally, that he himself traces in an essay about one of his English professors at Howard University. Speaking of this teacher, Baker observes: "He had crafted an Oxonian mask behind which one could only surmise black beginnings. . . . He enjoyed using philosophi-cal words that he knew would send the curious among us scurrying to the dictionary."[3]

Joyce A. Joyce, however, is not buying any of this. Her essay's con-clusion is worth reproducing:

> Since the Black creative writer has always used language as a means of communication to bind people together, the job of the Black literary critic should be to find a point of merger between the communal, utilitarian, phenomenal nature of Black literature and the aesthetic or linguistic— if you will—analyses that illuminate the "universality" of a literary text. Rather than being a "linguistic event" or a complex network of linguistic systems that embody the union of the signified and the signifier indepen-dent of phenomenal reality [i.e., a mere "text"], Black creative art is an act of love which attempts to destroy estrangement and elitism by demon-strating a strong fondness or enthusiasm for freedom and an affectionate concern for the lives of people, especially Black people. (343)

Taking up Joyce's remark that black creative art is "an act of love," Gates—borrowing some lines from Tina Turner—entitles his reply "What's Love Got To Do With It?" Unfortunately, Turner seems to have been thinking about sex while Joyce is thinking of agape. This proves to be only the first of Gates's problems. "I must confess," he replies, "that I am bewildered by Joyce Joyce's implied claim that to

engage in black critical theory is to be, somehow, antiblack. . . . I find
this sort of claim to be both false and a potentially dangerous—and dis-
honest—form of witch-hunting or nigger-baiting" (346). And he adds,
very plausibly, "It is merely a mode of critical masturbation to praise a
black text simply because it is somehow 'black'" (347). He then concedes that in the past black literature and criticism were put primarily
to practical rather than aesthetic uses, but today, "our increasingly central role in 'the profession'" has changed the nature of enlightened
black criticism.

> We critics in the 1980s have the especial privilege of explicating the black
> tradition in ever closer detail. We shall not meet this challenge by remain-
> ing afraid of, or naive about, literary theory; rather, we will only inflict
> upon our literary tradition the violation of the uninformed reading. We
> are the keepers of the black literary tradition. . . . (352–53)

> Let me state clearly that I have no fantasy about my readership: I write
> for our writers and for our critics. If I write a book review, say, for a popular
> Afro-American newspaper, I write in one voice; if I write a close analysis
> of a black text and publish it in a specialist journal, I choose another voice,
> or voices. Is not that my "responsibility," to use Joyce Joyce's word, and
> my privilege as a writer? But I do not think my task as a critic is to lead
> black people to "freedom." My task is to explicate black texts. That's why
> *I* became a critic. (357)

Gates then goes on to note that his work is in its own way political.
"How can the use of literary analysis to explicate the racist social text
in which we still find ourselves be anything *but* political? To be political, however, does not mean that I have to write at the level of diction
of a Marvel comic book" (358).

Houston Baker takes a very different approach. He begins by describing an earlier public conflict he had had with another black woman
scholar, Deborah McDowell, also "conservative" like Joyce, at the 1984
conference of the English Institute. He then expresses surprise mixed
with pleasure at *New Literary History* opening its doors to black studies
when it had previously been entirely Euro-American, but he is troubled
by the fact that this door-opener involved yet another conservative black
woman scholar who is attacking somewhat radical fellow black crit-

ics. He then goes on for several pages magisterially enumerating the inaccuracies and errors in Joyce's essay. Then he explodes his bomb:

> . . . it is impossible to believe that an essay focused on Anglo-American criticism as dreadfully flawed by factual mistakes as Professor Joyce's work on Afro-American criticism would have been accepted or printed by a major critical or theoretical journal. Why, then, was her essay accepted and published by *New Literary History?*
>
> The most charitable explanation is that the journal's editors were victims of a too casual reader's report. A less charitable, and, I think, more accurate view, is that many people share Professor Joyce's essential animosity toward recent modes of critical and theoretical discussion that have enlarged the universe of discourse surrounding Afro-American expressive culture. Their animosity springs from the fact that the new critical and theoretical modes marking investigation of black expressive culture so clearly escape the minstrel simplicity that Anglo-Americans have traditionally imagined and assigned (and that some Afro-Americans have willingly provided and accepted) as the farthest reaches of the black voice in the United States. (366)

Describing his own avant-garde interests and their failure to harmonize with either a mainstream or an academic majority, Baker castigates "black willingness to tread conservative/minstrel paths, and a multi-ethnic fear in the academy of new and difficult modes of critical and theoretical study" (368) and then concludes: "Further, to publish a grossly erroneous attack on Afro-American literary criticism in a journal traditionally devoted to Euro-American points of view and directed to a white audience could, I suppose, be profitable in an academic world where any attack whatsoever on anything Afro-American whatsoever is taken as a valuable sortie" (368–69).

Baker's response is preposterous to a self-discrediting degree when we consider the wide-ranging interests of *New Literary History* and *Critical Inquiry*, not to mention a multitude of other journals like *Cultural Critique, Signs*, and *Telos*, that thrive on avant-gardism and ethnic studies. Just as Baker is still able to fancy that he represents a real avant-garde when his work is in fact indiscriminately derivative and epigonic, he is equally able to pretend that black critics and criticism are still not flourishing, neither in the academy nor in the journals, even in 1986. Not an inch is conceded, nor will he even refer to the Modern Language Association and its meetings and journal, which have been nothing if not receptive to pluralism and minorities. But Baker's real problem is grandiosity, not Joyce A. Joyce or *New Literary History*.

Given the powerful replies of Gates and Baker, however, one would have supposed that Professor Joyce, lacking their big guns, would wrap up this conflict with a reply both inadequate and desperate. But it is one of the fascinating aspects of this debate's complexity that, despite what seems to me a vulnerable ambivalence in her position and her relatively inexperienced rhetoric compared to that of Gates and Baker (who are masters at this sort of thing), her reply is devastating. For this debate is not just about intellectual issues like avant-garde black criticism, or racial issues like the power or powerlessness of blacks in the journals and in the academy, or socioethical issues like attitudes of the races toward each other and toward themselves; it is also about matters like self-deception, hypocrisy, professionalism, and the political by-products of personal struggles for power and reward in the academy. When all of these are considered, the problems that even I find present in Professor Joyce's position seem of secondary importance in relation to the ethical cruces suggested by her reply, although the other principals may be too self-involved to have noticed it. "Touché," says the fencer in Thurber's famous cartoon, while the severed head of his opponent looks on rather surprised.

Professor Joyce's reply, subtitled "Unconsciousness and Unconscionableness in the Criticism of Houston A. Baker, Jr., and Henry Louis Gates, Jr.," launches into a direct confrontation: "I knew that my two Black colleagues would not respond with either geniality or comradeship," it begins. Then it slashes away at Gates's use of Tina Turner:

> This song represents the denial of love and the degeneration of values that begin with self-love and are reflected in the way one human being responds to another. . . . And equally insidious is the video that flaunts the Black woman as sex object for Black men *and* white men, as Turner, with bleached stylishly unkempt hair suggestive of the white blond . . . and wearing a tight leather skirt and jacket and very high heels that accentuate her shapely legs, struts down the street. This video and the song lure our young people into the world of glamour, rapacity, and ignorance.

Unaware that they are being manipulated, the young Black women who
imitate Tina Turner manifest the self-hatred and self-denial widespread
among contemporary Black Americans. (372–73)

Joyce comments on how Baker and Gates have "overstate[d] their
cases against what they see as my errors and misjudgments. Perhaps, in
the past few years, they have used the obfuscating language and ideas
of Derrida, Barthes, Paul de Man, Foucault, Kristeva, Althusser, Bakh-
tin, and others to cloak their difficulties. In Baker's case, I fear, the
problem is much worse than an inability to read. His distortions of what
I wrote and his more serious warping of what took place at the English
Institute are, simply put, unethical" (373). All of these objections have
more of truth than falsity about them but even more cutting is her remark that "Gates and Baker have two standards for judgment, one by
which they judge and adopt the ideas of European and American white
males and the other by which they adjudicate the work of Black women.
*They allow the one group greater latitude for metaphorical language
than they do the other*" (374, emphasis added). She points out to Gates
that his insistence that readers, particularly black ones, must work to
understand difficult prose (since he does not want to write at the level
of Marvel comics) is contradicted by his admission that he chooses different voices depending on whether he is writing for the black masses
or his colleagues. She raises questions about the reason the critic writes
and for whom he writes. After contrasting two pieces of black criticism, one straightforward, the other "academic" and avant-garde, she
observes that "instead of inundating our works [i.e., black literature]
with contrived references to fashionable scholars and philosophers who
have decided that literature and life no longer have meaning and thus
that existence is a game, the Black American critic . . . should be at
the vanguard of a worldwide Black intellectual movement in much the
same way as Du Bois, Wright, and C. L. R. James were" (378), in
order to relate black literature to actual life in the world rather than
to other critical "texts." Speaking of Baker's description of his project
in the introduction to *Blues, Ideology, and Afro-American Literature* as
"a minute beginning in the labor of writing/righting American history and literary history," she remarks: "We can only question then the

reasons for the contradiction between the intended aim . . . and the semantic disjunctions that typify the essays in the text. . . . The entire collection is suffused with poststructuralist jargon" (379, 381).

Introducing her peroration, she approaches the very heart of the matter at hand. "I hope to show that my views of Black literary criticism are inextricably and unembarrassingly tied to my identity as a Black person and that Gates's and Baker's responses are, by nature, inextricably related to an absence of identity" (380). She explains this more concretely by adding that Gates maintains "that his mode of critical theory is Black critical theory . . . and that my objections to his analyses of Black literature suggest that he is antiblack. A significant difference exists between being 'not' Black and being antiblack. Of course, the real issue, the one that Gates refuses to let surface . . . concerns whether being a Black person who writes about Black literature makes one a Black critic" (381).

Joyce's penultimate paragraph must be read in toto, since it is the most important one in her response:

> Finally, Gates and Baker agree (since they are "ideal readers" for each other) that they are "spokespersons who move across ethnic and gender boundaries and who have decisively relinquished the role of simpleminded conservative spokespersons on behalf of a putatively simpleminded expressive culture." These embarrassing words imply that those Black literary critics who worked to provide what is now the foundation of Afro-American literary criticism and whose ideas have been subsumed and reshaped by Gates and Baker are simpleminded. These final comments water the seeds that I have planted throughout this essay: While Black American literature and its criticism are rooted in an allegiance to Black people, Baker and Gates have "relinquished" that allegiance. The first sign manifests itself in the hostile, warlike, ungracious nature of their responses to my essay. Although Baker goes so far as to suggest that Deborah McDowell should not have challenged him (the vanguard) in a "mixed" audience [at the English Institute], he has, as we can deduce from his language, no hesitation in attempting to make me appear mindless and backwards in the eyes of white society. He himself brings up the issue of the readership of *New Literary History*. Both he and Gates broke the most important code of the signifying tradition: they failed to attack [another black] by subversion (to speak in such a way that the master does

not grasp their meaning). They failed to demonstrate love and respect for
a Black sister. They do not understand that Black political involvement
can be achieved even in the ivory towers of academe as well as on the
streets and that an interrelationship exists between the two. Political involvement, the commitment to struggle for the movement of Blacks into
all strata of society, means that neither should have censured *New Literary History* for accepting the work of a Black sister. They should have
been committed to strategies for revision rather than to the proliferation
of their individual ideas and to the protection of their egos. As literary
critics, they should have been committed to the future of a Black American criticism that gains its strengths through challenges and trials rather
than through censorship and bravado. (382–83)

The lessons to be learned from an exchange like this go far beyond
the ostensible issues—to global ones that are not even raised by the
principals. To begin with, Professor Joyce's view that the structuralist
and deconstructive methods of Gates and Baker violate the integrity of
black literature and transform it from the record of a human struggle to
a mere business operation for intellectuals can hardly be cast aside with
a professional sneer. Certainly other critics than she have also taken
this view. For example, in an article in *The Journal of the Midwest Modern Language Association*, Norman Harris criticizes both Gates and
Robert Stepto on similar grounds. "My thesis here is that the New Black
Formalism disfigures the literature it discusses while trivializing the
dreams and aspirations of Afro-Americans in the world."[4] Referring to
a somewhat arcane essay by Gates on Ishmael Reed's *Mumbo Jumbo*,
Harris remarks, "What Reed intended is at least open to question, but
what he accomplished seems a clear part of a continuing struggle on
the part of Afro-Americans to find the proper pose and voice to understand and change the world. In fact, the intertextuality in the novel
which Gates takes as a sign that it is a post-modernist novel may well
be hooked to similar techniques used by those who wrote slave narratives. . . . Indeed, Gates's view seems accurate only if we view the
novel as being directed at an essentially Euro-American audience. It
is quite possible that Reed was directing his work toward the various
black communities" (42). His essay concludes by noting that "the New
Black Formalism ought to consider the purposes of literary criticism

within the context of the spiritual (aesthetic) needs of black people" since Afro-American literature is "a literature that is so much more than words" (44).

Even more remarkable than this is an essay by Barbara Christian, also black, and a professor of Afro-American studies at Berkeley. In "The Race for Theory," referring to the academic hegemony of current theorists, she expresses concern that "theory" may be inappropriate for dealing with "emerging literatures." In what is virtually an echo of Professor Joyce, she notes that this hegemony is widely discussed, "but usually in hidden groups, lest we, who are disturbed by it, appear ignorant to the reigning academic élite." "Among the folk who speak in muted tones are people of color, feminists, radical critics, creative writers, who have struggled for much longer than a decade to make their voices, their various voices, heard, and for whom literature is not an occasion for discourse among critics but is necessary nourishment for their people and one way by which they come to understand their lives better."[5] As for the language of the reigning theorists, it "is repulsive to me and one reason I raced from philosophy to literature, since the latter seemed to me to have the possibilities of rendering the world as large and as complicated as I experienced it, as sensual as I knew it was." Her conclusions resemble both Joyce's and Harris's:

> Now I am being told that philosophers are the ones who write literature, that authors are dead, irrelevant, mere vessels through which their narratives ooze, that they do not work nor have they the faintest idea of what they are doing; rather they produce texts as disembodied as the angels. I am frankly astonished that scholars who call themselves Marxists or post-Marxists could seriously use such metaphysical language even as they attempt to deconstruct the philosophic tradition from which their language comes. And as a student of literature, I am appalled by the sheer ugliness of the language, its lack of clarity, its unnecessarily complicated sentence constructions, its lack of pleasurableness, its alienating quality. It is the kind of writing for which composition teachers would give a freshman a resounding F. (56)

One can well understand why Joyce, Harris, and Christian feel so deeply that this neoformalist criticism is a betrayal, an unclean and venal act in which the suffering and blood of black Americans—as well as a liberation that is still in progress—have been turned into a market commodity not completely removed from cabbage-patch dolls and rock videos. When the classic writings of Afro-Americans are appropriated as mere "texts," patterns of words for deconstructive analysis by upwardly mobile academics—some of whom, to add insult to injury, are themselves black—it is not impossible to regard this as a milder form of medical experiments on prisoners in concentration camps. It is an appropriation of lived life for other ends, a violation of the Kantian imperative, a failure to distinguish between "for itself" and "in itself," a blurring of the distinction between subjects and objects.

But set opposite this are a number of forces that Joyce and Harris fail to consider—those of self-consciousness, intellectuality, scholarship, history, knowledge—in a word, civilization. While thinking, analyzing, knowing, recording are violations of *being*, they are paradoxically the distinctively human activities that set us apart from the purely lived lives of animals. Professor Joyce's sense of herself as a betrayer when she defends James Baldwin's art over and above the aspirations of her black student is surely an epiphanal moment in the history of a consciousness, representing as it does a split in the self, a gulf between the obligations of blood and the obligations of mind. But if Knowing is a betrayal of Being, it is a betrayal that cannot be stopped without our ceasing to be human. Thoughts cannot be unthought, innocence cannot be reinstated, nor can purity be brought back (especially when "purity" itself is open to question). The belief that there are original pure thoughts or experiences that are subsequently defiled cannot be substantiated because we can never get back to thoughts or feelings to which nothing is prior. Our deepest and most sacred states of being derive from prior states, with nothing that is "given" absolutely. There is no inviolable self because the "purity" of the self has already been compromised by our first acts of thinking, by our first assimilations of the imprint of our environment. At what point then could we decide to say, "From now on thinking about this subject is prohibited"? For at that point, someone would be bound to ask, "Why stop here rather than somewhere else? Why is Thought Number Three evil but Thought Number Two sacred?"

Thus Joyce and Harris are both right and wrong when they object to the activities of Gates, Baker, and Stepto as sinister: the transformation of black literature into academic grist is indeed a sacrilege in the strictest sense. For here are these bourgeois mandarin types shedding crocodile tears about their black roots while at the same time cultivating those roots—with weird graftings superadded—for all they are worth, turning other people's flesh not into lampshades but into pelf, power, and professorships in the decadent academy.

Yet that is what knowledge is, however sinister its darker side. Nor is it for nothing that knowing has been connected with evil (though some people have believed it leads to a paradise happier far). In this conflict between Being and Knowledge, even Professor Joyce has already been compromised: having partaken of the Tree of Knowledge (as professor and critic), she is past pure Being and well advanced into the depradations of Knowing. Surely Gates is right when he says that it is wrong to praise a black text simply because it is black. "Does the propensity," he asks, "to theorize about a text or a literary tradition 'mar,' 'violate,' 'impair,' or 'corrupt' the 'soundness' of a purported 'original perfect state' of a black text or of the black tradition?" (350). In expressing his own love for the black tradition and its works, Gates gives us little grounds to doubt his sincerity, although he ambiguously adds, "I am as black as I ever was, which is just as black as I ever want to be" (358).

Still, if Joyce's and Harris's view is not *intellectually* as persuasive as they suppose, why do we feel that their objections are powerful nonetheless? We feel so, I think, because the black revolution is not yet over and it seems too early to academicize it in cold blood. We feel too that the various forms of postmodern criticism have their own serious problems, problems that can reduce any literature to inconsequence and that particularly distort the unique aspects of the Afro-American literary condition. With its elimination of the author, its view of words as engaged in a synchronic free play with no reference to a "real" world, its reduction of writing to self-canceling antinomies that ultimately say everything and nothing, its mandarin and technical jargon, its real character as a New Formalism that nevertheless derides the old formalism of "New Criticism," given all of these it seems outrageously, blindly, tastelessly inappropriate because, whether intentionally or not, it *does* appear to trivialize, as Norman Harris claims, the writings to which it fastens itself at the very same moment that these writings are working in the world.

When the chief practitioners of this variety of Afro-American criticism happen themselves to be blacks, but blacks who have left their roots far behind as they become ultra-bourgeois academic superstars; when for all practical purposes these black critics are "white" while retaining a privileged access to people whose plight provides the material basis for their own eminently successful escape—one does not have to possess unduly sensitive moral faculties to find grounds for protest. In reply to Gates's objection that he is not "antiblack," Professor Joyce explained that "a significant difference exists between being 'not' Black and being antiblack." By this, of course, she meant that Gates is essentially a white critic making use of black writings while reaping the benefits of his blackness. He himself refers to "our increasingly central role in 'the profession' " and adds that "I do not think my task as a critic is to lead black people to 'freedom.' My task is to explicate black texts. That's why *I* became a critic." But at the same time as they engage in such admirably candid confessions, both Gates and Baker are apt to veer back to a sort of "minstrelsy" of their own when it suits them. Thus, Baker, in the process of exploiting the resources of white bourgeoisification in the academy, in the act of escaping from "minstrelsy," can allow himself to charge *New Literary History* with publishing Joyce's essay because "any attack whatsoever on anything Afro-American whatsoever is taken as a valuable sortie." This switch from scapegoat to sage and back again is much too facile for comfort.

Professor Joyce is also quite right to be outraged by Baker's anger at being criticized at the English Institute by a black woman while he himself goes on "unconscionably" to abuse Joyce herself in the pages of *New Literary History*. For her, this is another instance of the way in which blackness is at one and the same time used to propel a rising career while protecting it from assaults, not only by whites but by fellow blacks as well. This selective blackness, with its patronizing treatment of women, is the real basis of Joyce's protest, for her criticism of Gates and Baker is essentially a charge of moral blackmail against members of her own "family," who do not hesitate to kick her down so that they can rise up.

Nevertheless, this ongoing debate derives most of its interest not from the rightness or wrongness of its principals' positions so much as from its exhibition of an evolving, conflicted consciousness. The case of Richard Rodriguez, whose writings describe his gradual separation as an intellectual from his Mexican-American family, his early achievement of fame as a token gifted member of a minority, and his surprising rejection of the academic perquisites that were heaped upon him, is not nearly so painful to witness. Rodriguez was unusually conscious of his own psychology as well as his environment and he quickly realized not only that you can't go home again, but that once you have chosen where you *are* going, you have to accept the consequences accompanying that choice. But in the present case, things have not worked out quite so well. Though Professor Joyce's love and loyalty with regard to her people can only command respect, and though her conscience as a professor can only be admired, her conflicting roles as black and as intellectual involve a psychic split that can never be healed without an alteration of perspective and a transvaluation of values. This is, however, a very common dilemma, experienced by everyone who has grown away from family because of rejection of ethnicity, change of social class, or increased education. In order to function as an intellectual, love—though one certainly does not like to say it—is simply not enough. (I think, however, that Professor Gates has blundered in citing Tina Turner on this matter, for it betrays his somewhat hardboiled and excessively "playful" postmodern sensibility—and there is a point at which "playful" melts into "irresponsible.")

Professor Joyce has, nevertheless, caught Gates and Baker at a very vulnerable point not only in their own careers but in the careers of black studies and black liberation as well. There is no doubt that their services to black studies have been immense. They have lifted them out of the "right-on" folk-sentimental mutual backslapping of the sixties and given respectability to a university department that more often than not was hard pressed to justify its existence beyond power politics. But they have not yet come fully to terms with bourgeoisification, not only its profound connection to white mainstream culture, but their own indebtedness to it, without which they would not even exist in their sometimes smug present incarnations. Like many other kinds of privi-

leged intellectuals, they have yet to appreciate the general desirability
of being middle class in America—even while enjoying its benefits—or
to realize the extent to which they have not pulled themselves into it by
their own bootstraps, even with all their superior gifts. Indeed, you do
not have to be a neoconservative to recognize that individual success is
less often due to prodigious gifts than to institutions that are already
in place when you appear on the scene, institutions that have come
about through *other peoples' efforts* rather than your own. Still, Gates's
accomplishments are remarkable enough for him finally to throw away
his two jumpsuits, to accept his bourgeois identity, to recognize Joyce's
valid objections to various rootless (and ruthless) aspects of postmodern criticism, particularly in their application to black literature, and
to acknowledge that both he and Professor Baker are now part of the
Establishment, estranged from any supposed moral purity they may
once have presumed to enjoy as blacks, while sharing the same obligations and liabilities as any other successful bourgeois professionals—
obligations that must be met not in some nebulous future when perfect justice reigns on earth and racism has disappeared, but right now.
Perhaps *that's* what love's got to do with it.

Part Three

· · · · · ·

Academic
Capitalism

11

. . . . . .

Public Intellectuals
and the Academy

Like the perennially moribund but never-quite-dead novel, the man
of letters is a genus always on the verge of extinction but never quite
extinct. In his well-known book on the subject, John Gross, tracing the
man of letters from the eighteenth century to the modern period, sees
him as a changing phenomenon that—whatever its current form in the
twentieth century—is nevertheless antiquated and obsolete.[1] For there
is no one quite the equivalent nowadays of Leslie Stephen, T. S. Eliot,
Edmund Wilson, or Lionel Trilling.

In the introduction to *Lionel Trilling and the Fate of Cultural Criticism*, Mark Krupnick contrasts the academicized criticism of today with
the literary journalism that flourished fifty years ago, pointing out that
critics like Blackmur, Tate, and Burke could be immensely learned,
though "not in the way of today's academic theorists. . . . The tren-
chancy of Tate and Philip Rahv owe [*sic*] a great deal to their connection with living history and to the fact that they were partisans,
controversialists on behalf of their opposing worldviews. The pressures
of history and the discipline of regular reviewing accounted for much
of the strength, as of the weaknesses, in this culture of journalism. . . .
They represented an avant-garde in literature and politics. Nowadays,
the avant-garde has moved into the universities."[2]

If we think of this old literary breed as consisting principally of non-

academic writers on literature and culture, we can, however, come
up with a formidable roster of present-day successors: Joseph Epstein,
Hilton Kramer, Gore Vidal, Joan Didion, Stephen Spender, Joyce Carol
Oates, Leon Edel, Cynthia Ozick, and V. S. Pritchett, to mention just
a few. Although some of these have had part- or full-time academic
connections, we think of them as essentially nonacademic. Nevertheless Krupnick finds that all is not well: "As the avant-garde abandoned
bohemia for the English department, literary journalism became the
refuge of humanistic orthodoxy, notably in the writings of neoconservative critics. That journalistic counterattack, conducted in the name
of humanistic values, has frequently taken the form of middlebrow
anti-intellectualism" (3). Although the majority of critics listed above
cannot be called "neoconservative" or "anti-intellectual," it is true that
all can be considered as more or less "conservative," not so much politically as in their adherence to fairly traditional intellectual paradigms
and their avoidance of "theory." In addition to writers like these, there
also exists today what Alvin Gouldner might have called a group of New
Class descendants of the traditional man of letters consisting largely
of specialist academics who are not too supercilious to write for a general audience. When these Persons Of Letters are taken into account,
we find ourselves with a fairly lively enterprise: the science essays of
physicist Jeremy Bernstein, the sui generis essays of biologist Lewis
Thomas, the poetry essays of Helen Vendler, the literary-political essays
of Richard Ohmann, the cultural essays of Frederick Crews, the shorter
historical pieces of Gertrude Himmelfarb, even some of the essays of
Terry Eagleton and Stanley Fish, when they can manage to tranquil-
ize their half-crazed hobby horses. Even so, it is true that free-floating
"public intellectuals" are less numerous than they used to be and that
the connection with academia involves certain constraints on performance and behavior such that none of these academics can boast the
magisterial or vatic qualities of a George Eliot or John Stuart Mill, a
Carlyle or an Edmund Wilson.

I take the phrase "public intellectuals" from Russell Jacoby, whose
book *The Last Intellectuals*, a remarkably wide-ranging synthesis of
sources across the humanities and social sciences, has sharply focused
these issues. Tracing the ways in which risk-taking bohemia and brazen

New Left have been replaced by the job security of the university, he writes: "Today nonacademic intellectuals are an endangered species; industrial development and urban blight [and now, one should add, gentrification of seedy neighborhoods] have devastated their environment. They [i.e., the old survivors] continue to loom large in the cultural world because they mastered a public idiom. The new academics far outnumber the independent intellectuals, but since they do not employ the vernacular, outsiders rarely know of them."[3]

Jacoby himself illustrates the dilemma facing intellectuals who resist academia while depending upon it in order to earn a living. His plight is described by Richard Bernstein, who interviewed him for the *New York Times* after the appearance of his book: "But Mr. Jacoby, even while making a stir, sees himself as he put it, as 'part of the problem.' At 42 years of age and with a Ph.D. in European history from the University of Rochester, he is a graying, unemployed member of the diploma-laden club whose collective failure he laments. And so, he is twice disappointed: first, that his generation has not produced its share of what he calls 'public intellectuals' and second, that his much-noted effort to point out that failure may have placed obstacles in his own academic path."[4]

I witnessed at first hand the sort of problem faced by Jacoby when I met a young San Francisco poet who lives on a pittance from odd jobs and occasional small grants from arts foundations. In previous years he had occasionally picked up part-time teaching in university programs concerned with English as a second language (TESOL), but as more and more Ph.D.'s have been created in this field, these odd jobs vanished. As for full-time teaching in a writing program, he reported to me his fears of turning into an "academic poet." Despite this, I told him, with considerable sense of guilt and betrayal, that he should read the want ads in the *Chronicle of Higher Education* for poets-in-residence because starving poets no longer had any cachet in our society. His fear was hardly an unrealistic one, as can be seen in an article by Kate Adams, "Academe's Dominance of Poetic Culture Narrows the Range of American Poetry." Adams observes that "when poets are dependent on universities for their salaries, they must participate in the economy of intellectual production that rules academe and will determine their position in its hierarchical structure."[5] The rewards that are offered by that structure "go only to a narrow constituency of poets." "Publication represents only the final and most obvious step in the complex process through which universities assert their control over the definition and distribution of poetic culture. Through the policies of the workshops and the granting of advanced degrees, through the editorial and aesthetic policies of the literary journals [which are tightly connected to the universities], through offering or not offering jobs, and through awarding or not awarding tenure, academe has a major influence on contemporary poetry."

The conclusion is bleak: "When poetry is institutionalized, its power as a medium of communication becomes attenuated, because it is cut off from audiences outside the university." Since the major audience consists mainly of other academics, poetic gifts have now been transformed "into a kind of institutional scrip, negotiable only within the walls of academe—a means not for giving [the benefits of poetry to a larger world] but for getting ahead."

As audiences for general culture dry up in an age of specialization, public intellectuals become an anomaly, since an academic job is now required in order to live decently, and this means catering to the needs of specialized readers who can use other people's writings to further their own careers. Jacoby is particularly vexed at what happened to the youthful rebels of the New Left of the sixties. "The New Left sprang into life around and against universities; its revulsion seemed visceral. Yet New Left intellectuals became professors who neither looked backward nor sideways; they kept their eyes on professional journals, monographs, and conferences" (140). Although Jacoby has some good words for much of the Marxist, feminist, and radical scholarship that resulted, his overall response is negative. Speaking of this body of writing, he concludes: "It is largely technical, unreadable and—except by specialists—unread. While New Left intellectuals obtain secure positions in central institutions, the deepest irony marks their achievement. Their scholarship looks more and more like the work it sought to subvert" (141). Commenting on a critic's description of Fredric Jameson's work as "the opening up of the individual text into that *hors texte* or unspoken (non-*dit*) ground of intolerable contradiction that it cannot acknowledge," Jacoby sounds very much like Jim Merod[6] on Jameson: What the critic "cannot acknowledge is that the real text is the advance and self-advance of careers" (168).

The point to which he keeps returning, however, is "that colleagues have replaced a public, and jargon has supplanted English. American Marxists [and other specialists] today have campus offices and assigned parking spaces" (180). Although he is understanding, even somewhat sympathetic about the new comforts that professionalism affords, he is unwilling to forfeit the virtues of the public intellectual. Thus, he laments that "to describe someone as a 'man of letters' in the 1980's is almost derogatory, hinting of village poets or family historians" (195), but like Krupnick he associates today's surviving specimens with "conservative journals, such as the *New Criterion, Commentary, American Scholar*" (196), which still honor men of letters. To that extent, he is favorably disposed toward these journals, particularly to the lucid writing that makes them both readable and actually read, vehicles of public prose. Moreover, they can be depended upon to criticize the failings of professionalism and the academic takeover of the arts. Their serious shortcoming, however, is that they insist the man of letters must stand apart from politics. Even this view might be acceptable if it were really honored in their own practice—but Jacoby finds them to be far from apolitical. "Not only do they imagine that at some point culture was uncontaminated by politics; but for them politics can only mean left-wing politics. Their own politics is not politics. Yet rarely have general periodicals devoted to the arts and scholarship been as emphatically political" as the aforementioned journals (200–201). After a long discussion that supports this claim with chapter and verse, Jacoby adduces their general principle: "Whoever pays the tab does the ordering. Culture and scholarship should celebrate capitalism because they are sustained by it. . . . Little irritates them more than left intellectuals who are not starving; social critics, in their view, should be poor, hungry, or sick" (207). It is more than a little ironic that Hilton Kramer, in a reductive and peremptory review of Jacoby's book in the *New Criterion*, should ignore its rare virtues and social conscience in order to dismiss it out of hand on the narrowest of political grounds.

For the moment, it is hard to see how the problem of the public intellectual will be resolved. On the one hand, the traditional man of letters, while not fully extinct, is clearly on the way out because the social formations that enabled him to flourish no longer exist. The virtual disappearance of bohemia and the spread of middle-class standards of comfort, health, education, and general well-being to the majority of the inhabitants of Western cultures, along with the unacceptability of poverty, have made it almost impossible for intellectuals to be independent of a secure source of income. Furthermore, the fragmentation of "culture" into myriad subcultures and the rise of mass audiences who have been bred by television rather than by "literature" means that no one speaks for the general society and that there are no longer eternal verities. The submerged minorities that made possible a prevailing culture by default continue to emerge, disrupting the skewed consensus, and the notion of a melting pot is in at least temporary disfavor. Obviously, this fragmentation cannot go on indefinitely, for it is not possible for road signs to be printed in twenty-five different languages. Some sort of "hegemony" has to prevail just to keep things operating. Though it is always possible that some people will feel their innermost being violated by the use of red traffic lights to signify STOP, mundane existence in the world requires finite and often arbitrary choices in order for any actions to take place at all—and some deep feelings have to be violated for civilization to continue. Since it *does* seem possible to avoid injustice while nevertheless favoring one choice over another for the sake of worldly existence, it also seems reasonable to expect that a relatively general culture is not only feasible but a dire necessity in order to avoid a return to the primal jungle. In such a culture, some people rather than others will necessarily function as spokespersons, but it is hard to suppose that there can ever be a return to any monolithic culture, short of totalitarianism. It is also hard to suppose that such a culture could again seem desirable.

If public intellectuals are bound to continue to speak to more specialized audiences than they did in the past, today's excesses of specialization are nonetheless far from satisfactory, at times participating in an eccentricity of fetish worship that has affinities with madness. The excesses of the Joyceans, the academic Marxists, the Bloomsbury cultists, and the deconstructionists can look startlingly like the myopic freaks and follies of extreme right-wing evangelicals or even the Ku Klux Klan and the American Nazis. What prevents a genuine identity between these two cultures is the extraordinary intelligence and sensibility of literary intellectuals and their ability—when pressed—to laugh at themselves, which right-wing extremists are generally unable to do (though it would not be hard to cite a few dour intellectuals).

In the course of chapters that follow, I expand the constituency of public intellectuals and suggest a role for them both within and without the academy. The operating principle is that noblesse oblige requires those with gifts to use them for the general welfare.

12

. . . . . .

Academic Capitalism
and Literary Value

In recent years we have witnessed a repeating cycle in which academic minorities and underdogs, once they ascend to the mainstream, necessarily acquire the same characteristics as the people they have displaced —just like other minorities in the so-called real world. That sweet little family-run business, once so sterling and reliable, becomes just another ruthless capitalist enterprise when success arrives, complete with false advertising, grandiose claims, international franchises, shady backroom dealings, and all the other familiar practices of monopoly capitalism. This is not to say that the supplanting of New Criticism and dry-as-dust scholarship by feminist, black, deconstructionist, and Marxist methodologies has not produced a lively, flourishing period for literary studies. On the contrary, the sheer quantity of intelligent writing is surely amazing, but whatever the virtues of these approaches may have been while they were fighting for their lives, the reality is rather different now that they have become the chief corporations of academic capitalism. What once served as correctives to monolithic but moribund methodologies have by now become "hegemonic" monoliths themselves, though they are apt nonetheless to affect an air of violated innocence. Clearly, the acquisition of power, the shift in role from underdog minority to reigning monarch, involves deep ontological laws that cannot be evaded. To acquire power is to dance to the already choreographed patterns of the power structure. Yet many of these new potentates continue to whine as pariahs even as they bark out categorical imperatives from endowed chairs at principal research universities.

Since so many of the powerful are incapable of realizing that they are now the odious power elite, it becomes urgent that they be reminded of this virtually inescapable preordination. Thus, it is reassuring to see in the past few years, even in journals like *PMLA* that normally roll with the punches, a manifest backlash against the new academic capitalism.

If anything was begging for a backlash, it was surely J. Hillis Miller's "Presidential Address" to the Modern Language Association in December 1986,[1] which stands out as a shamelessly entrepreneurial specimen of its genre, suffused, of course, with the requisite academic pieties. Although the rhetorical materials out of which it is constructed are a ragbag of whimsical academic ideas that Miller—a decentered and uprooted scholar (see Chapter 7 above)—worked up for the occasion, the heart of the address is an attack on the New Historicism prompted by Miller's own involvement in deconstruction. He tells us that he has been concerned of late with "the ethics of reading" and "if that phrase means anything, it must have something to do with respecting any text discussed, with accepting an obligation to read—to read carefully, patiently, and scrupulously, under the elementary assumption that the text being read may say something different from what one wants or expects it to say or from what received opinion says it says" (284). The reason that the New Historicism is becoming popular, Miller claims, is that there is a resistance to careful reading and to "theory" on the part of deconstruction's enemies.

Contrary to the universal belief that deconstruction denies inherent meaning to texts, Miller informs his audience that they are failing to read deconstructive texts carefully in order to find out what they are really saying; and despite the extraordinarily high level of skill and intelligence that characterizes academics in general, he tells them that virtually no one but himself and his friends grasps the essence of deconstruction. The reason that nobody understands it is the "blind refusal to read," which "flouts the minimal obligations of our profession." He then concludes by naming a dozen or so younger academics who are not guilty of these deficiencies of reading and understanding and who can thus carry deconstruction from its necessarily militant to its redemptively triumphant state.

Two later essays mount such an attack on this strange mentality that it is hard to believe deconstruction can ever recover its former questionable prestige. Robert Scholes, in "Deconstruction and Communication,"[2] begins with an idea that will be seen again elsewhere, that "the powerful appeal that Derridean thought has had for American literary critics has its emotional roots in a cultural reflex of sympathy for the outlaw" and a wish to escape from "stifling rules and responsibilities" (278), but Scholes regards the freedom as illusory. In a reading of Derrida's debate with John Searle over speech-act theory, Scholes whips out a supersharp sword on which to impale some of deconstruction's fondest dogma. He zeroes in on the very contradiction we found in Miller's address to the MLA—the deconstructionist complaint about being misread. Quoting a number of passages in which Derrida reproaches Searle for his failure to read him carefully and correctly, Scholes remarks, "We can find frequent instances of sympathy for the outlaw becoming righteous indignation when [Derrida's] own textual property is at stake" (281). "What Derrida says here, through his obvious pain and outrage at being misread, is that reading involves some observation of the generic and contextual features involved in the production of a text. . . . It is perhaps unfortunate that this conservatism emerges most vigorously when his own texts are being read," but, he concludes, "The really sacred texts are the ones we write ourselves" (282).

Scholes is relentless in exposing Derrida's hypocrisy: avoiding any reference to truth or falsity, in which deconstructionists do not believe, Derrida uses euphemisms such as "rigorous" and "scientific" in order to complain about the qualities his opponents lack when they (mis)read him. Like the rest of us, he resorts "to the 'language-police,' to science, rigor, or other euphemisms for the Law which he sometimes affects to be above—or below" (284). Scholes then goes on to expose the fallacies involved in Derrida's foundational notion of *différance* by showing how even this idea depends on fixities and conventions as well as on "reason" itself.

Why has so unconvincing a doctrine as deconstruction managed to retain a hold for as long as it has?

> In particular, for the generation whose sensibilities were shaped by the six-ties, the anarchistic irreverence of deconstruction holds a profound attraction. For those who still remember the slogans of the past well enough to think of themselves as having sold out, as having been co-opted by the establishment, the verbal or textual posture offered by deconstructive discourse is almost irresistible. Its appeal is so strong because it allows a displacement of political activism into a textual world where anarchy can *become* establishment without threatening the actual seats of political and economic power. Political radicalism may thus be drained off or sublimated into a textual radicalism that can happily theorize its own disconnection from unpleasant realities. (284–85)

John Ellis carries this line of argument even further. Remarking, like Scholes, that deconstructors regard not only outsiders as disqualified from criticizing deconstruction, but other insiders as well, he wonders "how one can argue that deconstruction cannot be characterized as other theoretical positions can, and then go on to attack a fellow-deconstructor's characterization in order to substitute one's own." He realizes that this is a common practice, like invalidating the author's intention as a norm for interpretation and then attacking other critics, as Miller and Derrida do, for misinterpreting their works.[3]

Ellis goes beyond these inconsistencies to find that unlike other critical methodologies, deconstruction requires that the "misreadings" and traditional methods that it attacks be retained for repeated assault rather than disposed of and forgotten about once they are supposedly routed. Deconstruction, oddly enough, needs to destroy the same opposition over and over again by "taking the traditional (obvious, literal, repressive, authoritarian, and so forth) view and standing it on its head—subverting, undermining, or opposing it" (268). Ellis offers a historical explanation for such perversity:

> There are two features of the French context of origin that seem relevant: the first relating to the academy, and the second to French intellectual life in general. As to the first: an unusual degree of rigidity and conservatism prevailed in French universities in the mid-sixties when de-

construction emerged. A version of literary history and biography which
had gone unchanged since the nineteenth century held complete sway in
the field; the theoretical turmoil of the last forty years in England and
America had barely touched French higher education. In linguistics, too,
Saussure's theory of language had given rise to structural linguistics in
England and America, but had scarcely made a dent in the old-fashioned
historical philology which still dominated the study of language in French
universities. . . . There was one truth, and it was contained in Gustave
Lanson's literary history of France, which students were required to com-
mit to memory. Any deviation from this basic truth provoked a massive,
unified reprisal. (270–71)

As for French intellectual life in general, "By long-standing tradition, the French intellectual has defined himself by opposition to the
dull-witted bourgeoisie and the official organs of the state (such as the
university) which are its expression. As a result, an outstanding characteristic of French intellectualism is an obsessive denigration of the
bourgeois and all his manifestations" (271). As for deconstruction, the
French intellectual's need to *épater le bourgeois* results in "denigrat-
ing the traditional reading for its own sake" while at the same time
keeping it alive "in order to mock it and run dazzling intellectual rings
around it, rather than let it pass into obscurity" (272). The importa-
tion of this obsessional exposure of bovine naïveté, according to Ellis,
is ludicrously inappropriate for American intellectuals and explains
their curious habit of constantly flogging the dead cow of traditional
readings. "There is, in fact, something logically very odd about this
mismatch between a critical theory that in its obsession with conformity could only have arisen in France, and its acceptance in America,
the pluralistically cheerful acceptor of diversity" (273), especially when
what American intellectual institutions really need at present is "a
greater degree of resistance to the acceptance into this chaos of yet
another ideology" (272).

In essence, Ellis—like Scholes—sees as central to American deconstruction its playacting of revolution and subversion. Since there is very
little intellectual authority to subvert in the United States and since
"le bourgeois" is, after all, ourselves, "The temper of deconstructionist
criticism is, in fact, remarkable for its conformism, rather than the re-

verse; deconstructive writings tend to go over the same ground and use the same vocabulary (logocentrism, difference, demystifying, and so on) without substantial modification or fresh analysis on each occasion. These are not the signs of a genuinely open, intellectually probing new movement" (275). Interestingly enough, if there *is* any sort of canonical authoritarianism operating today in literary studies, it comes as a fruit of deconstruction. Marjorie Perloff rather sharply unmasks this new tyranny in a little essay, "An Intellectual Impasse," that formed part of a debate about the canon in *Salmagundi*, where she remarked that "our literature faculties sometimes bear a painful resemblance to Swift's Acadamy of Lagado,"[4] and that a new but minority-skewed canon has replaced the old. Students, she feels, can now be depended upon to have read Kate Chopin or Terry Eagleton but are less likely to know Greek drama.

If Scholes and Ellis have done a number against deconstruction, Edward Pechter, in an elegantly written tour de force, this time in the redoubtable *PMLA*, takes on the New Historicism.[5] Although he agrees that new historicists fail to experience the text in all its fleshly concreteness, he and Hillis Miller share little if any other common ground. Pechter explains that the New Historicism puts texts back into their historical contexts in order to reveal the will and desire that produce and receive them. In so doing, new historicists want to expose the political interests, the power relations, that lie behind them. Everything, once again, is political. What he hastens to add is that far from setting literary "interpretations" into the concrete factual reality of history, such "factual" settings are themselves interpretations of past events that can never be known directly, interpretations that reflect the will and desire of the interpreters, like all other interpretation. "The histories being recovered are themselves transcendental signifieds" because "history speaks in our voice. History does not tell us what the text is, because we decide what history is" (298). Thus the new historicist is himself the product of politically determined forces and, like the texts he deconstructs in order to reveal their "political unconscious," he too is a political unconscious in action, reconstituting "history" for his own ends. Although Pechter does not explicitly say so, he implies throughout that just as deconstructionist and Freudian readings always produce the same set of meanings, regardless of the texts they address, so new historicists always find the same expression of power-struggle wherever they look. To read literary works under the domination of such totalizing theories inevitably becomes a bore, since no matter what evasions and arabesques the poet or novelist may employ (known in the past as "technique" or "poetics"), the (unconscious) message is always the same. Speaking of this school's "imperial new claims," and focusing on their obsessive themes (in this case as applied to Renaissance drama), he concludes: "When addressed to the left-liberal academic community, for whom the monarchy is an anachronism, feminism an article of faith, and colonialism a source of embarrassed guilt, these critical versions cannot help draining the plays of much of their potential to involve an audience." "One aspect of this draining strategy is the new historicists' tendency to deemphasize passages whose affective power seems unusually great" (299). He offers an explanation for this curious tendency: "by reducing the power of the text, detachment increases the observer's power over the text," and then he quotes the same passage from Frank Lentricchia that I have already used (see Chapter 8) to the effect that we must interrogate the text "so as to reproduce it as a social text in the teeth of the usual critical lyricism that would deny the social text power and social specificity in the name of 'literature.' The activist intellectual needs a theory of reading that will instigate a culturally suspicious, trouble-making readership." To this Pechter replies that "for many new historicists, the power over the text derived from this suspicion is instrumental to social change, part of the project of making the world a better place" (299). But unlike Lentricchia, Merod, and others, Pechter thinks that "there are simply more effective ways of proceeding" (300) if one wants to subvert the status quo than by practicing literary criticism.

Since Pechter's concern here is literary, he does not explore these other ways; rather, he wants to specify the consequences to literature of such a mentality.

> It would be foolish indeed (or saintly) to hold that benevolence is *the* human essence, the force that through the green fuse drives our flower. *But is it any less foolish to substitute the will to power?* [emphasis added] Getting beyond humanism is supposed to mean getting beyond such

essences, not merely exchanging one for another, replacing the flattering with the cynical.

. . . Acquiring power over the text will seem a costly achievement, since what it sacrifices is the potential power of the text—the power to open up new areas of experience, unfamiliar ways of being in the world. New-historicist procedures are designed to resist any such power, to work around or get beyond immediate textual impressions to arrive at a pre-determined point of theoretical understanding. . . . New historicist criticism is a criticism of recognition, of knowing again what one knew before. It is criticism that systematically deprives the text of its capacity to surprise, and who wants to go to a theater where there are no surprises? (301–2)

The new historicist critic wants "to master the text before it masters him" (302). Once again, it's you or me, you bastard!

Ironically pretending not to be ironic at all, my last critic, Richard Levin, refocuses the laser beam he had already used in his 1979 book, *New Readings vs. Old Plays: Recent Trends in the Reinterpretation of English Renaissance Drama*, in order to aim it at recent feminist readings of Shakespeare. In "Feminist Thematics and Shakespearean Tragedy," a rhetorical performance of exquisitely genteel brutality, he unmasks yet another variant of the critical upstaging of authorial power.

Examining a substantial selection of writings on Shakespeare's tragedies, Levin finds that "these critics agree that the plays are not really about the particular characters who appear there but about some general idea," and that "the themes employed in their interpretations are basically the same. Although the terminology may vary, these critics all find that the plays are about the role of gender in the individual and in society."[6] The pattern Levin discovers in this criticism is that the cause of the tragedy is invariably not in the characters of the drama "but in one of those two abstractions whose opposition constitutes the theme, nor will we be surprised to learn which one always turns out to be the guilty party" (126). In a word, the oppositions are male and female and the guilt always male. Levin quotes many examples whose tenor is that the tragedy is caused by "masculine consciousness," or the rejection of feminine values, or patriarchy itself, wryly observing that "of course, the characters themselves are unaware of the real cause of their

misfortunes . . . which seems a pity, for if they only knew they might
have given us some great last words. When the dying Desdemona is
asked by Emilia, 'Who hath done this deed?' she could have answered,
'Nobodie, twas the male order of thinges, farewell' " (127). Since the
characters in the tragedies themselves regard Lear and Othello, for instance, as exhibiting horrible and deranged behavior, Levin repeatedly
reminds the critics that it is impossible to attribute the catastrophes to
society's general acceptance of "patriarchal values." While the tragic
denouements "are all made possible by the kind of society in which
they occur . . . they are all regarded by that society as extraordinary
calamities (otherwise they would not seem tragic). It is hard to see,
then, how these plays could be blaming the patriarchal society for the
tragic outcome. It is even hard to see how they could be conducting
an enquiry into patriarchy, when the actions they focus on are clearly
meant to be atypical" (127–28).

Levin demonstrates how consistently the critics are enabled to blame
the tragedies on the male deficiencies of patriarchal society by selec-
tively omitting all contradictory evidence. Since most of the critics
praise the comedies for their "feminine" dominance (to which they attribute the happy endings), Levin reminds them that these comedies
also take place in patriarchal society. "It seems evident, then, that patriarchy cannot have any necessary causal connection to misery, when it
is just as capable of producing happiness" (128).

The extraordinary willfulness of the critics in imposing their own
desires upon the plays is one of Levin's most pressing objections:

> Moreover, the critics can always make their thematic concepts of gender
> fit the facts of the play, because the facts are defined by the theme, rather
> than the reverse. Erickson provides a revealing example of this process in
> his chapter on *The Winter's Tale*, where he asserts that Leontes's "sponta-
> neous outburst of jealousy" is "intrinsic to the male psyche." But no other
> man in the play ever shows a trace of jealousy, and all the men who com-
> ment on Leontes's accusation of Hermione take *her* side, which is not what
> one would expect if his feelings also resided in their own psyches. (130)

Finally, not only do these feminist critics tend to reduce or elimi-
nate the force of the play's characters *as characters* and supplant them

with thematic ideologies, they tend to ignore the dramatic elements of the plays altogether. The critics are uninterested in the tragic climax or its catharsis and their routine denigration of the tragic hero "tends to minimize emotional involvement with the characters in its concentration on an intellectual grasp of the thematic lesson" (131). In sum, "most thematists are much more interested in the intellectual theme they derive from a play than in its emotional effect" (132).

A general summary account of the limitations of the New Historicism by A. Leigh DeNeef can serve to underscore *the* problem that refuses to go away: the global demolition theories that are now so fashionable invariably demolish themselves along with their victims, although the theorist pretends not to notice. DeNeef speaks of "the tendency to substitute for a questionable notion of history an unquesioned notion of context,"[7] as if context were an objective fact rather than a construction of the theorist out of infinite possibilities. Thus the cult of "patriarchy" that Levin satirizes in his treatment of feminist Shakespearean criticism is for DeNeef simply one more example of the "enabling context[s]" that "assume a concreteness and a specificity that are, theoretically, hard to justify" (503). To put it even more destructively: "If we think again of the various feminist revisions currently under way, we might well inquire about the extent to which patriarchy is a historical 'context' of the Renaissance *or* of the late 1970s and early 1980s. Indeed, the most persistent topics of the new historicism—gender relations, the various appropriations of power and authority, the complex structures of identity configuration, the subversions of a literary subversiveness by a dominant ideology—would seem much more *our* issues than ones we have 'discovered' in the Renaissance" (505). And lastly, "I am not convinced by the new historicist's easy acknowledgement that the critic's work is as historically embedded as the text he or she is studying, for that acknowledgement rarely goes beyond a facile gesture. Until the critic puts his own pressures into play as concretely and precisely as those he is uncovering in the past, acknowledgement remains purely rhetorical" (507).

To look back upon these critics, as well as others who have appeared in the course of this book, is to witness the same overriding programs— why not call them "hegemonies" or "wills-to-power"?—rudely forced upon defenseless texts and abused readers. One need not believe in a doctrine of Magical Immediacy in order to feel that poems, novels, and plays *could* speak in something resembling their author's voice if an effort were made to help them to do so. Critical mediations need not issue in rapacious and violating ventriloquism. It *is* possible to suppose that some critics and scholars give us a much more accurate picture of and feeling for their subjects than others.

One of the most pervasive of these critical programs involves a relentless machinery to *épater le bourgeois*, a game that has reached the point of an academic pathology. Early on, perhaps, it was very amusing to see cream pies thrown in the faces of inflexible reactionaries and doddering philologists. But when almost everyone is now bourgeois and the term itself practically meaningless, and when most of the "bourgeois" whom these critics attempt to astonish are none other than their fellow academics, a good deal of the force of this one-upmanship is dissipated. In what is now a rapid turnover of marketable ideas in the academy, a turnover similar to the one in technology ("You're still using that ancient 4.77 mhz computer?"), astonishing one's colleagues has less to do with "truth" than with conspicuous production and consumption, a need to banish last year's models from the showroom floor. A speech like that of Hillis Miller to the MLA, with its crass intimation that only a chosen few can even begin to understand deconstruction, is not at so great a remove from the glory of being the only yuppie in your condo to own a Ferrari. If "only a few" can understand the arcane mysteries unaided, and if the gratifications of preening exclusivity cannot last forever, then clearly a great opportunity arises for the self-appointed elite to empower franchised agents to produce intelligible versions for the unwashed, giving rise to the Derrida, Foucault, and Jameson industries, for example, while the innovators at the cutting edge gear up for next year's model, which is bound to reveal a fatal flaw in Foucault's heart, or at least a cosmic crux in Lacan. What remains unresolved is that these self-appointed elites are every bit as "bourgeois" as the victims they attack. Indeed, they are unwitting tools of the system they pretend to destroy, drones in the dissemination of the Gross Intellectual Product. What is particularly embarrassing is that they have already been described by Nietzsche: "There is from the very start something unwholesome about such priestly aristocracies, about their way of life, which is turned away from action and swings between brooding and emotional explosions: a way of life which may be seen as responsible for the morbidity and neurasthenia of priests of all periods. Yet are we not right in maintaining that the cures which they have developed for their morbidities have proved a hundred times more dangerous than the ills themselves?"[8] Nor is it so impossible to envision a "poisonous eye of resentment" (again from Nietzsche) lurking behind the unceasing mockeries of these powerless intellectuals out for a powergrab.

Yet most of the reigning methodologies participate in this need to stun the bourgeois: deconstruction, by showing that the meaning apparent to the vulgar is thwarted by an opposite meaning (to which only the elect are privy); New Historicism and Marxism, by insisting that what looks like behavior emanating from a freely choosing "subject" is in fact being generated by an economic or cultural substratum (which is really under the control of the critic, who determines its essence from his power-carrel in the library); feminism, by showing that "nature" is really "culture," and that almost all of culture, except that which is defined by feminists, is vicious. In moderation, each of these methods yields usable results, extending and refining human consciousness. It is even possible to have a sneaking fondness for some of the perpetrators, but it is the global nature of these claims, their malicious "monologic" quality, their dependence on a guilt-ridden bourgeois-as-victim that forces one to suspect unstated, unacknowledged needs in their proponents, needs perhaps surprisingly similar to those they scorn in others. (Liberal guilt was one of the great discoveries of modern times, providing a sort of psychochemical weapon whereby you can knock out your enemy and take his exact place in the structure of things—without experiencing any guilt of your own.)

It is sometimes objected that criticism is not necessarily weakened by the fact that the critic practices the very vices he attacks in others.[9] According to this view, the operating principle ought really to be "Do as I say rather than as I do," but that may be too sanguine a hope. For when the new historicists, the feminists, the Marxists, et al. attack hegemony while struggling to obtain it for themselves, do they not invite a deconstructionist new historical analysis to be practiced upon them, in an infinite regress that undermines each analyst? If the ostensible attacks against hegemony are not really against hegemony at all, but simply against *who exercises* the hegemony; if hegemony is acceptable *as long as I exercise it,* then what the critic *does* becomes as important as what he *says,* because what he *does* is ultimately what he is really saying. Values, after all, are revealed in action as well as, if not more truly than, in speech. Indeed, Gramsci himself, the patron saint of academic Marxists, endorses this view: "And is it not frequently the case that there is a contradiction between one's intellectual choice and one's mode of conduct? Which therefore would be the real conception of the world: that logically affirmed as an intellectual choice? or that which emerges from the real activity of each man, which is implicit in his mode of action? *And since all action is political, can one not say that the real philosophy of each man is contained in its entirety in his political action?*" [10] (emphasis added). If we are genuinely to learn the lesson of Jamesonian analysis, it is impossible not to apply that analysis to Jameson himself, for when the operating principle is that one must never take ostensibilities as realities, how can we then continue to privilege the ostensibilities of the analyst? The analyst must himself be unmasked. The only alternative to this conclusion is that the contemporary obsession with unmasking should be discarded because of the self-invalidating infinite regress it necessarily brings on.

If bourgeois-bashing entails a fake war against vice that unwittingly raises questions about the ethics of scholarship, there is another program connected with today's ideologies—the decarnalization of art— that raises problems of aesthetics. Levin, Pechter, and even Miller complain about the new historicists' unconcern with the emotional power of literary texts, their habit of playing it down, or ignoring it altogether. If any of us were to think about our first reading experiences, what would we principally recall if not the way in which we were taken over by a thrilling and relentless force that somehow transformed our way of being in the world? Yet when we read Jerome McGann on Emily Dickinson, or Jameson on Conrad, or Susan Gubar on Charlotte Brontë, is not this affective power transformed, for the most part, into sociology? Or philosophy? Or psychoanalysis? Or polemic? Or into an

entrepreneurial act, as when McGann sets up impossible historical requirements before we can read anything at all, requirements, in fact,
that only he can satisfy, rendering him indispensable, like those shock-
ingly expensive parts one is forced to buy from the manufacturer when
the washing machine breaks down? (See Chapter 13 for a discussion
of McGann.) It seems understandable, in this light, why it has become
popular to think that there is no such thing as "literary works," that
such hypothetical works differ in no way from "nonliterary works," that
everything is potentially literature if people choose to treat it as such,
even, presumably, the telephone directory. Since no essence can be
found for "literature," it is supposed that literature does not exist, only
"writing," just as the deconstructionists assume that without "presence" in the use of signs, real communication is impossible. Yet people
continue to understand each other and equally continue to have powerful emotional experiences, not only from music and art but from novels
and poems as well. But in choosing to ignore this reality, the entre-
preneurs of each critical methodology can feel justified in taking all
knowledge as their province, feeding their indiscriminating machines
with seemingly unlimited raw materials.

I would like to propose, however, that many of the critics who have
been considered in these pages do not actually deal with "literary
works" at all. That is to say, literary works exist but these critics have no
traffic with them. Rather, they are dealing with alternate productions
derived from what look like the same texts as the literary ones but that
are in reality sociological, psychoanalytic, and political data isomor-
phic with the literary texts but *effectively* (and *affectively*) quite different
existents. When Jameson examines Balzac, he is not examining the
novels we actually read, but other texts that look exactly like them. Just
as Andy Warhol turns a Campbell's soup can into art, Fredric Jameson
turns art into a Campbell's soup can.

Although literary works may have no essence, what we choose to call
literature invariably has an emotional power produced by a skill with
language that we conveniently call "literary skill." When that power
is not present, or when it is not invoked, the texts in question cease
to be literature. In our current political climate, the emotional power
has been stripped from literary texts in order to turn them into some-

thing else, something utilitarian rather than "aesthetic," something over which the critic has power, rather than the reverse. As these texts become "decarnalized," removed from the type of sensuous world we associate with music and the visual arts and translated into philosophy, history, or blueprints for changing society, they can be regarded simply as "writing," like all other texts, and analyzed irrespective of their defining and enabling characteristic, i.e., their emotional power. I would add to this that deconstruction, even with its attendance upon the flesh of literature, takes place in a nonliterary atmosphere because it believes too strongly in the "free play" of language. This belief in free play, insofar as it accompanies a disregard for intentions of an author—as irretrievable and, in any case, unimportant—is incommensurate with the emotional impact that comes from the expression of a willing, desiring "subject." Thus, to use a familiar example, the computer-generated "poem" that washes onto the shore in a bottle is not a specimen of literary art no matter how much it may resemble a bona fide poem because it cannot be the expression of an affective consciousness. Without affect, sensuousness, and desire, no "literature" is possible in the everyday sense of the word, and when these qualities are removed from a critical consideration of art, we are not in the world of art at all. Jameson's ingenious examinations of the novels of Balzac, Gissing, and Conrad, whatever they may be, are not examples of criticism of the novel, because the works *he* examines are not novels, only simulacra of the texts of novels, psychosocial documents, like the garbage cans sifted through by sociologists for news about American domestic life.

Literary works can still be discussed, however, without a relapse into sentimentality or impressionism, yet without sacrificing the insights obtainable from psychology, history, philosophy, and politics. No pure aesthetic realm divorced from real life needs to be posited as an atmosphere for the experiencing of "literature." (And, in any case, the aesthetic realm is the most practical realm of all: the sensuous life that is the ground of our being.) The chief disabling characteristic of recent criticism, the practice that most consistently alienates the reader from any possibility of emotional union with the work, is the assumption that it is the sophisticated critic's task *not to heed the voice of the author*. To heed it, according to this practice, is to be a too-willing victim of the work's power, to be turned into swine by the charms of Circe. Rather, the sophisticated critic wants to unmask and disable the voice of the author in order to show what it really is, in all its bogus, shabby, self-deceiving, and fake authenticity. To truly read Milton, in this vein, is to hear the rationalizations of a licentious, puritanical misogynist. To read Charlotte Brontë is to acknowledge another victim of patriarchy and class struggle. To read Virginia Woolf is to recognize the muffled protests of someone steamrolled by Victorian medical advisors and a tyrannically repressive husband. The critic shouts as loudly as possible so that the voice of the author will not be heard over the more enlightened din of his or her own voice, a voice that speaks more truly because it is not taken in by the power of the author.

Reading novels or poetry in this new Realm of Freedom manufactured by bourgeois-stunning criticism is a self-dividing experience in which one is trained to discountenance the voice that is doing the speaking while paying strictest heed to the voice-over, the supertitles, provided by the critic, a voice-over that speaks the true subtext, the *real* message of the poem. The poem is a coded vehicle and not a performance, according to this dispensation, and thus requires no emotional response, union with the speaker, or "sympathy," which would result in uncritical subjection to authorial power, a fall into ideology. Rather, the audience must rush up onto the stage and unmask the players, wash the greasepaint from their faces, cleanse their mouths with soap, deliver a homily to the actors—and close down the theater! For all art is fraud, deception, and bad faith. The mission of the neoplatonic critic is to reveal the rhapsodist for what he is—someone possessed by madness, whose mind is no longer in him. The warbling flutes spell danger, poetry is a form of music, and music leads to the irrational, to unconscious strivings for power (from which the critic is free). The neoplatonic critic prefers Ideas to representations, because representations are deceptions. The truth is in the Idea, if only you can find it, and that is the *business* of the critic.

But most of today's theories are themselves representations of reality and they are necessarily *mis*representations. I say this not because of some privileged position from which I can compare their representations with a reality that is not itself a representation. I say it because today's theories reject the whole idea of accurate representations of reality. Yet I have no serious objection to this; what I do reject is the farce of theories offering themselves as "true" while simultaneously rejecting the possibility of accurately representing the truth. According to virtually every regnant methodology, it is *power* that establishes "truth" through the force of hegemony. At least the pragmatists are honest about this and avoid hypocrisy: they do not pretend to a truth divorced from usefulness. The other dominant methodologies are varieties of religious fanaticism, violating with insouciance the law of contradiction in their requirement of blind faith in their adherents, while denying the existence of a reality in which such faith would be plausible.

At the same time, they are draining the affective power from works of art, arrogating all such power to themselves as puritanical intellectual tradesmen amassing academic capital. Poets, novelists, artists, and musicians certainly pose their own problems, and uncritical veneration of them seems foolish, but to pretend that they are little more than dumb tools of transitory hegemonies is to deny them the power that they still can have over us, a power that still seems eminently desirable, a source of enlightenment and pleasure. But pleasure is now a form of false consciousness, of nostalgia, of embracing one's chains. Rather, ye shall know the New Historicists[11] and they shall make you free.

But free for what?

13

. . . . . .

Critical Situations:

A Literary Manifesto

for the Nineties

Like everyone else—it is said—the critic is a "situated" individual who makes his pronouncements from a personal and social context rather than ex cathedra, however much it may appear to the contrary. His "cathedra," in other words, is not a Transcendental Chair of Criticism but a rickety antique picked up at the neighborhood rag-and-bone shop, where everyone else is also rummaging for components of a personal identity. The Cultural Materialists, however, would go even further: "Person me no persons," they insist. For "persons," it turns out, are just upscale euphemisms for Bourgeois Subjects of History, "subjects" for short. Subjects, unlike persons, are "subjected" to the material forces that produce them and can make little or no claim to "autonomy," which is just another bourgeois myth to be exploded. To wit:

> The fiction workshop is not a "neutral" place where insights are developed, ideas/advice freely exchanged, and skills honed. It is a site of ideology: a place in which a particular view of reading/writing texts is put forth and through this view support is given to the dominant social order. By regarding writing as a "craft" and proposing realism as *the* mode of writing, the fiction workshop in collaboration with humanist critics ful-

fills its ideological role in the dominant academy by preserving the subject
as "independent" and "free." In the fiction workshop the writer is postu-
lated as an independent person who discovers the secret of writing and the
meaning of the world through the discovery of her/his unique "self." The
main cultural purpose of the dominant fiction workshop in the present
pedagogical regime is in fact to teach the student how to discover the
"self," and the cultural politics of this self-discovery, as we have indicated,
is to construct a subject who perceives herself as self-constituted and free
so that she can then "freely" collaborate with the existing social system, a
system that assures the continuation of patriarchal capitalism.

The academics who have freely come to these conclusions, because
they themselves are not bound by any ideologies except the ones that
dictate "her/his" as a possessive adjective and "she" as a generic pronoun, are Donald Morton and Mas'ud Zavarzadeh in "The Cultural
Politics of the Fiction Workshop," a madcap exercise in *Cultural Critique.* Even extremist draughts like theirs can have some merit, if you
know how to water down the hemlock enough to swallow it and survive.
Of course, very few of us intellectual sorts ever really supposed we were
fully autonomous or that we had invented ourselves; and we certainly
acknowledge that had we been born in another time, another place, or
from other parents, we would be other people with other truths. Except
for occasional megalomania, most of us feel only too subjected to forces
material and otherwise, and so we are largely ready to buy into the
notion that what we say and do is "situated." That is why it was Dosto-
evsky and not I who wrote *The Brothers Karamazov.* My own situation
just was not right for it.

So the critic too is a situated being, not a transparent Intelligence,
and his psoriasis (as we learn from John Updike) or crack high will
probably enter into his critical judgments. Indeed, after the initial
romance with an innovational critic—like, say, Roland Barthes or Paul
de Man—a reaction invariably sets in and we are then informed that
what seemed like a transcendent voice from the cosmos was little more
than a certain admixture of clay, a very personal sexual or political
psychogenesis. (This is the price one must pay for immoderate initial
claims and the trendy commoditized hero worship that haunts the fast
lane of the critical scene.) But there is always a danger of pursuing such

ideas as "situation" too far. While the critic's time, place, parents, and personal history may all be factors in his sensibility and judgment, just how much value can such a corrective yield? At what point must we leave off inventorying his multitudinous kinks incarnadine in order to acknowledge that the critic can sometimes speak for more than himself alone, more than his limited intellectual community—and indeed must do so to be really worth our attention? The danger of intellectual extremism, of overpushing bright ideas like "situation" and "subject," is that it makes useful thinking altogether impossible. Whole corpuses of work, if you go on like Fredric Jameson or Morton and Zavarzadeh, become little more than itches that the writer can't help scratching. (Has anybody inquired what itches Morton and Zavarzadeh are scratching?) On the other hand, for the critic to claim perfect validation as an utterly open consciousness (a state that would be hard to distinguish from imbecility) he would have to become an exact duplicate of the consciousness he is assessing. In which case, why not abandon the redundancy of criticism and let the novelist or poet speak for himself?

The skilled critic, then, can engender new insights that exploit his "situation," which becomes an enabling rather than a crippling disposition of his mortality. Lamentably, there is no automatic or objective method for producing good criticism, even if you use "she" as a generic pronoun or speak of subjects instead of people. What is more, some of the extreme Marxists would insist that there is no method at all for being "creative," nor is there even any creativity—since for them nothing is possible beyond an expression of the existing superstructure of society. But if the fashion of the moment encourages many of today's critics to sing about their situational chains instead of the literary text, the implication even here is that they are freely and creatively doing so. For who is ready to confess that he too is just another wind-up toy of the gods?

Three major situations appear to dominate present-day critical practice: academic, aesthetic, and (for want of a better term) secular; and more often than not any given practitioner is likely to represent more than one of these. The academic critic is predisposed to theory; the aesthetic critic to technique or poetics; and the secular critic to matters of ethics, politics, and "truth." The richest criticism would ideally combine all three, but in the real world such a combination is not often found.

In choosing a few recent specimens to use as representative instances of current practice, I need to indicate that their only significant common feature is their date of publication: the last years of the 1980s. Although most cultural criticism now seems to emanate from an academic hothouse in which exotic plants are kept alive by ideological steroids, aesthetic and secular critics have not yet disappeared altogether. Two poet-critics who have recently assembled collections of essays about poetry, J. D. McClatchy and Robert Pinsky, can serve as useful instances, though like many poets and fiction writers today they also have academic careers in university writing programs. This connection provides one of the principal differentia of contemporary aesthetic critics from those of previous generations, since some academic qualities are bound to rub off, though usually not those of a theoretical sort. Rather, today's aesthetic/academic critic is likely to be more rigorous, scholarly, more widely read than his impressionistic and sometimes precious forebears, and to be markedly less afflatus driven, using knowledge of literary history and biography to place individual poets and poems within a larger framework. Occasionally, he will even flirt with theory. In a word, although academia may often work harm upon the poet-professor's own poetry and stories, its influence can at times be good when it comes to criticism.

J. D. McClatchy's *White Paper* reveals a critic of considerable erudition, with a daunting knowledge of modern poetry in English as well as a good deal from other periods and languages, existing for him in a kind of immediate random access memory, so that he reads with vast quantities of writing always present in his mind. His sensibility of the sounds, meanings, allusions, and syntax of verse is about as fine-tuned as one is likely to come upon, and he makes good use of biography and atheoretical criticism to increase the density of his poetic accounts.

These are much-needed talents in a world now dominated by theory, but the difficulties and limitations of McClatchy's essays persistently undercut these gifts, reducing their usefulness to all but a handful of poetry professionals. For nonspecialist readers—however literary and intellectual they may be—who care for poetry but do not much care about the cerebrations of the poetry workshop, the strain of these essays is likely to be too great, for McClatchy is guilty of drastic overreading of poems, one of the most lamentable by-products of his well-stocked mind. The problem of overreading, obsessively encouraged by the reign of New Criticism (a tiger that one sometimes cannot dismount), is that the critic—like a too-solicitous parent—takes over the proper functions of the reader, creating diffidence instead of strength, a sense that "I can't do it without you." Unfortunately, the reader may very well also feel that he cannot do it even *with* the critic, whose sensibility, subjectivity, and particular mix of aesthetic response and literary knowledge may be too alien to lend itself to reproduction in other psyches. A reader would have to be reborn—in this case as McClatchy—to be able to respond to any given poem with the sensuous or intellectual particularity that he brings to bear upon the poems he reads for us. What is so perplexing about these overreadings is that much of the time McClatchy is aware of what he has done—and sensing that the whole enterprise is about to collapse before our very eyes, he begins to take it all back! By then, however, it is too late to salvage critical authority.

Speaking of Elizabeth Bishop's "The End of March," he writes: "First, then, the title itself, 'The End of March.' It seems only to designate the poem's setting, or season. But 'end' also means both 'purpose' and 'goal.' And if we take 'march' to stand in for 'walk,' then the title directs us. . . . There is even an (unintentional but apposite) allusion to a phrase from one of her earliest poems, 'The Imaginary Iceberg,' where she speaks of the 'end of travel.' " Then, ruminating about the poet walking on the beach, he remarks: "On her beach walk, the poet's eye, as it looks out on and creates the horizon, divides the elements into sky and sea. The sky comes to be the lion's element. The sea, which is said to be 'the color of mutton-fat jade,' is the lamb's. We might further construe the season as Eastertide [why?], and so the paschal lamb is its sign. This is, after all, a poem with a 'dead man' (the sodden ghost of string), a kind of tomb, and then at its conclusion an extraordinary, 'majestic' resurrection—a risen Son who destroys death, or bats down a kite with its cross-shaped frame" (58).

All of this is extraordinary license enough to anyone familiar with Bishop's poem, an almost total manufacture of free associations, but insult is added to injury when McClatchy then comments, "These symbols (or perhaps, because she was not a believer, it would be better to call them motifs) wait in the wings of the poem, but never, I think, make enough of an appearance to merit much notice. Bishop is telling another kind of story." Pages later, in the course of discussing the room of her own that the poet envisions in several stanzas of this same poem, McClatchy, in a burst of rather startling irrelevance, feels obliged to tell us with respect to "stanza," that "the very word is one for 'room'" (62) in Italian! Similarly, in an excessively long account of James Merrill's "An Urban Convalescence," a poem that describes a walker in New York City who laments the destruction of old buildings for the sake of new, he suddenly begins to talk about James's "The Beast in the Jungle," for little more reason than that its central character is named John Marcher, about whom he remarks, "Marcher—whose very name links him with Merrill's walker[!]—is blocked from life . . . and suffers, as Merrill's speaker does not, a terrible failure of human energy. Both men are ill, though" (265). We are relieved to learn they have even that much in common.

Finally, it is worth quoting a section of this Merrill poem in order to provide the actual flesh upon which McClatchy explicates. As the New York walker returns home after witnessing a wrecking company's destruction of a neighboring building, which then sets off a train of thought about a woman he knew years before, he meditates:

> So that I am already on the stair,
> As it were, of where I lived,
> When the whole structure shudders at my tread
> And soundlessly collapses, filling
> The air with motes of stone.
> Onto the still erect building next door
> Are pressed levels and hues—
> Pocked rose, streaked greens, brown whites.
> Who drained the pousse-café?
> Wires and pipes, snapped off the roots, quiver.

Although no portion of this poem contains explicit references to the Orpheus myth, and it is highly doubtful whether there are even implicit references, McClatchy comments as follows:

The memory of the woman that draws him deeper into the past only to undo it had demonstrated how private experience is shaped by myth—the lesson of art itself. The woman's resemblance to Eurydice tells us a great deal about the man who so remembers her. The strain continues here, if we imagine the speaker imagining himself as Orpheus [Does a later reference to a visit to Paris and the Champs-Elysées warrant all this?] climbing the stair of Hades, that realm of roots. Orpheus' music made the stones dance; here his "air" [Does Merrill really pun here on air as song?] dances with "motes of stone." Later, having failed, he faces a maenad-like "shrieking," his "eyes astream" like Orpheus' singing head. *But this, perhaps, is to bring to the forefront what was only meant to be lurking. A specific myth is less important than the cast of mind* [emphasis added]. (263–64)

What can one say about habits like these, except to urge the critic to abandon them as quickly as possible, lest aesthetic criticism become even more obscure than literary theory.

While McClatchy's book is an example of aesthetic criticism at its purest, Robert Pinsky's *Poetry and the World* starts out in the aesthetic mode but then, as its title would suggest, shifts gears so boldly that the overriding final impression is secular. There are a number of alarming moments, however, in which *his* obsession with etymologies and an inclination toward overreading begin to produce the same kind of diminishing returns we have seen in McClatchy. "The title of 'An Ordinary Evening in New Haven' uses in the first word after the article an exotic root (with echoes of church government) to denote the idea of routine, echoed by the Germanic second word with its similar meaning—'making things even'—so that these two words together may perhaps by contrast awaken just a little of the sense of freshness and hazard sleeping in the last two: new, haven" (127). Speaking of Jefferson's "Life, Liberty and the Pursuit of Happiness," Pinsky remarks: "In that instance the plain domestic roots 'life' and 'hap,' with their Germanic hominess, bracket the Latin and French overtones of 'liberty' and 'pursuit' with their flavors of law, the hunt, and books" (126). Not many readers are constituted to take very much of this sort of thing, which is potentially open-ended and disintegrative; nor will it offer much appeal as a model to the literary academics who are most in need of being weaned away from "theory." Fortunately, however, before these verbal worryings become irreversibly destructive, Pinsky's real powers as a secular critic begin to do their work. In "Responsibilities of the Poet," Pinsky asks what if anything the poet owes to society and replies that the poet is under no obligation to court readers who have no interest in poetry. His audience ought to consist of those who are already "hungry for one's art" (84). Although he himself does not use the term "Horatian," his sense that poetry is built upon the feelings of the body and upon a need for transforming ideas (i.e., ideas that transform) is a variant of Horace's pleasure and enlightenment. The poet accomplishes this transformation by serving as a mediator between the traditions inherited from the past and the edificational needs of future generations—he is a preserver/transformer of culture, a witness. There is an especially striking paragraph in which Pinsky describes these functions:

> The need to notice, to include the evidence as a true and reliable witness, can be confused and blunted by the other, conserving responsibility of mediation between the dead and the unborn. And just as society can vaguely, quietly diffuse an invisible, apparently "apolitical" political ideology, culture can efficiently assimilate and enforce an invisible idea of what is poetic. In a dim view of the dialectic, it seems that society's tribute to poetry is to incorporate each new, at first resisted sense of the poetic, and so to spread it—and blunt it—for each new generation. Even while seeming not to taste each new poetic, the world swallows it. (88)

What gives this passage its distinction is its palatable naturalization of a familiar Marxist point of view without the fanaticism of hardline faux-revolutionary programs (cf. Morton and Zavarzedah) that undermine valuable insights through overstatement. This leads Pinsky to what is perhaps the essence of his insight: "Only the challenge of what may seem unpoetic, that which has not already been made poetic by the tradition, can keep the art truly pure and alive. Put to no new use, the art rots" (88). Thus the imperative to preserve and change the inherited traditions becomes a usable updating of the Hegelian/Marxist concept of *Aufhebung*. Put another way, "Real works revise the received idea of what poetry is; by mysterious cultural means the revisions are assimilated and then presented as the next definition to be resisted, violated and renewed" (89). The rest of the chapter goes on to demonstrate the achieving of this transformation by several specimen poems.

In what is perhaps the best essay in the book, "Freneau, Whitman, Williams," Pinsky begins by asking, "What is, or would be, a democratic poetry? What is the relation of an art reborn in European courts to [American] vernacular culture?" (101) Through revelatory use of poems by these three poets (complete with texts), in other words through "readings" of a very persuasive kind, Pinsky is able to show how Freneau refashioned the eighteenth-century prosody he inherited from Pope into a mingled dialect, half Augustan, half American, and how Whitman and Williams did likewise with their own inheritances. Supporting his accounts with proppings from Parrington and other historians of America, Pinsky gives a convincing concrete demonstration of his principles of poetic *Aufhebung*. In the chapter that follows, "American Poetry and American Life," he carries this further along with poems by James Wright, Jean Toomer, and Wallace Stevens, building a gripping episode around Anne Winters's "Night Wash," a poem about nightlife in a New York laundromat, again with complete text provided. He concludes that "their work brings the speech and behavior of their American social setting into an energetic, self-calibrating struggle with all that poetry was, just before they came to it" (131).

In the final section of his book, Pinsky makes inventive use of autobiography to illustrate how he himself as a poet has been put together from his own situations, with the implication—or hope—that he too has digested, synthesized, and surmounted the traditions that produced him. (His most concrete materialization of this is his own long poem, *An Explanation of America*.) Besides giving us several accounts of his roots in American Jewish culture in Long Branch, New Jersey, accounts saturated with specificities about his recalcitrance as a high school student, his gangster Grandpa Dave, and the threadbare quality of immigrant religious life in a provincial American city, Pinsky devotes two chapters to his experiences in Poland as a poet-on-the-road for the State Department. Here, as in most of his biographical recollections, he develops his preoccupation with "situation," the possibilities for resistance to its determinations, and the relation of such resistance to human freedom. Observing that "the appetite for poetry has the same mystery as all of the cravings that could be called, old-fashionedly, the human appetites," he muses that "[my] appetite for art also seems to free me from the social facts about me, that I was born in 1940 to Milford and Sylvia Pinsky, in Long Branch, New Jersey, and so forth. If social facts control us, control is (it is banal to say) what appetite pushes against" (159, 160). This concern with the question of freedom from one's determining situations becomes pressingly intense for him in Warsaw, where he somehow finds himself an implicated spectator of an episode of Polish anti-Semitism just before—with some nervousness—he is about to read a poem of his own that happens to allude to this very same ethnic prejudice. He becomes annoyed when his Polish poet-auditors laugh at his dismissal of American anti-Semitism as now being little more than a case of bad taste rather than anything as serious as the Polish variety (since, after all, his own family had done quite well in America). "But the annoyance on my country's behalf was superficial compared with the deeper annoyance that they [the Polish auditors] were telling me who I was—that I was perhaps a more historically determined creature than I might conceivably choose to be" (168). In this wonderful essay, subtitled "Form and Freedom," Pinsky uses his Polish material to urge us toward the conclusion that form in art is a resistance to the domination of "situation"—or, as he puts it, "Perhaps it is the exhilaration of any form to push against some confining expectation." One of his examples is Ginsberg's "America, I'm putting my queer shoulder to the wheel," which he glosses with, "Perhaps form, in its truest manifestations, must be an appetite, an appetite for being autonomous and oneself, more bold and naked than any external preconception of oneself. A poem may be the least confused, most free thing one says (or hears) because it is the most deliberately physical, and so the most naked. Form expresses the craving to be free of imposed, controlling abstractions. It is a made, bodily abstraction to challenge the abstraction of circumstance" (168–69). Morton and Zavarzadeh would probably roll on the floor with laughter at such a bourgeois humanist conclusion—but then Morton and Zavarzadeh are pretty funny themselves. (They decide that Nadine Gordimer is a "collaborationist" with the South African government because she is trying to improve a decadent system, whereas a true revolutionary—e.g., Morton and Zavarzadeh?—would "dismantle" the system altogether.) Pinsky's autobiographical speculations provide his most forceful case for a connection between poetry and the world, and his vision of aesthetic form as the challenge of Desire against the pressure of Necessity is one attempt to spell out the nature of that connection. Although it is not my intention to set him up as a paradigm, his ability to connect poetry with the world on both a theoretical and a "bodily" level is a useful reminder that criticism does not *have to* retreat from life into a microcosm of rarefaction and specialization, and that a secular criticism is not only possible but necessary for literary revitalization.

There are now so many different schools of academic criticism that none can claim preeminence, but one of their most shared characteristics is a gratingly entrepreneurial commitment to professionalization that excludes any concern for nonspecialist "general" readers. This commitment works on the unstated assumption that poems and novels have all along been written for an elite cohort of postmodern literary specialists (even when they were written by Chaucer or Defoe) rather than for any larger readership of the unwashed, and that the keys to understanding them have only now been forged. Certainly Morton's and Zavarzadeh's essay about the writing workshop reveals an ethos as single-minded and blindered as any right-wing evangelicalism that consigns the majority of mankind to perdition. Like born-agains who "know" they are "saved" and who perceive the rest of mankind as spectrally insubstantial, these politicized academics operate in their own self-enclosed little universe of discourse outside of which the rest of the human race might as well be damned if they are not already—though in fact they *have* been, by the professors themselves.

A more mainstream case of academic self-enclosure can be found in the writings of Jerome J. McGann, a romanticist, bibliographer, and textual historian of impressive skill and erudition for whom the audience of bona fide readers of literature would appear to have reached the vanishing point, possibly leaving McGann alone, on whom perforce we must now very heavily depend. In the course of a recent jeu d'esprit in which he assumes the pseudonyms of "Anne Mack and J. J. Rome,"[1] we are presented with an intentionally parodic dialogue between several professors which is interrupted by a full-length essay by Jerome McGann himself, which the professors then go on to discuss. It is this essay within an essay—entitled "Byron's 'Fare Thee Well!' "— that provides even more instruction than McGann could possibly have intended.

The central aperçu of this raid on Byron, which resembles much of McGann's other writing, is that far from being a self-contained construct of the sort the New Critics claimed a poem to be, Byron's poem— and all other literary writing as well—is more than just a verbal text. It is also the actual physical editions in which it appeared during its history in all their concrete materiality: title page, page layout, type, introductory matter, size, binding, price, and circumstances of publication, as well as the relation of these editions to the history of their reception by actual readers, to the poet's life, and to memoirs and letters by him and pertaining to him. As McGann puts it, "People tend not to realize that a certain way of reading is privileged when 'Ode on a Grecian Urn' is read in *The Norton Anthology of English Literature*, and that it is a way of reading which differs sharply from what is privileged in Palgrave's *Golden Treasury* or in the *Oxford Book of Romantic Verse*" (625). The "poem" then is an accretion of its physical and critical history, its "circumstances of production" as well as its history of reception. McGann attempts to support this claim with an account of several incarnations of "Fare Thee Well!" during Byron's lifetime, including a privately circulated copy commented upon in writing by his wife, as well as an early nineteenth-century magazine's printing of the poem alongside another poem of Byron's whose presence on the facing page was intended by the editor to put "Fare Thee Well!" in a very bad light.

After interpreting the *real* meaning of the poem, McGann concludes:

Poetic works are not autonomous in either of the senses that the academy has come, mistakenly, to believe. That is to say, poems are neither linguistically self-contained, nor are they simply the expressed forms of a single—an authorizing and integral—imagination. The actual production of poems [the material publishing history described above] is one part of that social dialectic by which they live and move and have their being, one part of the communicative interchange which they always solicit.

The Byron example is especially instructive, I think, because it shows how those interchanges can never be brought under the control of the author. Poems are produced, used, and read in heterogeneous ways; unlike other forms of discourse, in fact, they require—they thrive upon—those diverse forms of life. Crucial parts of those interchanges are encoded in the bibliographical, productive, and reception histories of the poems we read. When we neglect those histories we simply condemn our readings to a culpable—because an unnecessary—ignorance. (626)

These remarks may seem plausible enough as general "truths" about reading, since we have all been trained to believe that knowledge is always better than ignorance. In practice, however, they approach the preposterous, as we can easily see by looking for their implications elsewhere in McGann's writings. In an earlier essay, for example, McGann tells us that when we read Emily Dickinson's "Because I could not Stop for Death," we need to know that "the journey being presented is not some unspecified drive in the country, but a funeral ride which is located quite specifically in relation to Emily Dickinson and her Amherst world. The hearse in the poem is on its way out Pleasant Street, past Emily Dickinson's house, to the cemetery located at the northern edge of the town just beyond the Dickinson homestead. Of course, these details are not verbalized into the Dickinson poem as explicit description. They are only present implicitly, as an originally evoked context which we—at our historical remove—can (and must) reconstitute if we wish to focus and explain the special emotional character of the work."[2]

The cumulative message of McGann's writings is that only a bibliographer, textual historian, and editor of romantic and Victorian poetry can ferret out all that is necessary to read poetry with understanding. The thinly veiled subtext of this message is that the only qualified reader of such literature must be McGann himself, since he is the one person who can meet the exact mix of qualifications he puts forth as a bare minimum. He is, in a word, the monopolistic entrepreneur of the means of production—or reproduction—of texts. What McGann does

not address, however, is that despite all his vast erudition and intelligence, in the final reckoning these readings are *only* his readings and
no one else's. Interesting as they may be, they are often unconvincing
and always unreproducible, since they are the product of a particular
scholarly history—his own. While it is true that all criticism is the product of a particular personal history, the difference between a highly
skilled critic and a mediocre one is the former's ability to transcend
his own particularity. In McGann's case, the use of scholarship and
history is less to *convince* us (the business of a good critic) than to assert his authority over us as a person with special access to truth. As
contributions toward an act of reading, his reports could conceivably
be enriching, because good criticism does add up to more than the
sum of its situations, but as sine qua non, as prolegomena to any future
reading, they are neither necessary nor sufficient for an adequate literary response, being only the somewhat arbitrary effects of a particular
psychological/professional biography. Nor does McGann acknowledge
the infinite regress they presuppose. Why, after all, is it necessary to
know that Emily Dickinson's carriage was really a hearse on Pleasant Street but not also necessary to know what the exact prescription
happened to be for Emily's glasses as she beheld the scene from her
window? Or whether she was suffering from toothache? Or whether
she had just had a quarrel with her father? Or exactly where she was
in the phases of her menses? These things are at least as important
as the sightlines of Pleasant Street from the Dickinson window. And
what about the particular mix of air pollutants on the day in question?
Now that it is gradually becoming known that such pollution can have
startling effects on one's physical and psychological moods, there is no
reason that an ecological criticism of literary texts should not also be
insisted upon.[3]

When we read the letters of George Eliot, for example, we discover
how she regularly needed to leave densely smogged-in London for
the "fresh air" of the countryside in order to get rid of her crush-
ingly oppressive headaches, headaches that made a difference to her
life and art. When we read the letters of Charlotte Brontë we find that
unbeknownst to her the industrial emissions of the factories in West
Yorkshire were affecting *her* psychological states. A study of air pollution in English literature would thus enable an immense amount of

insight, and if I were to undertake such a study with McGann-like im-
periousness, I could doubtless provide a pollution-derived reading of
post-Enlightenment English literature in comparison with which textual matters would fade into petty insignificance. I then would be able
to say, "The emissions of sulphur-dioxide and particulates from knit-
ting mills in Leeds had profound effects upon Branwell's depressive
tendencies and drug-addiction, which resulted in powerful episodes
of revulsion in his sisters' novels, while Charlotte's sexual restlessness
was desperately at the mercy of winds from the northeast. Her frantic
letters to M. Heger were the unmistakable effects of industrial fall-
out carried to Haworth during the temperature inversions that were
a commonplace of her daily life, in addition to the overdoses of toxic
water drawn from the graveyard-contaminated aquifer that lay beneath
Haworth Parsonage. Her 'romance' with M. Heger had less to do with
erotics than with pollution-induced narcosis and mania. Had she lived
in Cornwall, neither *The Professor* nor *Villette* would ever have been
written." Would I also be able—or want—to say that "a reader who
fails to take these facts into account will have only the most superficial
ideas about what is *really* going on in a Brontë novel"?

The possible revelations emanating from specialized knowledge are
infinite, but if one must play this sort of game in order to understand
"literature" properly, then the reading of poetry and fiction would be
a futile and misbegotten enterprise for which literally infinite preparation is required before one can even begin, since the number of critical
and scholarly specialties is as unlimited as the "facts" that each one can
discover. Once we discard the plausible notion that "literature" must
be capable of transcending the particulars that generate it, then only
God—and not even Jerome McGann—can appreciate Byron's "Fare
Thee Well!" Without such transcendence, poems would be little more
than case studies of the psychobiological quirks of their makers. As for
criticism, it too must be able to transcend its generating particulars,
because no reader can reproduce in himself the mental history of the
critic. The "art" of criticism is its ability to go beyond its own provenance, to build upon the reader's existing self, just as the "art" of the
poet is to speak for or to a large and varied constituency of readers,
not just his simulacra. In both cases, the "art" is a form of cunning
whereby limited resources are made to do manifold work. Moreover,

why should scholar-critics like McGann suppose that the information we *really* need to know in order to read a Byron poem can be found in written materials at all? Did famous writers live their lives solely in their writings or did they also talk to their wives in bed, meditate at stool, suffer from food poisoning, beat the hell out of their defenseless children, all the while living a secret life in a public or private underworld we know little or nothing about? Perhaps the *really* important information about their poems is embedded in these unrecorded and irrecoverable phenomena, not in the easily accessible letters to mistresses and publishers which fuel academic careers and provide such entertaining materials for critical one-upmanship. Is it not, after all, a remarkably funny coincidence that the very sort of information we need to have in order to read a Byron poem is just the sort of thing that McGann's lifelong specializations have bequeathed him—and that put us all so much in his debt? This is God, Church, and Apostolic Succession all wrapped up in one, and it takes lots of faith to swallow it.

To turn from Jerome McGann to Margaret Homans's *Bearing the Word: Language and Female Experience in Nineteenth-Century Women's Writing* is to move from a sui generis critical scholarship to a type of feminist criticism that the past decade has produced by the truckload. (The vehicle's tires are getting rather bald, its engine about ready to throw a rod.) Indeed, it is disheartening to see so much intelligence thrown away on sterile make-work that (fortunately) has little chance of permeating outside the confines of a very parochial New Scholasticism whose audience consists almost entirely of academic feminists. If the Old Scholasticism treated such matters as the substance of angels, the nature of the Trinity, and the machinery of Transubstantiation, the newer version is not far behind in its manufacture of quiddities. In her introduction, Homans deploys this new *summa theologica* to establish a rickety thesis about female writing and then grinds her way through chapter after chapter in order to apply it to a series of classic nineteenth-century texts by women, doing none of them any good, even if she is incapable of doing them any serious harm.

Relying heavily on Lacan and French feminism as modified by the American Nancy Chodorow, Homans's thesis is that after their oedipal phase boys flee the mother, who represents literal, unmediated experience ("the Literal"), in order to enter the Lacanian "Symbolic," the world of representation through language. For girls, however, whose connection with the mother is not interdicted by a "castrating" father, an irresolvable tension or conflict remains between the feminine Literal and the masculine Symbolic. Insofar as women want to participate in the patriarchal world, they must enter the Symbolic realm of figurative representational language, but a part of their psyche remains drawn to the unsublimated world of direct Literal experience.

Since this terse summary reduces rather than emphasizes the egregious scholasticism of such mythmaking, a passage from Homans's introductory chapter would be more to the point:

> If the daughter's preoedipal closeness to her mother is accompanied by a presymbolic language of presence, then when the daughter attempts to recreate her symbiotic closeness with her mother, she is also attempting to recreate that presymbolic language. The reproduction of mothering will also be the reproduction of a presymbolic communicativeness, a literal language. While men are satisfied with heterosexual attachments as figures for the mother because they are replicating a situation existing after entry into the symbolic order, and while, as far as repeating their relation to their fathers goes, women too are satisfied with figures for the father, it would be impossible for the daughter to find the lost relation to the mother in any figure for it, since the preoedipal bond to the mother preceded the entry of the daughter into the world of figures, the symbolic, and thus the preoedipal bond could not be reimagined in symbolic terms. Quite possibly, a new child is just such a nonsymbolic figure. (25)

After this introduction, Homans goes on to apply these relentless mechanisms. Speaking of *Wuthering Heights*, for instance, she has startling (but dead) information to offer us about the novel's narrator: "according to Lockwood, the too-powerful mother, or literal meaning, must be killed, or removed from textuality, and replaced by substitutes that resemble the original but without its threatening power and independence" (72). And then:

> But for Lockwood, writing is intrinsically valuable, far more so than nature is. Fully invested in the symbolic order, Lockwood understands the antithesis in symbolic language between word and referent and makes his

> choice for language. Cathy, an outlaw from patriarchal law, also under-
> stands that antithesis, but makes her choice for nature, the literal, and
> therefore implicitly for the unnamed mother. While Brontë obviously ap-
> proves of Cathy as a character more than she does of Lockwood, the
> problem is that a novel could never be written following Cathy's principles
> of writing; whereas a novel can be written, in fact is written, according
> to Lockwood's and Nelly's principles. . . . Brontë must transform herself
> from wild girl to male writer if for a woman to write is for her interests to
> become merged . . . with the interests of androcentric culture. . . . Brontë
> dramatizes something like the conflict sketched in the introduction to this
> book between, on the one hand, the tremendous appeal of the literal and,
> on the other, the threat that the literal poses to articulation within the
> symbolic order. (73)

One should add that, if a woman were to remain in the warm and nur-
turing amniotic fluid of the fetus, she too would be unable to write a
novel, or a book of feminist criticism, or even utter a word. The "literal"
would appear to offer somewhat restrictive *Lebensraum* for anyone with
aspirations beyond contented mousehood, but one wonders whether
these speculations have anything to do with human possibility at all
or whether this is a hopelessly self-indulgent gnosticism that for the
moment has happened to strike it rich in certain specialist academic
literary circles. The result may be a Lost Generation of women scholar-
critics who have chosen feminist entrepreneurialism over the possibility
of addressing a larger portion of the reading audience, including those
"sisters" about whose fate they pretend to be so solicitous.

Homans's world, at any rate, is the familiar world of post-Enlightenment intellectual mythmaking, always less plausible and more ideological than social myths that gradually evolve through a collective
unconscious. Like Hegel's Absolute Idea, Marx's Realm of Freedom,
and Freud's Primal Scene, the Literal versus the Symbolic has a certain cold-blooded manufactured cachet that lacks the animating juices
that keep slow-evolving myths functionally alive for at least a while.
Moreover, Homans's distinction has already lived out its life in a
more usable and well-known form. Essentially, her Lacanian-derived
synthesis has been domesticated for almost two centuries already, as

Wordsworth's "spots of time," Woolf's "moments of being," the sense-memory elicited by Proust's madeleine, Lawrence's distinction between primal sex and "sex in the head"—and we know it well in its more developed forms in Emerson, Heidegger, Marcuse, the sixties' counterculture, and all the other thinkers who distinguish between Being and Thinking, between unmediated and acculturated experience. Far from representing a distinctively female tension, as Homans would pretend, this polarity is the property of the entire human race, a fact that is artfully concealed by the mendacities of the "masculinist" scholarship of which Homans is no less an exemplar than any male scholar. (A comparable book could be written using male writers as case studies, and probably *has* been written.) As for the attractions of the Literal, there is no way for human consciousness to remain in the warmth of the womb or to retain the pitch of orgasm or the ecstasies of art for more than brief spots of time or moments of being, because consciousness involves a cutoff from the purely "instinctual" and unmediated lives of animals. Since Homans knows all of this quite well, the justification for tracing this swing between the poles of Being and Thinking, Literal and Symbolic, Nature and Patriarchy in the works of nineteenth-century women writers is never made quite clear, for it is a swing that is neither avoidable nor proprietarily female. Not only does she concede that in order to write, her women writers had to leave the world of the Literal (simply to be alive as a person this must be done by everybody)—she concedes that in order for herself to have a career as a scholar, she too must live in the world of language and the Symbolic. (Given such a sullying compromise, however, the silence of "the Literal" has much to recommend it.)

Instead of telling us so little that is newly illuminating about Emily Brontë and others, and telling it so badly, Homans might have done better to produce a purely autobiographical essay giving us some insight into the psychological conflicts of today's woman academic and the pressures of careerism in the academy. Emily Brontë, after all, despite her imputed tensions, did manage to produce an enduring *Wuthering Heights* without the pampering bourgeois amenities of contemporary academic life; but the unplowed field that requires ground-

breaking exploration is the reason for so many of today's women scholars' feeling the need to produce supererogatory "masculinist" books
like *Bearing the Word.*

The domination of theory in the academic literary world has produced a situation that could now be quite receptive to aesthetic and
secular criticism of a high order. Backlashes against deconstruction are
becoming routine; and in the light of recent events in Russia, China,
Germany, and Eastern Europe, American academic Marxism may now
be viewed as moving from its absurdist phase into its decadent/patho-
logical phase (vide: the "revolutionary" blather of Morton and Zavarzadeh regarding Nadine Gordimer, among other things). Further, if
poems and fictions continue to induce only theoretical and ideological
responses, "literature" will soon become little more than another sociological curiosity. Already the observation is repeatedly being made that
today's vanguard professors and their student disciples have lost interest in both literature and the affective experience it generates. What has
taken their place is the processing of texts—for which TV ads for Burger
King serve as well as *The Prelude*—in order to expose the "political
unconscious" that underlies them. In stripping bare these "texts," the
critic shows himself operating at a higher level of consciousness than
their creators, since only a greater can understand a lesser or can reduce a complex consciousness to a few general rules that reveal him to
have been only a self-deceived naïf. When Fredric Jameson has shown
us that Balzac was really writing about his horror of oncoming capitalism, and that Conrad and Gissing were in dread of the Other, whether
as ethnic or class-derived threats, what can we be expected to do but
read Conrad and Balzac (if at all) with contempt, Jameson with admi-
ration? Still, the inescapable question is: does anybody who is not a
masochist really want to read Fredric Jameson instead of Balzac?

As for aesthetic and secular criticism, they too are beset with dangers: maundering explications and appreciations on the one hand and
self-serving literary/political reductions on the other, of which there
are already more than enough. The overreadings of aesthetic criticism reach for polysemous reverberations that court infinity—and an
infinity of meanings would be the equivalent of no meanings at all,

since everything and nothing are indistinguishable. To refer again to Frederick Turner on reading as "performance," "the critics give us a divine plenum of possible interpretations, but this divine plenum is quite impossible to perform." [4] The playfulness of language in general and poetry in particular is, of course, one of their beauties, but too much playfulness negates meaning altogether, producing incomprehension and frustration, not richness. As Turner continues, "*Any* group of words has anarchic proclivities toward tedious ambiguity: to make them mean something definite is the miracle. . . . The chief virtue of poetry is to perform a definite act within the indeterminate potentiality of the world" (160). When the aesthetic critic goes wildly astray—introducing vagrant mythologies, improbable etymologies, and implausible biographical explanations—we begin to lose confidence not only in *his* ability to read, but in our own. Some of the tough-mindedness of academic theory—particularly its use of general ideas—would serve well to articulate and universalize aesthetic ruminations that often yield only a sort of numinous fuzz. Aesthetic criticism, to be effective, must strive to arrest the dizzying free play of language by rescuing poems and fictions from the blankness of infinity. This would not mean that we regard any single critic's readings as definitive or final or that linguistic utterances are unambiguous. Rather, the critic needs to assume responsibility for what he says about a work without taking cover in facile ambiguities that mask his own incomprehension. Criticism is, after all, not a science but an art; yet the multiple escape clauses of ambiguous overreading engage in a pretense of scientificity on which they cannot make good. If it *is* true that linguistic utterances are at the mercy of infinite free play, then no amount of specifics will get any closer to that infinity, since when it comes to infinity, a miss is as good as a mile. Whether it is true or not—and at any given moment in time and place it does not appear that words *can* mean anything and everything—the critic ought not to be in competition with the poet. He should be otherwise engaged than in writing a sort of poem himself: different discourses require different rhetorical skills.

Alternately, the kind of criticism that we think of as secular must try to perfect the art of relating poetry to the world without simply degrading it into a vehicle for peddling a world, as the Statue of Liberty's raised torch is used in television commercials to sell underarm deodorants and ice cream cones. Although a return to the styles of Lionel Trilling and Edmund Wilson is not possible, these critics can serve as examples of what is meant by "public intellectuals." Yet today, instead of focusing on what is still useful in this class of critics, the fashion is to show how Trilling, for instance, was dominated by an elitist politics that he himself was unaware of (like Conrad and Balzac), the conclusion being that Trilling's accomplishments are somehow invalidated by his happening to have had his "own" point of view. Today's unmaskers of earlier hegemonies are subjected (i.e., made into subjects) by their own politics and their own hegemony, so that unmaskings of this sort can again only lead to infinite regresses, since everyone is ultimately unmaskable, most temptingly the unmasker himself. Secular critics will have to learn how to avoid being terrorized by the intellectual McCarthyism of today's magisterial cultural criticism, which discovers not pinkoes but neoconservatives under every bed.

With regard to theory, a critical program for the nineties would need to recognize that though theory cannot hold center stage forever, it is not yet ready to let go. Since even today's aesthetic and secular critics are more likely than not to be academics, their proximity to the sources of theory can make it possible for them to adapt theory and history for aesthetic and secular ends, which far from doing themselves any harm, would provide the toughening up that is needed to make other academics take them seriously. It is important for poets and fiction writers who aspire to criticism to deghettoize themselves from the writers' programs that swathe and shield them from the world and to shake off the stigma such programs attach to aspiring critics, who are perceived by "real" critics (i.e., theorists) as only poet-critics or novelist-critics, with the implication—not wholly undeserved—of ditherings with the infinite or infinitesimal. Whereas aesthetic criticism can return us to the originary flesh of poems and stories, a flesh that is being brushed aside by theory and New Historicism, to do so will require an artful balance of sentient particulars with illuminating general ideas. Unless aesthetic critics can capture the interest of literary academics and intellectuals, they will remain segregated and without real influence, except among other poets and novelists, because their audience is too limited, like the audience for much of poetry itself. Theoretical academics, however, whether they know it or not, need aesthetic and secular critics very badly since most of the time their own criticism is inadequate for dealing with literature, however stimulating as ideas. It would be to everybody's deeper advantage for the present segregation to come to an end, because it now exists mainly for the promotion of professionalism, not art and its dissemination.

Of course there is always the possibility that nobody really wants this segregation to be lessened or terminated, that the professionalism of both poets and theorists is too ingrained and self-directed, too tied up with success in the academy, so that there is little attraction in appealing to larger constituencies. If that is the case, the feeling of professional well-being may ultimately prove illusory, for as the bubbles of specialization get larger, thinner, and more filled with air, the dangers of their bursting increase. Audiences can be fractured only so far, until finally everyone is talking and no one is listening. The Modern Language Association complains that the number of special interests has increased to such a point that more than half the requests for special sessions at the annual convention have to be turned down. Even now, the annual convention runs close to eight hundred sessions in the course of approximately three days. Admittedly, attendance at these sessions varies enormously, but if you apportion eight hundred sessions among an audience that fluctuates between six and ten thousand academics (many of whom attend no sessions at all), you get an average audience of somewhat modest size. Soon the speakers will be talking only to God.

Now that most of the arts are hatching their eggs in the nests of academia, the problem of too many nests (and one is tempted to say, a certain quantity of rotten eggs) cannot be solved by handing them out to the general television-watching public. Robert Pinsky is quite right to say that he writes poetry for readers of poetry and not for haters of poetry, whom it is not his responsibility to entertain. But with most of the arts having gone academic, there exists a huge population of highbrow intellectuals who are either academics themselves or graduate students or bright undergraduates, as well as a complex audience of independent intellectuals of a type suggested by Daniel Bell. This audience, he remarks, "comprises not the creators of culture but the *transmitters:* those working in higher education, publishing, magazines, broadcast media, theater, and museums, who process and influence the reception of serious cultural products. It is in itself large enough to be a *market* for culture, purchasing books, prints, and serious music recordings."[5] The audience for the arts is in reality quite vast, but as long as specialists refuse to make concessions to other specialists with related but different specialties, this vast audience will remain fractured and incommunicado. Literature and its critics will have only themselves to blame for their marginality if they persist in believing that concessions to other intellectuals entail a sullying of the purity of their art. This "purity" is largely bogus, in any case, and when the academy can no longer afford to reward it through professional perks, such exclusiveness will turn out to have been a death wish that was not so necessary after all. If Althusserian Marxists can talk only to Althusserian Marxists, Lacanian feminists only to Lacanian feminists, and New Formalist poet-critics only to New Formalist poet-critics, then as far as "literature" is concerned it is back to Babel once again.

14

. . . .

Oppositional
Opposition

A major inference crying out for recognition in the course of these chapters is that the Academic Revolutionary is a fraud. Guaranteed a job for life through the tenure system regardless of subsequent performance, supported by dependable paychecks from the bureaucracy he pretends to scorn, relieved of some of the multiple anxieties of mortality by means of health insurance and a pension, and addicted as much as everyone else—if not more—to the perquisites of capitalism's shameless cornucopia, the revolutionary academic is no revolutionary at all. He is, rather, an exemplary specimen of capitalism in action. The marketplace of ideas, once only a metaphor, has literally become just that, a system of commodities. The Information Society, as Lyotard has so aptly insisted, is an exchange of ideas that is largely an Exchange of Ideas (as in "Chicago Mercantile Exchange"), where information commands a price and is traded like pork-belly futures.

The academic professional performs his function in the thick of this marketplace, enjoying it like crazy—flying around to conferences, aspiring to upper-middle-class tastes, benefiting from the cunning of technology (whether as computers, compact-disc players, xerography); indeed, today's academic is completely dependent on printouts, on-line retrieval systems, electronic bibliographies, so much so that one can hardly imagine academia functioning without them, any more than one can imagine a contemporary supermarket without a scanner at the check-out. Today's academic is an artifact of capitalist technocracy.

By fancying himself to be a revolutionary, the "radical" academic superadds real vice to his relatively venial enchantment with technology and high living. It is surely a painful irony that his culture hero should be someone like Gramsci, who really was a revolutionary and paid a heavy price for it, his major work having been written from a place that few academics will ever experience first hand, except perhaps as a penalty for drug pushing or murdering a spouse. Kierkegaard, had he lived in contemporary America, could have had wonderful new/old material for attacks against moral inauthenticity. Instead of exposing religious hypocrisy (e.g., the agent of Christ blesses the guns rather than protesting the war), he could have turned to its modern academic counterpart: phony radicalism. The radical academic exhibits the verbal trappings and forms of Marxist renunciation while acting as paradigmatic acquisitive capitalist: he needs a 32-bit computer to write his jeremiads against technology and the marketplace, as well as grants (from government or private enterprise) for trips to European watering places where he can give and hear papers about hegemony and patriarchal oppression—all the while pretending to bite the hand that is paying his per diem. Or as Irving Howe has succinctly put it, "Marxism has gone to the universities to die in comfort." [1]

The Academic Revolutionary is not just an oxymoron but an ultimate betrayer of authentic ideals. In acting out with such precision the roles assigned to him by capitalist ideology while attacking the false consciousness of everyone else, he is pretty much in the same class as the television evangelist who pretends to be amassing millions for Jesus, even as he lives a life of luxurious debauchery.

Being a false revolutionary seems much worse than being a passive tool of oppression, for it is hard to be vigilant about vice while seeing oneself as always already virtuous. As for capitalism, though it has played a major role in producing the darker side of the American academy, its achievements are not *entirely* bad when seen against the range of past history, with its poverty, disease, and lives short and brutish. Like everything else, capitalism needs to be constantly subjected to criticism—its horrors are manifold, like the horrors of life itself—but total repudiation in the midst of wallowing enjoyment is worse than uncritical acceptance.

Finally, as if failure to acknowledge the hands that feed us were not bad enough, the use of literature as a weapon to fight this war against capitalism and patriarchy is too often a violation of the creative skills and larger consciousness behind the novels and poems that give us so much psychological nourishment. This is not to say that poets and novelists are transcendent, ahistorical souls uncontaminated by the clay of human deficiency and therefore beyond criticism or reproach. Works of literary genius emerge from the same human soil as everything else, and nothing is finally sacred, but reductive readings produce crabbed and crippled forms of aesthetic response, constricting rather than expanding consciousness. To read *Wuthering Heights* (as I have already indicated) according to current political paradigms is to abort its multivalent and disturbing resonances by turning them into mere confirmations of today's vanguard political positions, positions that will rarely issue in worthwhile action, since a cheap sense of virtue (and marketability) is the "radically" operative motivation. If the reduction of art to politics is an evil in the totalitarian state, it is not so much less an evil when performed by ineffectual bourgeois intellectuals fueled by priestly resentments. If you believe in noblesse oblige, it comes off as rather worse.

Who could have guessed that academics would come to be as guilty of the commodification of culture as TV moguls and monolithic bookstore chains? But *this* betrayal of the clerks is more blameworthy than ordinary vulgar doublecross, because the pretensions are so much greater. In the long run, atypical professors like Allan Bloom and E. D. Hirsch (whether we like their views or not)—as well as less categorizable thinkers like Russell Jacoby—may turn out to have contributed more to forcing intellectual issues into the forum of the real world than self-professed revolutionaries, who ultimately seem so domesticated and unthreatening, so easily defanged with dollar bills. Now, with the disappearance of the traditional person of letters, academia must also make an effort to supply the "independent intellectual" in addition to the partisan specialist (since we are all academics now), though it is difficult for most professors to be significantly "independent" because they are as corporately "bespoke" in their way as office personnel in theirs. It is just the *illusion* of independence that is stronger in their case, for how independent can you be when the demands of specialization lead you deeper and deeper into narrow professionalism's profound unfreedom?

For the present, at any rate, genuinely radical academics can be neither wholly Marxist nor feminist, neither wholly black nor Third World. The only radical position plausible right now is skeptical non-alignment, using a bit of this and a bit of that. Today's vanguard intel-lectual must learn to live without grandiose cosmic beliefs, entertaining local, temporary, and flexible viewpoints that can accommodate them-selves to quotidian realities while resisting transcendental afflatus and bombast. This would be the only genuine heroism available to him, short of operating in the real world like Gramsci (who in today's com-fortable America might very well find himself incarnated as a fat-cat professor suited to a David Lodge novel). He claims, after all, to have accepted Nietzsche's message that God is dead, and he has welcomed Derrida's modification of that message in the form of an assault on logocentrism. If it is no longer possible to believe in a center, whether as God, Essentialism, or Foundationalism, then fanatic insistence upon favored ideologies as ultimately true or right is no longer tenable and is today's most reprehensible form of intellectual hypocrisy. While one can and ought to "believe" in the truth or rightness of things in relation to the present needs of society, global theoretical assurances are simply preposterous, however plausible they may seem at any given moment to transient political interests. The categorical imperatives of radical feminism, for example, are no more in touch with What Is than patri-archy (though feminism has a great deal to offer and the best feminists know how to offer it), and when antirepresentationalists nevertheless go on to tell us how things *really are*, beating us over the head with their own essences, foundations, and representations, their mendacity is too serious to be brushed off with laughs.

Although one would have expected the fruits of Nietzsche and Der-rida to involve the embrace of radical skepticism, an abandonment once and for all of eternal verities, the big surprise is the trendy re-vival of polytheism, with biodegradable gods popping up all over the place. These gods rise and fall in the twinkling of an eye, as the

needs of the academic job market produce sacred new truths to propel nascent careers. If today's consumers must throw out last year's
cordless telephones because the newer models enjoy better transmission (and unlike theoretical artifacts, consumer appliances really do
get better), so today's academic consumers must throw out Stephen
Greenblatt (though he can still be peddled to undergraduates) because
the New Historicism is entering its inevitable down-market phase. If
the claims had been kept moderate, if the tenets of antirepresentation-
alism, antilogocentrism, and deconstruction had been synthesized as
functional components of a generally skeptical understanding, the passionate conversions of true believers followed by rapid losses of faith
would not have been necessary. Each theoretical movement has left
us with worthwhile alterations of consciousness—but must we accept
any of them as comprehensive accounts of the way things are, as their
hard-sell proponents would have us believe? It is not really a question
of accepting or rejecting theorizing altogether, as frequent debates on
the subject propose, but a matter of recognizing the *constructedness* of
theory, its pragmatic and instrumental nature. Theories can help us to
deal with experience by providing models for behavior, in the way that
thinking of the letter "H" can help us to shift the gears in a manual
transmission, but theories cannot provide us with ultimate truths.

Today's radical intellectual, then, is in the final instance not radical
enough, falling as he does into recidivist patterns of doctrinaire credu-
lity. Though the doctrines themselves may be new, the mentality that
generates them is old, tiresome, and effete. What is still to be learned
is the art of playing it cool—as neither leftist nor rightist, neither specialist nor nonspecialist, neither feminist nor antifeminist, but an amal-
gam of all of these: a critical intellectual. If "independence" is remotely
possible for a creature who emerges from the primal mud, from his own
genes, and from social and domestic history, then nonalignment looks
to be the only Promethean way, and today's Prometheus can expect to
have his entrails gnawed by all sides, since he or she would be opposed
to them all and thus fair prey.

Nevertheless, for *now* the radically radical stance could hardly be
clearer: alignments must be resisted so that *real* opposition may thrive.

Notes

Introduction

1. Randall Jarrell, "The Age of Criticism" in *Poetry and the Age* (New York: The Ecco Press, 1980), 81.

2. Helen Vendler, *The Music of What Happens* (Cambridge and London: Harvard University Press, 1988), 1–2.

3. Jacques Derrida, "But, beyond . . . (Open Letter to Anne McClintock and Rob Nixon)," *Critical Inquiry* 13 (1986): 155–70.

4. Jean-François Lyotard, *The Postmodern Condition: A Report on Knowledge*, trans. Geoff Bennington and Brian Massumi (Minneapolis: University of Minnesota Press, 1984), 27.

5. Ralph W. Rader, "Literary Permanence and Critical Change," *Works and Days* 4 (1986): 9–10.

6. Peter J. Rabinowitz, "Our Evaluation of Literature Has Been Distorted by Academe's Bias Toward Close Reading of Texts," *Chronicle of Higher Education*, April 6, 1988, A40.

7. Mark Walhout, "Textual Virtue: A Review Essay," *Journal of the Midwest Modern Language Association* 21 (1988): 65.

8. Robert von Hallberg, "American Poet-Critics Since 1945," in *Reconstructing American Literary History*, ed. Sacvan Bercovitch (Cambridge and London: Harvard University Press, 1986).

9. Frederick Turner, *Natural Classicism: Essays on Literature and Science* (New York: Paragon House Publishers, 1985), 156. See my "Ethical, Rational, Political, Poetical: What the Essay is Doing Now," *The Georgia Review* 41 (1987): 426–36, for an account of some of Turner's limitations as a guru.

CHAPTER ONE
Sparrows and Scholars

1. For a lucid and meticulous survey of the spectrum of subjective or reader-response criticism, see Steven Mailloux, "Reader-Response Criticism?" *Genre* 10 (1977): 413–31.

2. The problem has been exacerbated by Marxist, feminist, and New Historicist criticism, which aims to "correct" patriarchal and bourgeois readings of culture and texts while generally assenting to the doctrine that there are no correct readings of anything.

3. Jacques Derrida, "Structure, Sign, and Play in the Discourse of the Human Sciences." This essay, along with many others outlining structural thought of the 1960s, can be found in *The Structuralist Controversy: The Languages of Criticism and the Sciences of Man*, ed. Richard Macksey and Eugenio Donato (Baltimore: Johns Hopkins University Press, 1972).

4. Geoffrey Hartman, "The Recognition Scene of Criticism," *Critical Inquiry* 4 (1977): 415.

5. Since this was written, the situation has become even more complex. The current interest in literary canons has resulted in a rapid shuffling of the texts to be regarded as "sacred." This revaluation, however, has been more explicitly and consciously political than in the past. Along with these new sanctifications has also appeared a new debunking, a characteristic of some Marxist and New Historical criticism, which aims to expose venerated authors as unwitting tools of their societies.

6. Mas'ud Zavarzadeh, *The Mythopoeic Reality: The Postwar American Nonfiction Novel* (Urbana: University of Illinois Press, 1976), 224–25.

7. Stanley Fish, "Literature in the Reader: Affective Stylistics," *New Literary History* 2 (1970): 123–62. It is also reprinted with minor alterations in Fish's *Self-Consuming Artifacts* (Berkeley: University of California Press, 1972). Fish is aware of and discusses the problem of conventions of reading, both in this essay and elsewhere, but these conventions are not clearly related by Fish to his "affective stylistics," a term and conception with which he becomes increasingly dissatisfied in his later writing, in which he moves away from "subjectivity" to the idea of "interpretive communities."

8. Herbert Marcuse, *One-Dimensional Man* (Boston: Beacon Press, 1966), 179, 182.

9. Herbert Marcuse, *Eros and Civilization* (New York: Vintage Books, 1962), 168–69.

10. Theodore Roszak, *The Making of a Counter Culture* (Garden City, N.Y.: Doubleday, Anchor Press, 1969), 229.

11. Fish, *Self-Consuming Artifacts*. For illuminating examinations of the matter of conventions of reading and their relation to meaning and interpretation, see Jonathan Culler, *Structuralist Poetics* (Ithaca: Cornell University Press, 1975); Morse Peckham, *Man's Rage for Chaos* (New York: Schocken Books, 1967); and John M. Ellis, *The Theory of Literary Criticism: A Logical Analysis*

(Berkeley: University of California Press, 1974). Perhaps the most well-known treatment is E. D. Hirsch, Jr., *Validity in Interpretation* (New Haven: Yale University Press, 1967).

12. Norman Holland, *Poems in Persons: An Introduction to the Psychoanalysis of Literature* (New York: W. W. Norton, 1975), 98, 117.

13. It forms a quite literally ironic footnote to this passage to add that at least two critic-scholars who took up this essay after its original appearance accused me of rejecting postmodern critical theory because of my nostalgia for traditional religious beliefs. G. Douglas Atkins, for instance, in a chapter on J. Hillis Miller in *Reading Deconstruction, Deconstructive Reading* (Lexington: University Press of Kentucky, 1983), 66, quotes the above paragraph and adds: "Fromm's attack [on deconstruction] evidently stems from a desire to salvage transcendence," and he later refers to my "condemnation" of contemporary nihilism. Having no personal stake in traditional religious beliefs, I naturally find Atkins's description rather surprising. My aim in this account of "deconstruction" was to point out self-contradiction and hypocrisy: these nihilistic theories are never even slightly observed in practice and, as I insist in subsequent chapters, they exist in large measure as part of the intellectual's need to shock the bourgeoisie. An interesting project for investigation might be to find out why today's academic intellectuals have so powerful a need, especially when they are so bourgeois themselves.

14. Roland Barthes, *The Pleasure of the Text*, trans. Richard Miller (New York: Hill and Wang, 1975), 3.

15. Cary Nelson, "Reading Criticism," *PMLA* 91 (1976): 813.

16. Cary Nelson, *The Incarnate Word: Literature as Verbal Space* (Urbana: University of Illinois Press, 1973), 4.

17. Hartman, "The Recognition Scene of Criticism," 409–10.

18. Gerald Graff, "Fear and Trembling at Yale," *American Scholar* 46 (1977): 476. A year later, Graff's "The Politics of Anti-Realism" appeared in *Salmagundi* 42 (1978): 4–30, exploring in depth the role of Marcuse and the New Left in the shaping of the aesthetics of the seventies. Graff's earlier essay, "Aestheticism and Cultural Politics," *Social Research* 40 (1973): 311–43, provides even more enlightenment in this matter. Finally, his book, *Literature Against Itself: Literary Ideas in Modern Society* (Chicago: University of Chicago Press, 1979), incorporates several of his previous essays into substantial new material to mount a forceful attack on various trendy assumptions about literary meaning and value.

19. Charles Altieri discusses the impracticality of Derrida's extreme view of language in two essays: "The Hermeneutics of Literary Indeterminacy: A

Dissent from the New Orthodoxy," *New Literary History* 10 (1978): 71–99, and in "Wittgenstein on Consciousness and Language: A Challenge to Derridean Literary Theory," *MLN* 91 (1976): 1397–1423. Although these essays have their helpful moments, they introduce new problems as replacements for the old. I take them up in the next chapter.

20. Despite the passage of time since this was written, this contradiction between theory and practice has not disappeared. It surfaces again in recent attacks on deconstruction. See Chapter 12 below.

21. But a new and ingenious wrinkle has been added by Jean-François Lyotard since the above was written. In place of the old humanistic goals of "truth" and emancipation of the individual, Lyotard finds "performativity"— "that is, the best possible input/output equation. The State and/or company must abandon the idealist and humanist narratives of legitimation in order to justify the new goal: in the discourse of today's financial backers of research, the only credible goal is power. Scientists, technicians, and instruments are purchased not to find truth, but to augment power." As far as data are concerned, "The performativity of an utterance, be it denotative or prescriptive, increases proportionally to the amount of information about its referent one has at one's disposal. Thus the growth of power, and its self-legitimation, are now taking the route of data storage and accessibility, and the operativity of information." According to Lyotard, he who owns the data banks owns the world! *The Postmodern Condition: A Report on Knowledge*, trans. Geoff Bennington and Brian Massumi (Minneapolis: University of Minnesota Press, 1984), 46, 47.

22. At present, political interpretations have been supplanting "private" ones, but the objections to them do not substantially differ from those against the "erotic" text.

23. And mere politics.

CHAPTER TWO
Literary Professionalism's Pyrrhic Defense of Poesy

1. Jacques Derrida, *The Languages of Criticism and the Sciences of Man: The Structuralist Controversy*, ed. Richard Macksey and Eugenio Donato (Baltimore: Johns Hopkins University Press, 1970), 247–65.

2. *The Basic Works of Aristotle*, ed. Richard McKeon (New York: Random House, 1941), 335, 383.

3. Charles Altieri, "The Hermeneutics of Literary Indeterminacy: A Dissent from the New Orthodoxy," *New Literary History* 10 (1978): 75.

4. Charles Altieri, "Wittgenstein on Consciousness and Language: A Challenge to Derridean Literary Theory," *MLN* 91 (1976): 1418.

5. Charles Altieri, "The Qualities of Action: A Theory of Middles in Literature," *boundary* 2 5 (1977): 325–26.

6. Charles Altieri, "The Poem as Act: A Way to Reconcile Presentational and Mimetic Theories," *Iowa Review* 6/3 & 6/4 (1975): 103–24.

7. Charles Altieri, "Presence and Reference in a Literary Text: The Example of Williams' 'This Is Just to Say,'" *Critical Inquiry* 5 (1979): 492, 497.

8. In "The 'Found' in Contemporary Poetry," *The Georgia Review* 23 (1979): 329–41, Jonathan Holden discusses a fashion among poets in the seventies of using prosy lines that sound as if they had come from news articles or advertisements. Not surprisingly, he uses "This Is Just to Say" as one of his illustrations, albeit an early one. Regarding some of the more extreme cases, Holden remarks: "In fact, I'm certain that by applying standard New Critical techniques one could invent a plausible justification for *any* collection of words assembled as verse, isolated on the page, and asserted as a 'poem.' Confronted with gibberish, one could import heavy concepts like 'entropy,' in order to argue that the poem was *about* its own incoherence, that its content was, like the content of all true poetry, inseparable from its form" (332). Indeed, a supreme trickster like Stanley Fish does just this sort of thing with his surprisingly compliant students, as he reports in *Is There a Text in This Class?* and the entire episode is criticized and parodied by Robert Scholes in *Textual Power*.

9. Two essays by Michael Fischer have been helpful to me here: "Why Realism Seems So Naive: Romanticism, Professionalism, and Contemporary Critical Theory," *College English* 40 (1979): 740–50, and "The Collapse of English Neoclassicism," *Centennial Review* 24 (1980): 338–59.

CHAPTER THREE
Public Worlds/Private Muses

1. Douglas Stalker and Clarke Glymour, "The Malignant Object: Thoughts on Public Sculpture," *Public Interest* 66 (1982): 3–36 (includes replies).

2. Samuel Lipman, "American opera: honors and performances," *New Criterion* 1 (1982): 59.

3. Joseph Epstein, "The Literary Life Today," *New Criterion* 1 (1982): 9.

4. Tom Wolfe, *The Painted Word* (New York: Farrar Straus Giroux, 1975), 69.

5. Tom Wolfe, *From Bauhaus to Our House* (New York: Farrar Straus Giroux, 1981), 82.

6. Derral Cheatwood, "Models of Accountability and Modern Art," *Journal of Aesthetic Education* 16 (1982): 71–84.

7. George Rochberg, "Can the Arts Survive Modernism? (A Discussion of the Characteristics, History, and Legacy of Modernism)," *Critical Inquiry* 11 (1984): 330–32 *passim*.

8. Martin Steinmann, Jr., Review of *The Horizon of Literature*, ed. Paul Hernadi, *Journal of Aesthetics and Art Criticism* 42 (1984): 348.

CHAPTER FOUR
Recycled Lives

1. Cynthia Ozick, "Mrs. Virginia Woolf," *Commentary* 56 (1973): 33–44. Although a slightly revised version of this essay was included in Ozick's collection, *Art and Ardor* (New York: Alfred A. Knopf, 1983), I prefer to use the original version.

2. Elaine Showalter, *A Literature of Their Own: British Women Novelists from Brontë to Lessing* (Princeton: Princeton University Press, 1977).

3. Phyllis Grosskurth, "Between Eros and Thanatos," *Times Literary Supplement*, Oct. 31, 1980, 1225–26.

4. In a recent essay of astonishing brilliance, Thomas C. Caramagno devastatingly rejects most of the psychoanalyzing of Virginia Woolf that has fueled so much of the Woolf industry (*PMLA* 103 [1988]: 10–23). The first two sentences of Caramagno's abstract of the essay are worth quoting: "Although recent scientific discoveries about the genetic and biochemical components of manic-depressive psychosis have radically revised our understanding of the etiology and psychodynamics of this illness, psychological studies of Virginia Woolf's life and work have generally remained tied to Freud's outmoded model of loss-induced neurosis. This model appeals to critics because it readily imposes coherence on often inconsistent biographical data, but it fails to account for psychotic breakdowns and *tends to disparage Woolf with its emphasis on the infantile and evasive aspects of art*" (emphasis added).

5. These replies ran from November 7, 1980, through January 23, 1981.

6. Since references to popular culture date so rapidly, it should be explained that Linda Lovelace was a star in pornographic movies. The range of response to her ran from moral condemnation to use as a defenseless exemplar of patriarchal exploitation of women. For intellectuals, she became a text that could be put to any convenient use.

CHAPTER FIVE
Leonard Woolf and His Virgins

1. Leonard Woolf's autobiography consists of five volumes: *Sowing, Growing, Beginning Again, Downhill All the Way,* and *The Journey not the Arrival Matters.* These were published in England by the Hogarth Press and in the United States by Harcourt Brace Jovanovich. I use the Hogarth Press edition, in the present instance, *Sowing,* London, 1960.

2. Woolf, *Growing* (London, 1961), 54.

3. Leon Edel, *Bloomsbury: A House of Lions* (New York: J. B. Lippincott Company, 1979), 179–80.

4. Leonard Woolf, *The Village in the Jungle* (Oxford: Oxford University Press, 1981).

5. Leonard Woolf, *The Wise Virgins* (New York and London: Harcourt Brace Jovanovich, 1979).

6. George Spater and Ian Parsons, *A Marriage of True Minds* (New York and London: Harcourt Brace Jovanovich, 1977), 81.

7. Leon Edel, "Leonard Woolf and *The Wise Virgins*" in *Essaying Biography: A Celebration for Leon Edel,* ed. Gloria G. Fromm (Honolulu: University of Hawaii Press, 1986), 16.

8. Selma S. Meyerowitz, *Leonard Woolf* (Boston: Twayne Publishers, 1982), 60.

9. Duncan Wilson, *Leonard Woolf: A Political Biography* (New York: St. Martin's Press, 1978), 11–12. Wilson remarks, "There is no sign from Woolf's autobiography or from other people's memories of him that he came up against racial prejudice in those personal relationships which were most important to him. His urge to reform society owed nothing to any social rejection of himself as a Jew."

10. Edel, *Bloomsbury,* 115.

CHAPTER SIX
The Lives and Deaths of Charlotte Brontë

1. Edward Chitham and Tom Winnifrith, *Brontë Facts and Brontë Problems* (London and Basingstoke, 1983), 12. This poem is in an unfinished state, but the basis of Winnifrith's claim can be gathered from a few stanzas:

> But wild and pathless was the space
> That lay our lives between,

And dangerous as the foaming race
Of ocean's surges green. . . .

I dangers dared, I hindrance scorned
I omens did defy;
Whatever menaced, harassed, warned
I passed impetuous by. . . .

I care not then how dense and grim
Disasters gather nigh
I care not in this moment sweet,
The hate, the love, the joy, the sweet

Though all I have rushed oer
The wrath I had passed oer
Should come on pinion strong and fleet

2. Elizabeth Gaskell, *The Life of Charlotte Brontë*, ed. Alan Shelston (Harmondsworth, Middlesex, England: Penguin Books, 1980), 30.

3. Winifred Gérin, *Charlotte Brontë: The Evolution of Genius* (London: Oxford University Press, 1967), 67.

4. Tom Winnifrith, *The Brontës and Their Background: Romance and Reality* (New York: Barnes and Noble, 1973), 6.

5. To Winnifrith's credit, he remarks several years later, in connection with the poem he discovered at the Berg Collection of the New York Public Library, referred to above: "I have previously poured scorn on those who have sought to draw parallels between the lives of the Brontës and their works, and upon those who have sought to draw conclusions about the novels from a study of the Brontës' juvenilia and poetry. The Berg manuscript as it stands makes this scorn a little premature." Chitham and Winnifrith, *Brontë Facts and Brontë Problems*, 11.

6. Margot Peters, *Unquiet Soul: A Biography of Charlotte Brontë* (New York: Pocket Books, 1976), 423–24.

7. Helene Moglen, *Charlotte Brontë: The Self Conceived* (Madison: University of Wisconsin Press, 1984), 39, 241.

8. Terry Eagleton, *Myths of Power: A Marxist Study of the Brontës* (London and Basingstoke: The Macmillan Press, Ltd., 1975), 4.

9. Winnifrith, *The Brontës and Their Background*, 50.

10. Sandra M. Gilbert and Susan Gubar, *The Madwoman in the Attic: The Woman Writer and the Nineteenth-Century Literary Imagination* (New Haven and London: Yale University Press, 1979), 13.

11. John Maynard, *Charlotte Brontë and Sexuality* (Cambridge: Cambridge University Press, 1984), 171.

12. Cited in Maynard, 218: Phillip Rhodes, "A Medical Appraisal of the Brontës," *Brontë Society Transactions*, 16, no. 2 (1972), 101–9.

13. Rosamond Langbridge, *Charlotte Brontë: A Psychological Study* (New York: Haskell House Publishers, 1972). Wild as this particular example may be, Langbridge's book is also filled with some brilliant insights. See her sixth chapter, "The True Story of Charlotte Brontë's Marriage."

CHAPTER SEVEN
Emily Brontë and the Strains of Modern Criticism

1. J. Hillis Miller, "The Critic As Host," *Critical Inquiry* 3 (1977): 439–47.

2. J. Hillis Miller, *The Disappearance of God: Five Nineteenth Century Writers*, 2d ed. (Cambridge, Mass. and London, England: The Belknap Press of Harvard University Press, 1975), 180–81.

3. J. Hillis Miller, *Fiction and Repetition* (Cambridge: Harvard University Press, 1982), 50.

4. Sandra M. Gilbert and Susan Gubar, *The Madwoman in the Attic: The Woman Writer and the Nineteenth-Century Literary Imagination* (New Haven and London: Yale University Press, 1979), 252–53.

5. James H. Kavanagh, *Emily Brontë* (Oxford: Basil Blackwell, 1985), 24–25. To avoid redundancy, I have decided not to discuss Terry Eagleton's chapter on *Wuthering Heights* (in *Myths of Power*) because there is little to add to what I have already said in Chapter 5. Eagleton's treatment of *Wuthering Heights*, if one can accept its reductive focus on capitalism, exhibits all his characteristic strengths and few of his weaknesses, making this a notable essay, though one regrets the narrowness of its focus. One has to appreciate real gifts even when they are accompanied by qualities that limit their effectiveness.

6. John Gray, "Fashion, fantasy or fiasco?" *Times Literary Supplement* 4482, Feb. 24–Mar. 2, 1989, 183.

7. Stevie Davies, *Emily Brontë* (New York and London: Harvester/Wheatsheaf, 1988), 6.

8. Q. D. Leavis, "A Fresh Approach to *Wuthering Heights*," in *Collected Essays*, Vol. I: *The Englishness of the English Novel* (Cambridge: Cambridge University Press, 1983), 263.

CHAPTER EIGHT
The Hegemony of "Hegemony"

1. Jim Merod, *The Political Responsibility of the Critic* (Ithaca and London: Cornell University Press, 1987).

2. Richard Ohmann, *Politics of Letters* (Middletown, Conn.: Wesleyan University Press, 1987).

3. Frank Lentricchia, *Criticism and Social Change* (Chicago and London: University of Chicago Press, 1983).

4. Fredric Jameson, *The Political Unconscious: Narrative as a Socially Symbolic Act* (Ithaca: Cornell University Press, 1981).

CHAPTER NINE
Literary Politics and Blue-Chip High-Mindedness

1. Henry Louis Gates, Jr., ed., *"Race," Writing, and Difference* (Chicago and London: University of Chicago Press, 1986). Page numbers in parentheses following quotations will be to this book rather than to the issues of *Critical Inquiry* in which these essays originally appeared.

2. John Carlos Rowe, " 'To Live Outside the Law, You Must be Honest': The Authority of the Margin in Contemporary Theory," *Cultural Critique* 2 (1985–86): 60.

3. The reference here is to some notorious remarks made by W. Jackson Bate about the trivialization of the MLA convention by its inclusion of sessions on minority literatures. "Signifying" is a vernacular black expression that refers to the making of satirical remarks—often directed against whites—by means of a relatively private ethnic argot. Gates discusses this phenomenon at length in his earlier essay, "The Blackness of Blackness" in *Critical Inquiry*, June 1983.

4. Jules Chametzky, "Ethnicity and Beyond: An Introduction," *Massachusetts Review* 27 (1986), 251.

5. Cornel West, "The Dilemma of the Black Intellectual," *Cultural Critique* 1 (1985), 122.

6. Ibid., 123.

CHAPTER TEN
Real Life, Literary Criticism, and the Perils of Bourgeoisification

1. Joyce A. Joyce, "The Black Canon: Reconstructing Black American Literary Criticism"; Henry Louis Gates, Jr., " 'What's Love Got to Do With it?':

Critical Theory, Integrity, and the Black Idiom"; Houston A. Baker, Jr., "In Dubious Battle"; Joyce A. Joyce, " 'Who the Cap Fit': Unconsciousness and Unconscionableness in the Criticism of Houston A. Baker, Jr., and Henry Louis Gates, Jr.," *New Literary History* 18 (1987): 335–84.

2. Houston A. Baker, Jr., *Blues, Ideology, and Afro-American Literature: A Vernacular Theory* (Chicago and London: University of Chicago Press, 1984), 61.

3. Houston A. Baker, Jr., "What Charles Knew: Homage to an English Teacher," *New York Times Book Review*, March 22, 1987, 3.

4. Norman Harris, " 'Who's Zoomin' Who': The New Black Formalism," *Journal of the Midwest Modern Language Association* 20 (1987): 39.

5. Barbara Christian, "The Race for Theory," *Cultural Critique* 6 (1987): 53.

CHAPTER ELEVEN
Public Intellectuals and the Academy

1. John Gross, *The Rise and Fall of the Man of Letters: A Study of the Idiosyncratic and the Humane in Modern Literature* (New York: The Macmillan Co., 1969).

2. Mark Krupnick, *Lionel Trilling and the Fate of Cultural Criticism* (Evanston, Ill.: Northwestern University Press, 1986), 2–3.

3. Russell Jacoby, *The Last Intellectuals: American Culture in the Age of Academe*, (New York: Basic Books, Inc., 1987).

4. Richard Bernstein, "Critic of Academe Fears Catch-22 in His Success," *New York Times*, Dec. 28, 1987.

5. Kate Adams, "Academe's Dominance of Poetic Culture Narrows the Range of American Poetry," *Chronicle of Higher Education*, May 18, 1988, A48. All quotations come from this page.

6. See Chapter 8 above.

CHAPTER TWELVE
Academic Capitalism and Literary Value

1. J. Hillis Miller, "Presidential Address 1986: The Triumph of Theory, the Resistance to Reading, and the Question of the Material Base," *PMLA* 102 (1987): 281–91.

2. Robert Scholes, "Deconstruction and Communication," *Critical Inquiry* 14 (1988): 278–95.

3. John M. Ellis, "What Does Deconstruction Contribute to Theory of Criticism?" *New Literary History* 19 (1988): 259.

4. Marjorie Perloff, "An Intellectual Impasse," *Salmagundi* 72 (1986): 129.

5. Edward Pechter, "The New Historicism and Its Discontents: Politicizing Renaissance Drama," *PMLA* 102 (1987): 292–303.

6. Richard Levin, "Feminist Thematics and Shakespearean Tragedy," *PMLA* 103 (1988): 126.

7. A. Leigh DeNeef, "Of Dialogues and Historicisms," *South Atlantic Quarterly* 86 (1987): 502.

8. Friedrich Nietzsche, *The Genealogy of Morals* (Garden City, N.Y.: Doubleday, Anchor Books, 1956), 165–66.

9. An entire essay is devoted to this argument by Oscar Kenshur: "Demystifying the Demystifiers: Metaphysical Snares of Ideological Criticism," *Critical Inquiry* 14 (1988): 335–53.

10. Antonio Gramsci, *Selections from the Prison Notebooks*, ed. by Quintin Hoare and Geoffrey Nowell Smith (New York: International Publishers, 1971), 326.

11. Or the Marxists, feminists, and deconstructors.

CHAPTER THIRTEEN
Critical Situations

1. Jerome J. McGann, "Marxism, Romanticism, and Postmodernism: An American Case History," *South Atlantic Quarterly*, 88 (1989): 605–32.

2. Jerome J. McGann, "The Text, the Poem, and the Problem of Historical Method," *New Literary History*, 12 (1981): 282.

3. See particularly: Harold Fromm, "Air and Being: The Psychedelics of Pollution," *Massachusetts Review* 24 (1983): 660–68. Also related are my essays "From Transcendence to Obsolescence: A Route Map," *Georgia Review* 32 (1978): 543–52, and "On Being Polluted," *Yale Review* 65 (1976): 614–29.

4. Frederick Turner, *Natural Classicism: Essays on Literature and Science* (New York: Paragon House Publishers, 1985), 156.

5. Daniel Bell, *The Cultural Contradictions of Capitalism* (New York: Basic Books, Inc., 1978), 20n.

CHAPTER FOURTEEN
Oppositional Opposition

1. Irving Howe, "The Treason of the Critics," *The New Republic*, June 12, 1989, 31.

Works Cited

Adams, Kate. "Academe's Dominance of Poetic Culture Narrows the Range of American Poetry." *Chronicle of Higher Education*, May 18, 1988, A48.

Altieri, Charles. "The Hermeneutics of Literary Indeterminacy: A Dissent from the New Orthodoxy." *New Literary History* 10 (1978): 71–99.

——. "Wittgenstein on Consciousness and Language: A Challenge to Derridean Literary Theory." *MLN* 91 (1976): 1397–1423.

——. "The Poem as Act: A Way to Reconcile Presentational and Mimetic Theories." *Iowa Review* 6/3 & 6/4 (1975): 103–24.

——. "Presence and Reference in a Literary Text: The Example of Williams' 'This is Just to Say.'" *Critical Inquiry* 5 (1979): 489–510.

——. "The Qualities of Action: A Theory of Middles in Literature." *boundary 2* 5 (1977): 323–50.

Aristotle. *The Basic Works of Aristotle*, ed. Richard McKeon. New York: Random House, 1941.

Atkins, G. Douglas. *Reading Deconstruction, Deconstructive Reading*. Lexington: University Press of Kentucky, 1983.

Baker, Houston A., Jr. *Blues, Ideology, and Afro-American Literature: A Vernacular Theory*. Chicago and London: University of Chicago Press, 1984.

——. "In Dubious Battle." *New Literary History* 18 (1987): 363–69.

——. "What Charles Knew: Homage to an English Teacher." *New York Times Book Review*, March 22, 1987, 3.

Barthes, Roland. *The Pleasure of the Text*, trans. Richard Miller. New York: Hill and Wang, 1975.

Bell, Daniel. *The Cultural Contradictions of Capitalism*. New York: Basic Books, Inc., 1978.

Bernstein, Richard. "Critic of Academe Fears Catch-22 in His Success." *New York Times*, Dec. 28, 1987.

Caramagno, Thomas C. "Manic-Depressive Psychosis and Critical Approaches to Virginia Woolf's Life and Work." *PMLA* 103 (1988): 10–23.

Chametzky, Jules. "Ethnicity and Beyond: An Introduction." *Massachusetts Review* 27 (1986): 251.

Cheatwood, Derral. "Models of Accountability and Modern Art." *Journal of Aesthetic Education* 16 (1982): 71–84.

Chitham, Edward, and Tom Winnifrith. *Brontë Facts and Brontë Problems.* London and Basingstoke: The Macmillan Press, Ltd., 1983.

Christian, Barbara. "The Race for Theory." *Cultural Critique* 6 (1987): 51–63.

Culler, Jonathan. *Structuralist Poetics.* Ithaca: Cornell University Press, 1975.

Davies, Stevie. *Emily Brontë.* New York and London: Harvester/Wheatsheaf, 1988.

DeNeef, A. Leigh. "Of Dialogues and Historicisms." *South Atlantic Quarterly* 86 (1987): 497–517.

Derrida, Jacques. "But, beyond . . . (Open Letter to Anne McClintock and Rob Nixon)." *Critical Inquiry* 13 (1986): 155–70.

———. "Structure, Sign, and Play in the Discourse of the Human Sciences." In *The Structuralist Controversy: The Languages of Criticism and the Sciences of Man*, ed. Richard Macksey and Eugenio Donato. Baltimore: Johns Hopkins University Press, 1972.

Eagleton, Terry. *Myths of Power: A Marxist Study of the Brontës.* London and Basingstoke: The Macmillan Press, Ltd., 1975.

Edel, Leon. *Bloomsbury: A House of Lions.* New York: J. B. Lippincott Company, 1979.

———. "Leonard Woolf and *The Wise Virgins*." In *Essaying Biography: A Celebration for Leon Edel*, ed. Gloria G. Fromm. Honolulu: University of Hawaii Press, 1986.

Ellis, John M. *The Theory of Literary Criticism: A Logical Analysis.* Berkeley: University of California Press, 1974.

———. "What Does Deconstruction Contribute to Theory of Criticism?" *New Literary History* 19 (1988): 259–79.

Epstein, Joseph. "The Literary Life Today." *New Criterion* 1 (1982): 6–15.

Fischer, Michael. "The Collapse of English Neoclassicism." *Centennial Review* 24 (1980): 338–59.

———. "Why Realism Seems So Naive: Romanticism, Professionalism, and Contemporary Critical Theory." *College English* 40 (1979): 740–50.

Fish, Stanley. "Literature in the Reader: Affective Stylistics." *New Literary History* 2 (1970): 123–62.

———. *Self-Consuming Artifacts.* Berkeley: University of California Press, 1972.

Freedman, Morris. "Appreciating Innovative Art." *Chicago Tribune*, December 6, sec. 11, p. 19.

Fromm, Harold. "Air and Being: The Psychedelics of Pollution." *Massachusetts Review* 24 (1983): 660–68.

———. "Ethical, Rational, Political, Poetical: What the Essay is Doing Now." *The Georgia Review* 41 (1987): 426–36.

———. "From Transcendence to Obsolescence: A Route Map." *The Georgia Review* 32 (1978): 543–52.

———. "The Hegemonic Form of Othering; or, The Academic's Burden." *Critical Inquiry* 13 (1986): 197–200. Republished in *"Race," Writing, and Difference*. Chicago and London: University of Chicago Press, 1986.

———. "On Being Polluted." *Yale Review* 65 (1976): 614–29.

Gaskell, Elizabeth. *The Life of Charlotte Brontë*, ed. Alan Shelston. Harmondsworth, Middlesex, England: Penguin Books, 1980.

Gates, Henry Louis, Jr. "The Blackness of Blackness." *Critical Inquiry* 9 (1983): 685–723.

———. "Editor's Introduction: Writing 'Race' and the Difference It Makes." *Critical Inquiry* 12 (1985): 1–20.

———. "Talkin' That Talk." *Critical Inquiry* 13 (1986): 203–10.

———. "'What's Love Got to Do With it?': Critical Theory, Integrity, and the Black Idiom." *New Literary History* 18 (1987): 345–62.

———, ed. *"Race," Writing, and Difference*. Chicago and London: University of Chicago Press, 1986.

Gérin, Winifred. *Charlotte Brontë: The Evolution of Genius*. London: Oxford University Press, 1967.

Gilbert, Sandra M., and Susan Gubar. *The Madwoman in the Attic: The Woman Writer and the Nineteenth-Century Literary Imagination*. New Haven and London: Yale University Press, 1979.

Graff, Gerald. "Aestheticism and Cultural Politics." *Social Research* 40 (1973): 311–43.

———. "Fear and Trembling at Yale." *American Scholar* 46 (1977): 467–78.

———. *Literature Against Itself: Literary Ideas in Modern Society*. Chicago: University of Chicago Press, 1979.

———. "The Politics of Anti-Realism." *Salmagundi* 42 (1978): 4–30.

Gramsci, Antonio. *Selections from the Prison Notebooks*, ed. by Quintin Hoare and Geoffrey Nowell Smith. New York: International Publishers, 1971.

Gray, John. "Fashion, fantasy or fiasco?" *Times Literary Supplement* 4482 Feb. 24–Mar. 2, 1989, 183.

Gross, John. *The Rise and Fall of the Man of Letters: A Study of the Idiosyncratic and the Humane in Modern Literature*. New York: The Macmillan Co., 1969.

Grosskurth, Phyllis. "Between Eros and Thanatos." *Times Literary Supplement*, Oct. 31, 1980, 1225–26.

Harris, Norman. " 'Who's Zoomin' Who': The New Black Formalism." *Journal of the Midwest Modern Language Association* 20 (1987): 37–45.

Hartman, Geoffrey. "The Recognition Scene of Criticism." *Critical Inquiry* 4 (1977): 407–16.

Hirsch, E. D., Jr. *Validity in Interpretation*. New Haven: Yale University Press, 1967.

Holden, Jonathon. "The 'Found' in Contemporary Poetry." *The Georgia Review* 23 (1979): 329–41.

Holland, Norman. *Poems in Persons: An Introduction to the Psychoanalysis of Literature*. New York: W. W. Norton, 1975.

Homans, Margaret. *Bearing the Word: Language and Female Experience in Nineteenth-Century Women's Writing*. Chicago and London: University of Chicago Press, 1986.

Howe, Irving. "The Treason of the Critics." *The New Republic*, June 12, 1989, 28–31.

Jacoby, Russell. *The Last Intellectuals: American Culture in the Age of Academe*. New York: Basic Books, Inc., 1987.

Jameson, Fredric. *The Political Unconscious: Narrative as a Socially Symbolic Act*. Ithaca: Cornell University Press, 1981.

Jarrell, Randall. "The Age of Criticism," in *Poetry and the Age*. New York: The Ecco Press, 1980.

Joyce, Joyce A. "The Black Canon: Reconstructing Black American Literary Criticism." *New Literary History* 18 (1987): 335–44.

———. " 'Who the Cap Fit': Unconsciousness and Unconscionableness in the Criticism of Houston A. Baker, Jr., and Henry Louis Gates, Jr." *New Literary History* 18 (1987): 371–84.

Kavanagh, James H. *Emily Brontë*. Oxford: Basil Blackwell, 1985.

Kennéy, Susan M. "Two Endings: Virginia Woolf's Suicide and *Between the Acts*." *University of Toronto Quarterly* 44 (1975): 265–89.

Kenshur, Oscar. "Demystifying the Demystifiers: Metaphysical Snares of Ideological Criticism." *Critical Inquiry* 14 (1988): 335–53.

Krupnick, Mark. *Lionel Trilling and the Fate of Cultural Criticism*. Evanston, Ill.: Northwestern University Press, 1986.

Langbridge, Rosamond. *Charlotte Brontë: A Psychological Study*. New York: Haskell House Publishers, Ltd., 1972.

Leavis, Q. D. "A Fresh Approach to *Wuthering Heights*." In *Collected Essays*,

Vol. I: *The Englishness of the English Novel.* Cambridge: Cambridge University Press, 1983.

Lentricchia, Frank. *Criticism and Social Change.* Chicago and London: University of Chicago Press, 1983.

Levin, Richard. "Feminist Thematics and Shakespearean Tragedy." *PMLA* 103 (1988): 125–38.

Lipman, Samuel. "American opera: honors and performances." *New Criterion* 1 (1982): 57–60.

Lyotard, Jean-François. *The Postmodern Condition: A Report on Knowledge,* trans. Geoff Bennington and Brian Massumi. Minneapolis: University of Minnesota Press, 1984.

McClatchey, J. D. *White Paper: On Contemporary American Poetry.* New York: Columbia University Press, 1989.

McGann, Jerome J. "Marxism, Romanticism, and Postmodernism: An American Case History." *South Atlantic Quarterly* 88 (1989): 605–32.

———. "The Text, the Poem, and the Problem of Historical Method." *New Literary History* 12 (1981): 269–88.

Mailloux, Steven. "Reader-Response Criticism?" *Genre* 10 (1977): 413–31.

Marcuse, Herbert. *One-Dimensional Man.* Boston: Beacon Press, 1966.

———. *Eros and Civilization.* New York: Vintage Books, 1962.

Maynard, John. *Charlotte Brontë and Sexuality.* Cambridge: Cambridge University Press, 1984.

Merod, Jim. *The Political Responsibility of the Critic.* Ithaca and London: Cornell University Press, 1987.

Meyerowitz, Selma S. *Leonard Woolf.* Boston: Twayne Publishers, 1982.

Miller, J. Hillis. "The Critic As Host." *Critical Inquiry* 3 (1977): 439–47.

———. *The Disappearance of God: Five Nineteenth Century Writers.* 2d ed. Cambridge, Mass. and London, England: The Belknap Press of Harvard University Press, 1975.

———. *Fiction and Repetition.* Cambridge: Harvard University Press, 1982.

———. "Presidential Address 1986: The Triumph of Theory, the Resistance to Reading, and the Question of the Material Base." *PMLA* 102 (1987): 281–91.

Moglen, Helene. *Charlotte Brontë: The Self Conceived.* Madison: University of Wisconsin Press, 1984.

Morton, Donald, and Mas'ud Zavarzadeh. "The Cultural Politics of the Fiction Workshop." *Cultural Critique* 11 (1988–89): 155–73.

Nelson, Cary. *The Incarnate Word: Literature as Verbal Space.* Urbana: University of Illinois Press, 1973.

———. "Reading Criticism." *PMLA* 91 (1976): 801–15.

Nietzsche, Friedrich. *The Genealogy of Morals*. Garden City, N.Y.: Doubleday, Anchor Books, 1956.

Ohmann, Richard. *Politics of Letters*. Middletown, Conn.: Wesleyan University Press, 1987.

Ozick, Cynthia. *Art and Ardor*. New York: Alfred A. Knopf, 1983.

———. "Mrs. Virginia Woolf." *Commentary* 56 (1973): 33–44.

Peckham, Morse. *Man's Rage for Chaos*. New York: Schocken Books, 1967.

Pechter, Edward. "The New Historicism and Its Discontents: Politicizing Renaissance Drama." *PMLA* 102 (1987): 292–303.

Perloff, Marjorie. "An Intellectual Impasse." *Salmagundi* 72 (1986): 125–30.

Peters, Margot. *Unquiet Soul: A Biography of Charlotte Brontë*. New York: Pocket Books, 1976.

Pinsky, Robert. *Poetry and the World*. New York: The Ecco Press, 1988.

Poole, Roger. *The Unknown Virginia Woolf*. Cambridge and New York: Cambridge University Press, 1978.

Pratt, Mary Louise. "A Reply to Harold Fromm." *Critical Inquiry* 13 (1986): 201–2.

———. "Scratches on the Face of the Country; or, What Mr. Barrow Saw in the Land of the Bushmen." *Critical Inquiry* 12 (1985): 119–43.

Rabinowitz, Peter J. "Our Evaluation of Literature Has Been Distorted by Academe's Bias Toward Close Reading of Texts." *Chronicle of Higher Education*, April 6, 1988, A40.

Rader, Ralph W. "Literary Permanence and Critical Change." *Works and Days* 4 (1986): 9–15.

Rhodes, Phillip. "A Medical Appraisal of the Brontës." *Brontë Society Transactions* 16, no. 2 (1972): 101–9.

Rochberg, George. "Can the Arts Survive Modernism? (A Discussion of the Characteristics, History, and Legacy of Modernism)." *Critical Inquiry* 11 (1984): 317–40.

Roszak, Theodore. *The Making of a Counter Culture*. Garden City, N.Y.: Doubleday, Anchor Books, 1969.

Rowe, John Carlos. " 'To Live Outside the Law, You Must be Honest': The Authority of the Margin in Contemporary Theory." *Cultural Critique* 2 (1985–86): 35–68.

Scholes, Robert. "Deconstruction and Communication." *Critical Inquiry* 14 (1988): 278–95.

Showalter, Elaine. *A Literature of Their Own: British Women Novelists from Brontë to Lessing*. Princeton, N.J.: Princeton University Press, 1977.

Spater, George, and Ian Parsons. *A Marriage of True Minds.* New York and London: Harcourt Brace Jovanovich, 1977.

Stalker, Douglas, and Clarke Glymour. "The Malignant Object: Thoughts on Public Sculpture." *Public Interest* 66 (1982): 3–36.

Steinmann, Martin, Jr. Review of *The Horizon of Literature*, ed. Paul Hernadi. *Journal of Aesthetics and Art Criticism* 42 (1984): 347–50.

Todorov, Tzvetan. "'Race,' Writing, and Culture." *Critical Inquiry* 13 (1986): 171–81.

Trombley, Stephen. *"All That Summer She Was Mad": Virginia Woolf: Female Victim of Male Medicine.* New York: Continuum, 1982.

Turner, Frederick. *Natural Classicism: Essays on Literature and Science.* New York: Paragon House Publishers, 1985.

Vendler, Helen. *The Music of What Happens.* Cambridge, Mass. and London: Harvard University Press, 1988.

von Hallberg, Robert. "American Poet-Critics Since 1945." In *Reconstructing American Literary History*, ed. Sacvan Bercovitch. Cambridge, Mass. and London: Harvard University Press, 1986.

Walhout, Mark. "Textual Virtue: A Review Essay." *Journal of the Midwest Modern Language Association* 21 (1988): 65–74.

West, Cornel. "The Dilemma of the Black Intellectual." *Cultural Critique* 1 (1985): 122.

Wilson, Duncan. *Leonard Woolf: A Political Biography.* New York: St. Martin's Press, 1978.

Winnifrith, Tom. *The Brontës and Their Background: Romance and Reality.* New York: Barnes and Noble, 1973.

Wolfe, Tom. *The Painted Word.* New York: Farrar Straus Giroux, 1975.

———. *From Bauhaus to Our House.* New York: Farrar Straus Giroux, 1981.

Woolf, Leonard. *Growing.* London: The Hogarth Press, 1960.

———. *Sowing.* London: The Hogarth Press, 1961.

———. *The Village in the Jungle.* Oxford: Oxford University Press, 1981.

———. *The Wise Virgins.* New York and London: Harcourt Brace Jovanovich, 1979.

Zavarzadeh, Mas'ud. *The Mythopoeic Reality: The Postwar American Nonfiction Novel.* Urbana: University of Illinois Press, 1976.

Index